Advance Praise for
Social Work in an Online World:
A Guide to Digital Practice

"Social work practitioners and managers are increasingly embracing the opportunities afforded by digital and online practice. *Social Work in an Online World* brings us a wealth of ideas and frameworks to help navigate this transition. The authors examine a myriad of opportunities for interventions, advocacy, support, and engagement. However, the text also challenges us to consider how the values of the profession, inequalities, and ethical considerations will shape our practices in digital and online spaces. Readers will be especially interested in the authors' ideas on how to use online and digital technologies to promote social justice, activism, and macro-level change."

Kenneth Burns, PhD, BSocSc, MSW, NQSW
Associate professor in social work
University College Cork, Ireland

✶ ✶ ✶

"Social work, like many fields, faced a disruptive challenge as the COVID-19 pandemic required a rapid move to technology-driven interventions and new systemic operations. *Social Work in an Online World* provides the much-needed practical guide to illustrate this shift. It is a must-read handbook that introduces readers to a range of opportunities to enhance social work practice with technology. Going beyond synchronous telehealth, the chapters provide a view of micro, mezzo, and macro digital practices with clear examples and materials to support implementation. Through each chapter there is a responsible balance of the promise and challenges of embedding technology, and an unwavering commitment to social justice. Wilkerson and O'Sullivan's book urges the field to continue our meaningful integration of technology and builds on the grand challenge commitment to harness technology for social good."

Stephanie Cosner Berzin, PhD
Vice provost, professor
School of Social Work
Simmons University, Boston, MA

"Using the six practice areas in the digital social work map (support, identity, community action, psychotherapy, education, and psychoeducation), the authors provide an excellent foundation for thinking about digital approaches to the field, with a constant focus on ethical standards for digital equity and data justice. The authors' detailed explanations of their processes and their engaging, informative, and approachable writing style make digital practice accessible for readers who may be new to technology or digital innovations. The lessons learned and challenges encountered provide valuable insights for practitioners who may be considering similar projects in their own school or practice."

Sarah Caliboso-Soto, EdD, LCSW
Assistant director of clinical programs
Associate professor of social work practicum education
Department of Children, Youth and Families
Suzanne Dworak-Peck School of Social Work
University of Southern California, Los Angeles

SOCIAL WORK IN AN
ONLINE
WORLD

A GUIDE TO
DIGITAL
PRACTICE

EDITED BY **DAVID A. WILKERSON**
AND **LIAM O'SULLIVAN**

NASW PRESS

National Association of Social Workers
Washington, DC

Mildred C. Joyner, DPS, LCSW, President
Anthony Estreet, PhD, MBA, LCSW-C, Chief Executive Officer

Cheryl Y. Bradley, *Publisher*
Rachel Meyers, *Acquisitions Editor*
Julie Gutin, *Project Manager*

First impression: April 2023

Library of Congress Cataloging-in-Publication Data

Names: Wilkerson, David (Social work professor) editor. | O'Sullivan, Liam, editor.
Title: Social work in an online world : a guide to digital practice / edited by David Wilkerson and Liam O'Sullivan.
Description: 1 Edition. | Washington, DC : NASW Press, [2023] | Includes bibliographical references and index. | Summary: "Prior to 2020, the field of social work was limited in its adoption of digital practice. With the onset of COVID-19, traditional, in-person service delivery was dramatically interrupted. What once appeared to be a crossroads for the field became an emerging and seemingly unstoppable shift toward modern technology-mediated forms of delivery. This volume addresses this shift and maps the changing landscape from analog to digital practice with varied client systems, system needs, and system levels (micro, mezzo, and macro). Going beyond online mental health service, which is largely individually focused and synchronously delivered, the authors offer a map of digital social work practice that can be expanded to include support, identity, community action, education, and psychoeducation. Readers wishing to adopt digital practices will be inspired to apply these standards in their own applications"—Provided by publisher.
Identifiers: LCCN 2022054513 (print) | LCCN 2022054514 (ebook) | ISBN 9780871015846 (paperback) | ISBN 9780871015853 (ebook)
Subjects: LCSH: Social service—Technological innovations. | Social work education—Technological innovations.
Classification: LCC HV40 .S619553 2023 (print) | LCC HV40 (ebook) | DDC 361.3/2—dc23/eng/20221114
LC record available at https://lccn.loc.gov/2022054513
LC ebook record available at https://lccn.loc.gov/2022054514

Printed in the United States of America

For Liam's aunt Bernie Rowan, MA (Ed), MSocSc, CQSW, who inspired him to enter the social work profession

* * *

For Marijane

Contents

Mapping Social Work Practice in an Online World

David A. Wilkerson and Liam O'Sullivan

In 2018, the Council on Social Work Education (CSWE) Futures Task Force considered the field of social work in the United States to be at a crossroads. At the time, the field's adoption of digital practice had been limited. Practitioner and educator reluctance was driven by challenges and barriers associated with technology, training, client acceptance, payer reimbursement, client privacy, risk management, and the perceived limitations of online delivery for developing a treatment alliance and conveying values like trust, empathy, and caring (Berzin et al., 2015; Harst et al., 2019; LaMendola, 2010; Ramsey et al., 2016; Smith, n.d.). However, following the onset of COVID-19 in 2020, traditional, in-person service delivery was dramatically interrupted globally. What once appeared to be a crossroads became an emerging and seemingly unstoppable shift toward modern technology–mediated forms of delivery.

Social Work in an Online World addresses this shift and maps the changing landscape from analog to digital practice. Additionally, while the mental health field has been at the center of this emerging landscape, digital social work practice occurs with varied client systems, system needs, and system levels (micro, mezzo, and macro). Therefore, in addition to psychotherapy, a map of digital social work practice can be expanded to include support, identity, community action, education, and psychoeducation.

Technology also brings a new set of ethical issues for mapping practice. Reamer (2018) described the evolution of online social work practice, the fundamental ethical questions raised, and the standards developed for social workers' use of technology. We expand on those standards, and in Figure 1, we illustrate a landscape of digital practice embedded within the core social work value of social justice. Social justice is applied in this map as digital equity as well as the more recently developed principle of data justice.

Figure 1: Digital Social Work Practice Map

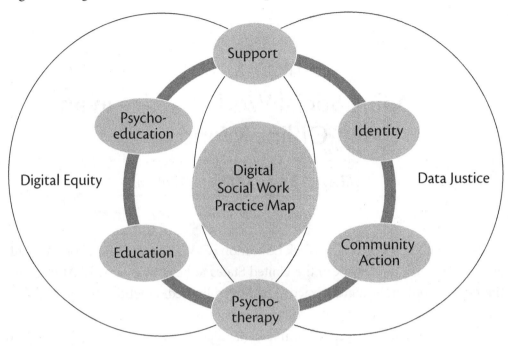

DIGITAL PRACTICE LANDSCAPE

We show six practice areas in our digital social work map: support, identity, community action, psychotherapy, education, and psychoeducation, as well as ethical standards for digital equity and data justice. Practice areas are illustrated in this guidebook by the work of social workers in the United States, Europe, and New Zealand. The chapters are joined by several through lines, but the impact of COVID-19 predominates.

Cyberfeminism

Apropos to our mapping goal, Funk and Fitch (chapter 1: Harnessing Technology for Social Justice: Radical Approaches to Digitally Revolutionize Social Work) introduce readers to a new digital social work practice identity of "cyberfeminist." They explore cyberfeminist social justice implications for digital practice at micro, mezzo, and macro levels. Numerous practice examples illustrate their theoretical perspective on an evolving landscape in which service delivery is being revolutionized and moving the field toward the CSWE Futures Task Force's scenario of "Social Work Leadership for a High-Tech World" (CSWE, 2018, p. 6). Their chapter also introduces the through line of COVID-19 in the digital practice landscape.

Support

Online support is an area that has seen significant growth since the advent of Web 2.0 and the proliferation of social media websites. Facebook was launched in 2004, YouTube in 2005, and Twitter in 2006 (White & Le Cornu, 2011). Online support groups operating in social media sites are a rapidly developing and expanding area within the digital practice landscape. Sometimes called "virtual communities," they are thematically diverse yet share a common focus on management of stress and uncertainty primarily through peer-to-peer support. Stressful life challenges and coping strategies are two key concepts associated with online support group work. Whereas stress and coping are normal parts of life, chronic stress creates numerous risks to mind, body, and spirit. Successful coping with chronic stress can be enhanced with support, and social workers have long been pivotal to the successful delivery of support services through group work. The growth of online support is based on information and communication technologies' ease of development and use. Operated through a variety of inexpensive and readily available synchronous and asynchronous technologies, online support systems provide the means for theme/topic specialization that would be largely unavailable in face-to-face settings.

In chapter 2, "A Team-Based Approach to Moderating Online Support Groups," O'Sullivan and Wilkerson provide a practice example for the area of "support" that illustrates the impact of COVID-19 for a reworking of the use of teams to deliver services. Initially unfunded and led by social work volunteers in Ireland, their support group uses the latest in online group functionality on a leading social media portal. The authors tell the story of the group's formation, including the advanced use of a volunteer, peer/professional moderator support group to remotely discuss practice/moderation dilemmas. When considering the alignment of the project with social work's principles and values, the authors suggest that digital equity and justice issues may limit participation for some clients and, in the case example described, family caregivers. However, the authors demonstrate that in some cases practitioners can actively support participants' digital literacy.

Digital Equity and Data Justice

The term *digital equity* refers to the social justice principle of technology access as a human right. In addition to the element of accessibility, digital equity includes digital literacy and digital citizenship. Helsper (2021) discussed digital equity and technology "divides" at three levels: (1) device and infrastructure accessibility; (2) technology literacy and skills; and (3) economic, social, cultural, and health outcomes that require digital equity.

Elswick, Peterson, Washington, and Barnes (chapter 3: Best Practices in Technology-Based Supports in Working with Children, Adolescents, and Families) provide an illuminating view of the use of a university–community collaboration to create an infrastructure for overcoming first and second levels of the digital divide for marginalized and oppressed families in the southeastern United States. As their work continues, it will be interesting to see its impact at the third level of economic, social, cultural, and health outcomes. The authors' work also illustrates the impact of COVID-19 on the development of digital social work practice in which digital inclusion is achieved through pioneering methods, including digital mentors and digital passports within a "social envelop" strategy.

The social justice principle of data justice was developed in response to the escalating *datafication* (digital information that is collected, organized, and translated into new uses that can be valued or monetized by parties other than the originators of the digital information) of society, subsequent human rights violations, and the ensuing need for data literacy and data citizenship skills to protect community members, especially members of vulnerable and oppressed groups. Taylor (2017) described *data justice* as "fairness in the way people are made visible, represented and treated as a result of their production of digital data" (p. 1). In chapter 4, "Advancing Data Justice," Ballantyne provides readers with a critical understanding of the uses of algorithmic data and artificial intelligence for governmental decision making and services delivery. Case studies illustrate the ways human rights violations occur followed by the author's recommended methods for data justice advocacy. Critical data literacy is described, and recommendations are provided for developing competency in its practice.

Community Action

Community action is defined as "collective action by community members drawing on the strength of numbers, participatory processes, and Indigenous leadership to decrease power disparities and achieve shared goals for social change" (Staples, 2012, p. 288). Many social work practitioners and academics, including some of this book's authors, are of the view that social work has lost its radical roots, often best epitomized by true grassroots community action/organizing and activism. It has been argued that social workers are all too comfortable in embracing government-endorsed and legislatively informed social control activities (e.g., probation, child protection) to the detriment of more radical activities. Fisher sees activism as being about "democratic grassroots analysis and action," which he believes is very much lacking in both traditional social work and in many radical social work perspectives (R. Fisher, professor and chair of community organizing,

University of Connecticut, personal communication, August 29, 2022). Fisher et al. (2018) argued that community efforts are fundamentally political, and whether groups like it or not, implicitly or explicitly, they are part of the social struggles of their historical context.

Clearly, group work is central to community action. Group dynamics were first theorized by Kurt Lewin nearly a century ago (Burnes & Bargal, 2017). Lewin determined that it takes the individuals who are the closest to a problem or an issue that needs to be changed to be involved in it for it to be effective and that—ultimately—it would take more than one individual within that community to create such a change.

Cuskelly and Ojeda (chapter 5: Online Opportunities for Community Action: Social Media as a Vehicle for Social Justice) describe online community actions and initiatives, informed by social work values, that focus on the macro-level change. They detail specific actions to take to promote digital equity and data justice. They describe how online collaboration with like-minded activists (but not exclusively social work practitioners) has effected legislative change and mobilized communities. They also discuss the risks of online misinformation and some governmental interventions to mitigate the worst effects of such misinformation. Their chapter provides useful tips for online activism as well as a tool kit for protecting practitioners from harm when placing themselves publicly online as part of their professional work.

Identity-Based Social Action

Digital practice overlaps into community action in significant ways. The foundation for identity-based social action is *self-concept*, in which we consider the integration of our personal and social identities. Developing a sense of self can be a lengthy process and a significant struggle, especially for members of oppressed and vulnerable groups. Identity-based social action focuses on the use of community action to achieve social justice for individual or intersectional aspects of the self-concept that have been threatened, attacked, or otherwise negatively impacted by a dominant community. In one example of identity-based social action, Richez and colleagues (2020) studied a Canadian Indigenous–led political movement that used social media to mobilize political action to address legislative policy on a range of Indigenous economic, health, and safety issues. Their work is available on the internet and presents an important study of the development of a digital movement and its outcomes.

Identity-based social action is a contentious aspect within the recent development of digital movements because of the use of social media by hate groups. Trading on the use of social media for self-concept development, they build racist movements, such as those based in White superiority ideologies (Faulkner & Bliuc,

2016). This highlights the potential negative power of social media to undermine what might be described as progressive causes. For those interested in the wider area of online macro social work activism, readers are referred to #MacroSW on Twitter (Cummings & Folayan, 2019).

Psychotherapy

We have noted that psychotherapy has been well represented in the digital practice map by virtue of the urgent need to resume behavioral practice following the pandemic lockdowns in 2020. Gregory and Werth (chapter 6: The Power of Online Synchronous Cognitive–Behavioral Group Intervention: A Get S-M-A-R-T Illustration) continue the through line of COVID-19's impact on digital practice with their work in the delivery of cognitive–behavioral therapy (CBT) for substance users through online, synchronous group delivery. Their chapter tracks the development of the program and describes the principles needed for developing a virtual therapeutic alliance with their treatment population. Practitioners will appreciate the knowledge these authors share on managing antitherapeutic client actions, handling the unexpected, and weighing the pros and cons of digital practice.

Education

Education is also located on the digital social work practice map because of its importance for student decision making regarding the adoption, readiness, and training for digital practice (Wilkerson et al., 2019). The Digital Professionalism Mapping Tool (Digital Professionalism Mapping Tool for Students, n.d.) is an example of a method used to explore student digital practice readiness based on their preferred patterns of engagement with the internet. A "visitor/resident" typology was developed with "visitors" preferring engagement for managing tasks and "residents" preferring engagement for interaction and identity management. The tool is used to map internet engagement in personal and professional virtual spaces and replaces older typologies like "digital native" and "immigrant" (White & Le Cornu, 2011). Taylor-Beswick (2022) applied the Digital Professionalism Mapping Tool for social work to understand students' experiences with digital skill gaps in their education.

Wolfe-Taylor, Khaja, and Deck (chapter 7: Bridging Education and Practice with e-OSCE Simulations) address the need to strengthen digital practice in social work education with their work on the development and uses of the e-OSCE. Before COVID-19, many social work faculty and administrators were critical of online social work education, and a specific focus of this criticism is captured in the remark, "You can't teach social work practice online!" The authors have refuted this criticism and identified ways to bridge the gap between education and practice using an online simulation–based educational opportunity for first-year MSW students. In their pilot qualitative case study, they identify students' evaluation of their self-efficacy, how they applied theory in practice, and what they identified as their strengths and challenges as they completed the e-OSCE experience. Additionally, students' feedback on the e-OSCE experience is explored.

Psychoeducation

The final location on the digital practice map is psychoeducation. Psychoeducation has a long history of analog practice and is still being developed for digital practice. Brown and Keesler (chapter 8: Creating a Digital School Safety Service: A Pathway from Traditional Analog to Digital Practice) demonstrate a school-based, mezzo-level application of psychoeducation that can overlap into community action. Their work demonstrates the potential for applying an aspect of psychoeducation—self-assessments—to achieve community-building outcomes in the mezzo setting of middle school to improve school safety.

Wilkerson (chapter 9: Digital Hybrid Psychoeducation: Model Development and Case Illustration) focuses on the further development of psychoeducation as a digital practice through the application of research with a digital hybrid psychoeducation program. The term "hybrid" is used to distinguish the alternating elements of digital individual and digital group work within the model. This differs from more commonplace uses of the term "hybrid," in which practice alternates between digital and on-the-ground spaces. The chapter addresses a gap in the development of intervention designs that enable peer support to contribute to the outcomes of online psychoeducation interventions. While many digital psychoeducation programs provide strong individual training components, the design for peer support is less well developed. Methods are described using case examples for engaging participants in peer support and also amplifying the individual training components within psychoeducation.

CONCLUSION

In this introduction, we have introduced readers to *Social Work in an Online World* with a digital practice map whose landscape reflects support, identity, community action, psychotherapy, education, and psychoeducation (see Figure 1). Each of the chapters represents a location in the landscape through which chapter authors provide a guided tour with their practice model. Authors contribute accessible theory and conceptualizations, practice examples, case studies, research, learnings, and reflections as well as the strengths and limitations of their approaches.

Social Work in an Online World seeks to expand the practice map beyond online mental health service delivery, which is largely individually focused and synchronously delivered. We outline a map for digital social work practice that includes group and macro work that occurs in many different environments (e.g., schools, healthcare facilities, nonprofit advocacy organizations, other community and population centers). In addition, we identify the core social work value of social justice as central to this map and as supporting the principles of digital equity and data justice.

A major through line in this work has been COVID-19. Like others who have discussed the pandemic and the resultant accelerated transition to digital practice (Earle & Freddolino, 2022), we can't deny the significant and likely enduring impact it has had on the delivery of online social work. Practices that were, at best, peripheral and criticized by mainstream social work are now commonly accepted. The pandemic's impact can also be observed by the support practitioners have received from many social work organizations and educators. A few of these include (a) the University College Cork's (n.d.) OSWP Tools through which practitioners share comprehensive tools for online professional social work practice; (b) the Social Care Institute for Excellence (SCIE), which provides e-learning for social workers using technology (SCIE, n.d.); (c) the British Association of Social Workers (BASW), which provides resources for digital social work practices (BASW, n.d.); and (d) Indiana University School of Social Work, which provides an online continuing education program on telepractice basics for social workers and educators responding to COVID-19 (Indiana University, n.d.).

These examples and the digital practice models presented in *Social Work in an Online World* demonstrate that a shift from analog practice to the inclusion of hybrid and digital practice is occurring and is largely positive for social workers and for those they seek to serve. However, for this shift to become truly transformative, the application of social justice principles of digital equity and data justice must become a standard for development. We hope that readers wishing to adopt digital practices will be inspired to apply these standards in their own applications.

REFERENCES

Berzin, S. C., Singer, J., & Chan, C. (2015, October). *Practice innovation through technology in the digital age: A Grand Challenge for Social Work* (Working Paper No. 12). https://grandchallengesforsocialwork.org/wp-content/uploads/2015/12/WP12-with-cover.pdf

British Association of Social Workers. (n.d.). *Digital capabilities for social workers.* https://www.basw.co.uk/resources/publications-policies-and-reports/digital-capabilities-social-workers

Burnes, B., & Bargal, D. (2017). Kurt Lewin: 70 years on. *Journal of Change Management, 17*, 91–100. https://doi.org/10.1080/14697017.2017.1299371

Council on Social Work Education. (2018, April). *Envisioning the future of social work: Report of the CSWE Futures Task Force.* https://www.cswe.org/about-cswe/2020-strategic-plan/strategic-planning-process/cswe-futures-task-force-report-four-futures-for-social-work/

Cummings, S., & Folayan, S. W. (2019, Winter). #MacroSW: Social work in these trying times. *The New Social Worker.* https://www.socialworker.com/api/content/e0d3a234-0a20-11e9-aeaf-120e7ad5cf50/

Digital Professionalism Mapping Tool for Students. (n.d.). *Video guide of using the Digital Professionalism Mapping Tool.* Retrieved September 12, 2022, from https://rise.articulate.com/share/Icj6kEGBZmacijjISnpOVR40du8sXiby#/lessons/UWU6_Hk8QXHjXdaHkF4az2m_nUl0hC1M

Earle, M. J., & Freddolino, P. P. (2022). Meeting the practice challenges of COVID-19: MSW students' perceptions of e-therapy and the therapeutic alliance. *Clinical Social Work Journal, 50*, 76–85. https://doi.org/10.1007/s10615-021-00801-3

Faulkner, N., & Bliuc, A.-M. (2016). "It's okay to be racist": Moral disengagement in online discussions of racist incidents in Australia. *Ethnic and Racial Studies, 39*, 2545–2563. https://doi.org/10.1080/01419870.2016.1171370

Fisher, R., DeFilippis, J., & Shragge, E. (2018). Contested community: A selected and critical history of community organizing. In R. A. Cnaan & C. Milofsky (Eds.), *Handbook of community movements and local organizations in the 21st century* (pp. 281–297). Springer.

Harst, L., Lantzsch, H., & Scheibe, M. (2019). Theories predicting end-user acceptance of telemedicine use: Systematic review. *Journal of Medical Internet Research, 21*, Article e13117. https://doi.org/10.2196/13117

Helsper, E. (2021). *The digital disconnect: The social causes and consequences of digital inequalities.* SAGE.

Indiana University. (n.d.). *Telebehavioral practice basics for social work educators & clinicians responding to COVID-19.* Retrieved September 12, 2022, from https://expand.iu.edu/browse/socialwork/courses/telehealth-basics-for-social-work-educators-behavioral-health-clinicians-responding-to-covid-19

LaMendola, W. (2010). Social work and social presence in an online world. *Journal of Technology in Human Services, 28*, 108–119. https://doi.org/10.1080/15228831003759562

Ramsey, A. T., Wetherell, J. L., Depp, C., Dixon, D., & Lenze, E. (2016). Feasibility and acceptability of smartphone assessment in older adults with cognitive and emotional difficulties. *Journal of Technology in Human Services, 34*, 209–223. https://doi.org/10.1080/15228835.2016.1170649

Reamer, F. G. (2018). Ethical standards for social workers' use of technology: Emerging consensus. *Journal of Social Work Values and Ethics, 15*, 71–80. https://jswve.org/download/15-2/articles15-2/71-Use-of-technology-JSWVE-15-2-2018-Fall.pdf

Richez, E., Raynauld, V., Agi, A., & Kartolo, A. B. (2020). Unpacking the political effects of social movements with a strong digital component: The case of #IdleNoMore in Canada. *Social Media + Society, 6*, Article 2056305120915588. https://doi.org/10.1177/2056305120915588

Smith, M. L. (n.d.). What my LED ball reveals about the future of technology and social work: A farewell aloha. *The New Social Worker.* http://www.socialworker.com/api/content/77ec673e-f007-344d-a6eb-d9321c457efe/

Social Care Institute for Excellence. (n.d.). *Building rapport and establishing meaningful relationships using technology in social work.* Retrieved September 12, 2022, from https://www.scie.org.uk/care-providers/coronavirus-covid-19/social-workers/building-rapport-with-technology

Staples, L. (2012). Community organizing for social justice: Grassroots groups for power. *Social Work with Groups, 35*, 287–296. https://doi.org/10.1080/01609513.2012.656233

Taylor, L. (2017). What is data justice? The case for connecting digital rights and freedoms globally. *Big Data & Society, 4.* https://doi.org/10.1177/2053951717736335

Taylor-Beswick, A. M. L. (2022). Digitalizing social work education: Preparing students to engage with twenty-first century practice need. *Social Work Education.* https://doi.org/10.1080/02615479.2022.2049225

University College Cork, Ireland. (n.d.). *OSWP tools.* Retrieved September 12, 2022, from https://www.ucc.ie/en/appsoc/aboutus/activities/oswp/oswptools/

White, D. S., & Le Cornu, A. (2011). Visitors and residents: A new typology for online engagement. *First Monday.* https://doi.org/10.5210/fm.v16i9.3171

Wilkerson, D. A., Wolfe-Taylor, S. N., & Kinney, M. K. (2019). Adopting e-social work practice: Pedagogical strategies for student decision making to address technology uncertainty. *Journal of Social Work Education, 57*, 383–397. https://doi.org/10.1080/10437797.2019.1661920

CHAPTER 1

Harnessing Technology for Social Justice: Radical Approaches to Digitally Revolutionize Social Work

Kristin Funk and Dale Fitch

No social work endeavor is worthwhile unless it achieves the goal of social justice. This chapter focuses on issues of equity and social justice in the planning and delivery of technology-mediated services (TMS). Information technology delivers important advantages, and the role of radical digital social work interventions is to guide the design and development of equitable TMS. Social workers can work with communities and populations to create nonhierarchically based, customized interventions across macro, mezzo, and micro levels of service. This chapter considers several solutions that intersect with technology-based sociotechnical system design augmented by a *cyberfeminism approach*, that is, the critical perspective that technology and virtual spaces should be used to empower and equalize to promote social justice.

CONCEPTUAL FRAMEWORKS

Before engaging in the delivery of TMS, careful consideration must be given to the way those services are designed before they are delivered. Some design considerations must address technical aspects guided by our professional values. The technical considerations can be ideally informed by sociotechnical systems theory (STS), while cyberfeminism frames social justice and equitable outcomes that form the basis for our values.

STS

STS has been used in a broad range of organizational applications over the decades (Clegg et al., 2011; Mumford, 2000; Pasmore, 1995). While a full explanation of

STS is beyond the scope of this chapter, the following illustration addresses those factors that social workers should consider when engaging in TMS. Specifically, all work with technology is situated in organizations comprising humans. In addition, while technology is ideal for managing data and facilitating communication within organizations, it is not capable of creating knowledge or instilling values. Technology can facilitate relationships, but it cannot replace them; it can convey feelings, but it cannot understand them. Technology can only serve larger human goals; it can never supplant them.

Schematically, the sociotechnical system comprises two subsystems: (1) the social subsystem and (2) the technical subsystem. The social subsystem includes the components (a) Structure and (b) People, and the technical subsystem includes the components (c) Technology and (d) Tasks. Most important to understand is that these four components must continually interact for the whole system to perform most efficiently. (For a diagram of this relationship, see https://is.theorizeit .org/wiki/Socio-technical_theory; see also Larsen & Eargle, n.d.)

For example, the *Structure* is the agency, organization(s), or interagency collaboration in which *People* work. *Technology* broadly includes everything we use to get our work done, which ranges from pen and paper to computers and the internet. Most important are the *Tasks* we perform to serve the needs of our clients. Represented thusly, no single component of the diagram is more important than the other. Conversely, the extent to which any component fails to be addressed is the extent to which the overall system will fail to achieve its goals. It is vital to understand that technology is not a replacement for humans; indeed, humans are the driver for all technology interfaces.

As such, humans can introduce radical (i.e., the opposite of how things have always been done) practice innovations. By doing so, these radical approaches will "disrupt" traditional approaches. STS must be contextualized in the larger environment. As discussed throughout all the practice applications in this text, COVID-19 has changed the environment for everyone, including how we deliver our services. To regain some control over those services, STS may help us function more efficiently to address that disruption.

Social Justice and Cyberfeminism

While social justice is a concept that most social workers have at least heard of, if not practiced, cyberfeminism might be new. The development of cyberfeminism was grounded in the perspective that sought to decouple the use of technology from traditional gender roles and constraints (Braidotti, 2003; Chatterjee, 2002; Hall, 1996; Haraway, 1990). Beyond gender roles, cyberfeminism challenges us to examine all defined social roles from a critical perspective. In the context of digital social work, cyberfeminism calls for the breaking down of hierarchical role constraints within agencies and creation of opportunities for greater flexibility within interagency collaborations. The script of leadership becomes flipped, if you will, and collaborative decision making can become the norm.

Moreover, the deconstruction of the roles that perpetuate power and privilege is one of the hallmarks of cyberfeminism and its contribution to our understanding of how we should view its use. For example, the traditional power dynamic (i.e., role) of provider and client is one in which the provider, though offering support, dictates the mode and delivery of services. By deconstructing the power dynamics, cyberfeminism suggests the client and therapist eliminate the hierarchy and make shared decisions regarding treatment or that the client requests certain modes of service delivery that the provider can choose to provide.

Social justice in the context of technology can be understood more directly— that is, how the use of technology is constrained by one's social identity, whether that identity is grounded in one's sociodemographics (McNutt, 1998, 2018) or by one's defined social roles (see cyberfeminism). Regarding identity being grounded in one's sociodemographics, those sociodemographics are associated with technology access, affordability, and the larger societal infrastructure dictating whether one's house or neighborhood even has access to the internet. Regarding identity being defined by one's social roles, do we employ a "diverse" range of ways in which to engage our clients? Do social workers have limited access to technology based on their "role" in the organization? Are they also constrained in its use by that role?

In 2016, the United Nations General Assembly declared internet access a basic human right (Sanders & Scanlon, 2021). Yet here we are several years later, and only some progress has been made in bridging the digital divide (see chapter 3 for a definition) in Europe, Latin America, and the United States (Sieck et al., 2021; Tomczyk et al., 2019), while the rest of the world continues to lack widespread access. In addition to directly advocating on this issue, this chapter also demonstrates that digital access is a fundamental building block for engaging in social work practice. Jointly, social workers should also be able to engage in online interventions *if* evidence demonstrates their efficacy.

Analog, Digital, and Hybrid Delivery

Combining STS, cyberfeminism, and social justice should result in a more nuanced understanding of how technology can be used to facilitate and enhance social work practice. Returning to the Tasks in the STS diagram (see "Diagram/

Schematic of Theory," 2016), our profession has been dominated by an *analog* mindset when delivering services. That mindset is embodied by three criteria:

1. Services are delivered at a physical location.
2. The social worker and client are at this location.
3. The social worker and client are at this location at the same time.

If any one of these criteria is not met, then social work cannot be performed. Over the past several years, COVID-19 has caused service delivery to disrupt those criteria. We have had to fundamentally rethink and redo the provision of social work services. Conversely, not all social work practice is now performed online—that is, we are not entirely *digital*. Whether intentional or not, we engage in a *hybrid* practice. We may still meet with a client at the same time, but this meeting may take place online. We still communicate with clients, but it may be through an email or secure message. Social workers may still go to the office, or they may work from their home office. Although clients and practitioners are not sharing the same traditional analog sense of time and space, they are not necessarily divided. Digital and hybrid approaches can transcend time and physical space, and the clients and practitioners share this digital space.

Once the possibility of delivering hybrid services has been experienced by both clients and social workers, how could we go back to analog delivery again? More importantly, if we did, would we be violating social justice principles in the process? The following practice examples examine social work practice from this analog versus digital mindset mindful of the STS framework, cyberfeminism, and social justice.

CONCEPTUAL FRAMEWORKS AND THEIR SOCIAL WORK PRACTICE CONTEXTS

We commonly understand that social work practice takes place in micro-, mezzo-, and macro-level contexts. The other chapters in this book provide detailed examples of those practice modalities. This chapter, instead, seeks to achieve two objectives: (1) explain how our conceptual frameworks factor into the design of the delivery of those services and (2) provide evidence of the effectiveness of those services. Evidence-based literature contains hundreds of examples that we could have cited. Instead, we reference those publications that illustrate the application of our framework.

Micro-Level Practice

This section includes examples from telehealth (including hospital social work), telebehavioral health, crisis management, psychoeducation, and health education. Most of the research in this area has been cross-sectional studies that limit the generalizability of the findings. However, of the studies selected, the variables of most interest were those reflective of STS and social justice issues related to access.

Telehealth

Per STS, typical Tasks involved include assessment, diagnosis, treatment, and referral. Without technology, these tasks must be performed in person with one provider seeing one client at a time while they are in the same location. Data can be gathered via paper and shared if physically copied, faxed, or stored in a location where others can access it. A digital approach allows the following: online telehealth visits; communication via secure messaging; remote symptom monitoring to collect data (e.g., smart watch, smartphone apps); and asynchronous follow-ups using text, email, discussion boards, and so on. Although these tasks are possible, the question remains as to whether they are effective or efficient. Fortunately, the research literature helps to answer that question.

Much of the research literature has focused on the displacement of "in-person, human contact" (Cristofalo, 2021) when technology is used. While social workers readily acknowledge the value of these in-person interactions, we give little consideration for *hybrid relationships*, that is, in-person contact supplemented by technology-facilitated communications. Always expecting clients to meet with us in person presupposes that clients always want to meet with us in person when a phone call or email may suffice. Telehealth visits also allow greater flexibility in accessing services and increasing intervention satisfaction since clients are not asked to make multiple trips to the clinic (Cooper & Zerden, 2021). This study also found that although in-person communications at on-the-ground clinics decreased due to COVID-19, social workers increased their electronic communications with nurses and medical assistants, thereby increasing the number of clients with whom they were working.

Whether clients meet with social workers in person or not, the emphasis should always be on the clients' health outcomes. For example, in their randomized intervention, Gellis et al. (2014) found significant improvement in client problem-solving skills and self-efficacy in managing their medical care along with significantly fewer emergency department visits. Participants also reported improved access to care and a heightened sense of security. This access to care is especially important for clients who live in rural or remote areas. Here, too, the research literature speaks to the use of technology-facilitated interventions. Cornell et al. (2021) reported data from 144 sites with a focus on rural practice settings for veterans who have limited access to U.S. Department of Veterans Affairs healthcare providers. The practice modalities included in-person and telephone along with video telehealth. While in-person encounters decreased over the study period (yet continued when medically necessary), telephone and video telehealth visits increased, resulting in an overall net increase in client encounters. Some sites also saw an increase in the number of requests for video services over telephone services.

Similar findings were reported on a positive psychology intervention for hemodialysis clients with depression (Hernandez et al., 2018). The intervention was delivered entirely online through a website the clients accessed while they were receiving dialysis. Results indicated a significant improvement in depressive symptoms with a reported effect size (Cohen's d) of .67 for all clients and an effect size of 1.4 for those clients with elevated depression scores on the pretest. Although client feedback included recommendations on how to improve the website interface, the intervention was well received overall. Most importantly, a benefit for the hemodialysis social workers was that it increased their capacity to deliver this intervention to clients because the content was online and did not have to be delivered in person, which left time for other tasks or follow-up on issues raised by the intervention. Other studies found a reduction in emergency department visits and an increase in primary care visits (Franceschini et al., 2021).

Training to support workers when using new technologies must be a continual administrative priority for healthcare organizations (Cornell et al., 2021; Cristofalo, 2021; Gellis et al., 2014). Because the organizational context has changed, it is, indeed, incumbent on administrators to provide the training necessary to deliver clinical interventions. In the United States, this is especially important when staff need to ensure clients that compliance with the Health Insurance Portability and Accountability Act of 1996 (also known as HIPAA) has been met (Cooper & Zerden, 2021; List et al., 2021).

Client access to technology must always be considered. However, the answer does not have to be a computer in every home with broadband access (at least not immediately). A hybrid approach of a healthcare home visitor with that technology capability coming in person to the home mitigates both of those situations (Cristofalo, 2021). Additional healthcare data would be generated and accessed by providers via telemetry (Gellis et al., 2014), or the home visitor would facilitate a virtual visit with the rest of the healthcare team during that visit (List et al., 2021).

While social workers must expect to examine issues related to efficacy, training, and access, systems theory would condition one to expect the unexpected. That is, even though our organizations are heavily influenced by our environmental context, changes in organizational practice can also influence that environment. For example, Franceschini et al. (2021) found that the shift to online services resulted in an increase in interorganizational service delivery due to all community agencies' becoming more dependent on one another to meet the increased community needs. As a result, the possibility of being able to gather broad-based data across all these agencies helped inform community needs, identify community resources (to avoid duplication), and identify advocacy opportunities where existing policies needed to be modified.

Telebehavioral Health

The Tasks associated with behavioral health include assessment, diagnosis, and treatment, with information and referral to a lesser degree. The analog components of behavioral health are well established: one provider working in person with one client (i.e., individual, group, or family) at a time in a scheduled 50-minute visit that takes place in a physical location where both are present and that necessitates client travel. Therapist–client communication only occurs during these visits. Of course, there are variations to this modality, but this form of intervention predominates behavioral health treatment.

A more digital approach to behavioral health would incorporate technology and might include online video sessions, secure email or texting communications outside of sessions, or bibliotherapy with discussion boards. A hybrid approach might include initial in-person session(s) integrated with any or all the digital techniques. The research literature with telebehavioral health is much more robust (hundreds of published articles, many of which are randomized clinical trials), and the following studies reflect those studies that illustrate pertinent aspects of STS and social justice.

The biggest difference between an analog and digital or hybrid approach is the synchronous or asynchronous component. An analog approach is entirely synchronous because it requires that the therapist and client be at the same place at the same time. A digital approach can still be synchronous when the therapist and client are still meeting at the same time, but they do not have to be in the same place. A totally asynchronous approach does not require working together at the same place and time.

Asynchronous modalities have been growing over the years as technology and the software it supports has become more ubiquitous in our lives (Chan et al.,

2018). These modes include text messaging, store-and-forward messages, asynchronous video, computerized guided therapy, mobile device momentary assessment (e.g., Google Pixel Watch, Fitbit), mobile device sensors, mobile app–based psychotherapy and psychoeducation (apps that help people track and journal or provide therapy), and computerized guided therapy containing independently completed modules that can be guided by a clinician.

The evidence on the efficacy of asynchronous or hybrid approaches is robust. In the first study of its kind, Yellowlees et al. (2021) reviewed outcomes of 160 clients randomly placed in synchronous versus asynchronous telepsychiatry services. The outcomes were similar. However, the asynchronous modality provided the following benefits: can be scaled (a provider can engage with several clients asynchronously and increase their care among more clients); can reduce bandwidth or internet access issues, thus potentially reaching more and more diverse client populations; and can be done in the client's primary language.

Additional studies have examined specific interventions addressing common issues. Fernandez et al. (2021) found that video-delivered psychotherapy (VDP) was no less efficacious than in-person per this meta-analysis. VDP is the closest analog to in-person psychotherapy. Most efficacy was found when the VDP addressed anxiety ($g = 0.99$), depression ($g = 1.29$), and PTSD ($g = 1.00$), especially when using cognitive–behavioral therapy (CBT). For example, the effect size of VDP using a CBT intervention was 1.34, noting that CBT might lend itself well to virtual delivery because it is standardized, is "less dependent on the dynamics of the client–therapist relationship," and "subtleties in the interaction might be less consequential in an intervention like CBT" (Fernandez et al., 2021, p. 10)—for example, using CBT to treat insomnia (Sweetman et al., 2021). Other systematic reviews have also found medium to large effect sizes when using CBT to treat depression (Berryhill et al., 2018).

Social Justice and Telebehavioral Health

Across all these studies and modalities (Chan et al., 2018; Fernandez et al., 2021; Yellowlees et al., 2021), STS and social justice principles become readily apparent. The interventions are time efficient (i.e., need not be scheduled for a certain time or amount of time, do not take the same amount of time as a synchronous appointment), thereby reducing costs to access. Additionally, digital services can help providers treat "hard-to-reach" clients—for example, those with PTSD, social phobia, personality disorders, and other mental health issues that can keep clients potentially homebound. Both clients and providers report wanting to use digital services, especially via smartphones and apps, which people tend to have more than laptops or computers.

The preference for these modalities was especially striking for clients and providers who reflect diversity in terms of populations and issues for which social stigma and discrimination were prominent. One notable study examined a group of Chinese adolescents in an internet-based depression program versus control group (Ip et al., 2016). The effect size was .36, indicating the internet-based program was effective. The authors suggested benefits of internet-based interventions included better standardization, scalability, and cost-effectiveness.

While clients in many cases clearly prefer internet-based services, concerns still linger whether providers find this mode of delivery inferior to in-person delivery, especially related to the secondary gain some providers receive from analog interactions. However, those secondary gains need to be critically examined. Providers working in situations in which funding is low, staffing is sparse, and clients are spread out or difficult to reach have found that digitally based services can address all these gaps (Dearinger, 2020; Jaffe et al., 2020). Providers reported that the ability to scale their services, especially during a public health emergency, was particularly helpful for them. Digital services allowed providers to continue serving clients despite shutdowns, quarantines, or other physical barriers (Jaffe et al., 2020) that would otherwise have left remaining providers with a large burden of care. Additionally, providers noted their no-show rates improved tremendously as the barriers of space and time were eliminated (Resnick, 2020; Sklar et al., 2020). Other social work providers found that telehealth improved their rapport and relationships with clients (Glenn, 2020; Sklar et al., 2020) by encouraging practitioners to be more present and intentional with language, expressions, and affect. These are new findings during the pandemic and postpandemic. However, researchers have been noting the benefits to and satisfaction of providers engaging in telehealth since at least 1998 (Fitzmaurice, 1998; Stamm, 1998). These seminal articles also point out that telehealth enabled providers to increase their ability to see more clients, demonstrating the longevity of these themes.

The research evidence is clear that client outcomes are comparable whether services are delivered in person or online for many modalities and client issues. Clients prefer online services in many situations, and providers have reported satisfaction in delivering those services in that manner. Therefore, when decisions arise as to whether it is appropriate to deliver online interventions, then we simply need to consider this: The services need to be tailored to those served!

Crisis Management

People experiencing crises have used the telephone for decades to access help. Not surprisingly, crisis interventions and management were one of the first services to experience the benefit of delivering services online. While this review is not exhaustive, social justice issues predominate, and the use of online technology has been found to be especially helpful to reach out to underserved or stigmatized populations and those individuals who live in rural or remote areas.

Online services have been especially helpful for the LGBTQ+ population (Fish et al., 2020). One study examined the usefulness of synchronous and asynchronous text-based crisis support services. The researchers examined qualitative data from the Q Chat Space, a national, anonymous, weekly facilitated online chat-based support group program. Online services were available to LGBTQ+ youth when other resources were not due to mandated physical distancing during COVID-19. Q Chat Space participants doubled during state shutdowns. Likewise, the Trevor Project also reported a doubling of the volume in crisis services during the pandemic. The findings indicate that text-based services were more helpful to this community because of youths' concerns about their confidentiality and fear of being overheard by family they were sheltered in place with. Results also have indicated the need for these online services to support LGBTQ+ youth because of their unique challenges and needs (e.g., needing to having connections with an affirming community for the sake of their mental health).

Access issues were illustrated by a crisis line service (Lifeline Australia) in remote locations in Australia (K. Williams et al., 2021). Due to internet access issues, this service relied on basic text messaging since the Australian population has widespread access to mobile devices. Survey results found that 87.9 percent rated the program as easy or very easy to use, and 83 percent reported they would recommend the service to others. With reference to hybrid technology use, this service was found to be "not a replacement for telephone services or face-to-face counseling but may serve as a valuable initial contact for further services" (K. Williams et al., 2021, p. 33). By being able to text when in distress and receive immediate support, help-seeker outcomes can be improved, especially in the areas of reduced psychological distress, increased coping and self-care, increased sense of belonging, and reduced high-risk behaviors (e.g., suicide, self-harm, violence, substance use).

Due to the high vulnerability risks of the populations with the following circumstances, we believe all social workers should be aware of some of the better-known applications that serve these individuals:

Aspire: Domestic violence app disguised as a newsfeed to help protect survivors; provides a section that allows a person in distress to discreetly send a premade message (and, if enabled, the location of the person in distress) to trusted contacts; app also has a "quick escape" button that automatically changes the screen to news if privacy or safety becomes an immediate issue while using the app. https://www.whengeorgiasmiled.org/aspire-news-app/

Crisis Text Line: Text-based connection with trained crisis counselors available in the United States, Canada, United Kingdom, and Ireland by text (text START to 741-741) and online. https://www.crisistextline.org

Lifeline Australia: A 24-hour suicide prevention service for Australians that is accessible via phone (13 11 14), chat, text (0477 13 11 14), or website. https://www.lifeline.org.au/

NHS [National Health Service] 111: Access to urgent medical and mental healthcare by phone (111) in the United Kingdom or online; services are offered in large print, easy print, British Sign Language, audio only, or via a translator for accessibility. https://111.nhs.uk/

National Human Trafficking Hotline: U.S.-based service that reports ability to respond to clients globally; service in 200 languages with phone, webchat, and text (text BEFREE to 233733) options to help human trafficking survivors; website has a "quick exit" button that takes users to The Weather Channel (https://weather.com/) if needed. https://humantraffickinghotline.org

PFLAG: U.S.-based organization for parents, families, and allies of LGBTQ+ individuals with a repository of crisis intervention resources available for those struggling with suicide, running away from home, HIV/AIDS, domestic violence, assault, and substance use; some resources are specifically for LGBTQ+ communities; others are topic based for the general public. https://pflag.org/hotlines

Trevor Project: Provides text (text START to 678-678), phone, and webchat options and an international online community ("TrevorSpace") for LGBTQIAP+ individuals; website alerts users to a quick exit strategy for privacy or confidentiality by pressing "Escape" three times if on a computer, or, if on a mobile device, tapping three times anywhere, which will shut down the website or app and remove all Trevor Project information from the user's cache. https://www.thetrevorproject.org/get-help/

The value of these services is easily apparent. All these applications have been built with privacy and security concerns at the forefront of their design. To enhance their impact, it would be helpful to reexamine the STS Tasks domain across these practice contexts. Many individuals who experience crisis situations initially present for help-seeking in healthcare settings. Social workers in that setting should readily provide information about these apps, as appropriate, to their clients. In turn, referrals can be made to behavioral health counselors in their communities. Next, we review how technology can be used to make those referrals.

Information and Referral

Two unassuming words—"information" and "referral"—seem insignificant until we realize that no services would ever be provided if people did not have "information" about those services and some type of "referral" had not been made. Telephones have facilitated these referrals for decades, sometimes augmented by fax services. While technology has been used, it is still analog in function—that is, telephones require that people be present at the same time. Faxes are also images of information requiring all the pertinent information on that paper to be recorded (or keystroked) again for it to be used by the receiving party in their own information systems. A more digital approach would be e-referrals that do not require synchronous communication (although not automatically precluded) and the transmission of information in a digital format that does not need to be keystroked again (Fitch, 2009). In addition, the information and referral Task intersects numerous types of professions, practice fields, and geographical and organizational contexts (Darracott et al., 2019) and has ramifications beyond social work.

Several studies have examined these factors across a range of populations and issues: individuals with dementia and their caregivers, including those living in rural and remote areas (Longstreth et al., 2020); foster youth in kinship care (Rushovich et al., 2017); an early intervention program for at-risk children (Dunst & Bruder, 2002); mental health services for elder LGBTQ+ individuals (Marmo et al., 2021); and smoking cessation (Kegler et al., 2015; Mullen et al., 2016; R. S. Williams et al., 2016). A scoping review of healthcare systems from around the world has shown effectiveness in the use of these technologies with positive benefits in terms of the quantity and quality of referrals along with improved workflow efficiency and productivity (Azamar-Alonso et al., 2019). Specific to Tasks, e-referrals provide the means for any authorized person in the system to be able to view the content of the referral, its status in real time, and the delivery of more timely services. At the community level, practitioners are able to participate more collaboratively with healthcare personnel in care and service coordination, thereby improving overall care planning (Warren et al., 2011).

In contrast to the successful adoption of e-referrals in the healthcare sector, child welfare continues to experience an uneven rollout of this technology. For example, and pertinent to STS, Los Angeles County experienced barriers associated with its technological infrastructure and other workload demands (Dellor et al., 2015). Specifically, not all workers had access to the internet or workstations where meetings were taking place with clients. Regarding workload demands, workers did not believe they could take the time to learn the new system due to the need to respond to emergency cases.

Both problems could be solved through administrative remedies by providing tablets with Wi-Fi access and the time for training on the new system, especially if making timely referrals might reduce future crisis situations. Perhaps building on lessons learned from prior projects, such as Dellor et al.'s (2015), a new project in Ohio is seeking to establish a cross-system intervention involving child welfare agencies and substance use treatment organizations (Bunger et al., 2020). A key component of this rural-based project is the ability to make e-referrals. Specific to barriers encountered in prior research, this project places interorganizational policies related to cross-system collaboration at the forefront. E-referrals, performed by specifically trained personnel, will occur in one system to be distributed to the appropriate agencies (instead of building separate referral systems for each agency). Addressing the STS domains of the policy context (i.e., the Structure of the interorganizational context), worker training, facilitation of tasks, and easy-to-use technology indicate a more likely than not successful outcome, with those results forthcoming.

When issues with e-referrals do arise, rarely is technology the primary problem. For example, in the Dellor et al. (2015) qualitative study, issues with the electronic health record were not mentioned (as they were in Hysong et al., 2011, for example). Instead, all issues could be addressed through administrative remedies—specifically, the need for updated policies, well-defined roles, clarified procedures and protocols, and sufficient personnel. Interestingly, regarding sufficient staffing, the e-referrals system shed light on staffing issues unbeknownst when working with paper-only systems. Conversely, settings that did have sufficient personnel noted improvements in kept follow-up appointments.

As described by Ramanadhan et al. (2020), direct care providers, such as health aides and case managers, are typically at capacity with meeting declared needs, and they have little ability to engage in prevention efforts that they know could decrease the demand for healthcare services. The ideal would be a community–clinical partnership that could address this objective. Ramanadhan and colleagues used social network analysis to explore the factors that facilitated such a partnership along with the barriers that were encountered. Unsurprisingly, referrals, both paper and electronic, were the most significant contributor to the partnership. Pertinent to this chapter were the STS components—specifically, the ability of technology to facilitate the delivery of community services in a timely and efficient manner. As with other studies, the barriers were unrelated to technology. Rather, they centered on training and support, development of new protocols, and sufficient staffing to deliver the services (a point to which we return to later in this chapter). Related to the protocols, concerning was the experience of resistance to the evolution of service delivery. As the community partners became more involved in identifying the need for health services, the very nature of how services needed to be delivered was going to have to change. Confidentiality and privacy issues related to client information that crossed sectors among healthcare providers, community partners, schools, and so forth were challenged because the new amount of information that was being shared had never been previously experienced.

Noteworthy is that in almost all the studies cited, social justice issues were paramount: The service was provided to an underserved or stigmatized population that had difficulty accessing services either due to location or other transportation barriers. Technology also shed light on workforce issues—specifically, role expectations not previously examined and an issue of central focus in cyberfeminism.

Psychoeducation and Health Education

Psychoeducation and health education is the final micro-level practice context that may rise in prominence in coming years. When approached from an analog perspective, psychoeducation and health education can be rather time consuming for the provider because these services present several barriers for the participant in terms of time and place constraints. A more digital or hybrid approach addresses both constraints.

Online psychoeducation with parent management training is a quintessential component of case management for many at-risk families. Using an online psychoeducation group with asynchronous peer support discussion groups, Wilkerson et al. (2020) explored the impact of using both on parenting and oppositional defiant disorder (ODD). The effect size was significant from pretest to posttest for an increase in parental self-agency and a decrease in the likelihood of ODD. Use of asynchronous elements can increase results and encourage more participation if synchronous services are a barrier—for example, reducing stigma barriers by allowing participants to remain anonymous, reducing relationship barriers through the noncoercive nature of participation, and reducing programmatic barriers through an asynchronous online platform that could transcend logistical barriers.

Similarly, web-based psychoeducation was found to be effective with people who experience pathological dissociation (Fung et al., 2020). The small to moderate effect size of the Web-based psychoeducation group was found to decrease comorbid symptoms ($d = .31$) and result in an increase in clinical recovery ($d = .25$). However, there was no significant decrease in dissociative symptoms (effect size $d = .09$). Pertinent to STS, clients could access services online that might not be in their communities, and these online services were found to be cost effective by eliminating or reducing travel costs. The asynchronous delivery meant that more people could be reached and in a timelier manner.

Mezzo-Level Practice: Community Development and Community Organizing

Much of what has already been discussed clearly interfaces with mezzo-level social work. Indeed, most of the articles cited referred to community prevention, collaboration work, interorganizational task forces, and so on. Instead of reiterating those uses in this section, this discussion focuses on the transformative aspects of technology on social work practice at the mezzo level.

One of the original pioneers of social work technology, Walter LaMendola has examined its use over the decades (LaMendola, 1985, 2010, 2019; see also VanDeMark et al., 2010). Specific to mezzo-level work, he found that technology interventions can incorporate different senses of presence, maximize flow, evoke empathy, and increase engagement (LaMendola, 2019). Technology does not have to be a lifeless, cold interface for human interaction. It can enhance human relationality, which is at the core of community development work. By circumnavigating the constraints of time and place, it can be an ideal tool to create human networks that are diverse, disruptive, and persistent. These new practice roles and contexts are the hallmarks of cyberfeminism and portend what some may consider radical social work, a theme to which we return in the conclusion to this chapter.

Perhaps unconstrained by historical modes of practice, social work students recently had to radically adapt to new educational modalities considering COVID-19 restrictions. Nowhere was this impact felt more urgently than in our field education classes. Fortunately, students, together with intrepid instructors, found ways to acquire their practice competencies while still meeting the needs presented in their communities. One such project found students engaged in community development work to address a community-identified need (domestic violence) through meetings and the development of a guide (Davey et al., 2021).

Social media continues to grow in importance as a digital organizing tool (Lee, 2020). Although "community" organizing is constrained by geography, digital organizing allows social workers to organize around issues. Lee (2020) discussed vicarious trauma for macro-level social workers due to exposure to negativity posted on social media, news, and so on. Lee also pointed out that internet technology can be used for community development, such as awareness raising of social issues, community building, activism, and organizing.

Macro-Level Practice

John McNutt has been the longest-running proponent of the use of technology to achieve the goals of equitable social policy. Early on, as the internet began to enter everyday life, McNutt quickly surmised that a digital divide would result and separate those in poverty from the benefits of this technology (McNutt, 1996, 1998). He encouraged social workers to be actively involved in providing education and training on how to use the internet along with providing the means to access technology and the internet. More recently, he has demonstrated how technology can be used to perform all types of macro practice: advocacy, collaboration, citizen empowerment, social justice via Twitter, support of the work of community action agencies, and use of social media for child advocacy, among many other practice illustrations (McNutt, 2018). Cases for the use of technology to achieve macro goals have demonstrated the use of blogs to achieve social justice, mobile apps to access government benefits, and Twitter to facilitate macro communities of practice (Goldkind et al., 2018).

Detailed examples for these practice areas are beyond the scope of this chapter; however, we highlight two notable applications. The first example involves the use of technology to perform advocacy associated with domestic violence. One of the biggest assets of using technology to perform domestic violence work is that it is *spaceless*—that is, geography does not constrain the advocate from performing their work or keep clients—especially those who live in rural or remote areas—from accessing services privately and confidentially (Harris et al., 2020). Harris and colleagues described their collaborative that brought together three Australian agencies: (1) the Women's Services Network, (2) Domestic Violence Resource Centre Victoria, and (3) Women's Legal Service of New South Wales. True to many components of a hybrid approach, the training and services were offered online and in person, depending on the user's situation and needs. Legal policies were updated or revised to accommodate online services, and workers were retrained to use the technology. Most importantly, an app was developed to help survivors collect and store evidence necessary for protection orders and other legal proceedings. Harris discussed broad advocacy goals that can be achieved via Twitter—for instance, #WhyIStayed and #WhyILeft, both of which have had a profound impact on the narratives we associate with domestic violence.

The second example, from Spain, provides empirical evidence on the use of Facebook to support social networking, both in person and online (Castillo de Mesa et al., 2018). As found in studies from other professions, the online world is not a substitute for the in-person world in terms of power and reputation (i.e., online interactions cannot convey power and reputation in the same way face-to-face relationships do). On the other hand, online connections have made for many more opportunities to network and enhance social capital compared with in-person relationships alone. In essence, the ability to network and collaborate when time and distance are not barriers is greatly facilitated through the use of online social networking. Many more case studies on how technology can be used to facilitate macro practice can be found in recent textbooks, such as *Teaching Social Work with Digital Technology* (Hitchcock et al., 2019) and *Digital Social Work: Tools for Practice with Individuals, Organizations, and Communities* (Goldkind et al., 2018).

PRACTICE IMPLICATIONS

Social Justice

As stated at the beginning of this chapter, no social work endeavor is worthwhile unless it achieves the goal of social justice. As such, none of these technology-facilitated or evidence-based practices are possible without internet access for the clients we seek to serve. Indeed, the very people who lack adequate internet access (e.g., low-income households, racial and ethnic minorities, those with lower levels of education, rural/tribal communities) are the primary populations served by social workers (Sanders & Scanlon, 2021). Some U.S. states are taking concrete steps to address this issue, as is illustrated by California's Internet for All Now Act, originally passed in 2017 and signed into law in July 2021. Funding in the amount of $6 billion (about $18 per person in the United States) was made available to leverage private–public partnerships to bring broadband access to these very populations. To find similar initiatives, social workers should consider collaborating with local and national organizing groups (see the National Digital Inclusion Alliance website, https://www.digitalinclusion.org/).

STS

The practice implications discussed thus far are fully in line with the tenets of STS illustrated in Figure 1.1.

As articulated by Pasmore (1995), these practice implications would include the following:

- The practice context affects technology use so that this use cannot be understood divorced from the practice setting. The converse of this tenet is also worth noting: Technology cannot be haphazardly transferred among practice settings if it does not fit the use for which it was intended.

- Noting that the need for "fit" is too paramount and as a reflection of the diverse practice settings in which social work takes place, the resulting complexity dictates that "top–down" hierarchical control is not possible. Control over the design of technology must be driven locally by managers who oversee those domains with input from the end users. The resulting organizational structure should be more "democratic" or pluralistic to meet both the end user's and client's needs.

- The corollary to this tenet then becomes obvious: "Teams are a viable basic building block for organizational design in many instances" (Pasmore, 1995, p. 16). Such an assertion should be obvious to social workers who practice in emerging or complex situations. Interdisciplinary teams are the go-to Structure for meeting difficult to achieve objectives.

Figure 1.1: Illustration of STS Tenets

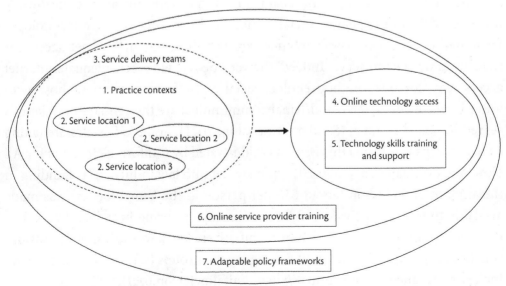

- Likewise, any technology designed to serve the needs of those teams should be flexible and adaptable beyond the scope of any one agency.

- Being adaptable requires learning new skills that may lead to new types of positions being created.

The COVID-19 pandemic that emerged in 2020 required numerous adaptations to the service delivery system, with many services and programming moving to virtual delivery. In retrospect, many of the adaptations that were spurred on by the pandemic should have occurred much sooner, such as the delivery of online therapy. However, organizations' penchant to maintain the status quo prevented such an adaptation, even though it is now clear that doing so before the pandemic would have made the pandemic transition more seamless. Anticipating such, Pasmore (1995) went on:

- Any such change also requires evolving changes in the support systems that make such a change sustainable. As we previously discussed, service provider training in the delivery of services has to be matched by the provision of changes in broadband access along with security or privacy enhancements to the technology used.

- Many COVID-19 innovations occurred before policy was even written, demonstrating that meeting client needs is not entirely dependent on "hierarchical arrangements being in place" (Pasmore, 1995, p. 16) before the innovation occurs.

- Most importantly, "organizations must develop evolutionary competence, which permits design arrangements to change as the system matures" (Pasmore, 1995, p. 16). Simply put, adherence to these STS principles means that social workers and the agencies in which they are employed must evolve as the social environment in which human behavior occurs evolves and develops. Having the technology tools necessary to fit the Tasks in those new contexts needs to be designed by the users of those tools, and social workers are best situated to provide input on those designs.

As mentioned in Ramanadhan et al. (2020), funding for prevention services can be problematic if they are not directly linked to "billable hours," the lifeblood for many organizations. However, due to COVID-19, Medicare, Medicaid, and many commercial providers recognized virtual visits as billable hours, resulting in increased billings (Cooper & Zerden, 2021). Whether alternative funding strategies become more commonplace (e.g., medical care homes, value-based healthcare), it is most important to remember that it was the use of technology that shed light on what could be achieved at the interorganizational or community level. Furthermore, practicing across state or jurisdictional boundaries is not necessarily prohibited. Specific steps on how to do so can be found in Barsky (2017).

Truly communicating and collaborating across practice sectors through integrating data can lead to new theoretical insights, practice innovations, policy redesign, and research initiatives. Rarely are technology issues the roadblock to serving clients during these demanding times when virtual and hybrid modalities are in clear demand. Instead, practitioners are oftentimes confronted by policy barriers that preclude collaboration via the sharing of information (Franceschini et al., 2021; Ramanadhan et al., 2020). Either through not understanding how data can be encrypted and protected or a blind allegiance to how things have always been done, today's leaders and administrators should instead be obligated to stay ahead of the curve, listen to practitioners, and provide them the permission they need via policies and procedures to get the job done. Specific steps on how agencies should approach their use technology should include policies on information access, security and encryption, procedures for information breaches, the use of social media, and information system backups (Barsky, 2017).

CONCLUSION

If one were to take all these radical approaches together, thereby disrupting traditional social work practice, by definition, one could assert that the practice of social work would be "revolutionized" with the goal of breaking down practice structures into service delivery that is more client centered and context sensitive. By deconstructing hierarchical roles and power structures, social work services can be provided from a place of equity and representation. This breaking down (but not throwing away) and recontextualizing of social work practice, the roles whereby individuals engage in such practice, and the policies by which they operate must be imperative for social work, moving forward. As noted by López Peláez (2018):

> Changing realities mean social work must assess and diagnose problems and carry out interventions in a different way. Indeed, the advent of the internet and social media has revolutionized the way people communicate and social work users should recognize the fact that the use of verbal and written communication has radically changed their jobs. (pp. 814–815)

To wit, perhaps it is time for a new job title: cyberfeminist social worker.

REFERENCES

Azamar-Alonso, A., Costa, A. P., Huebner, L.-A., & Tarride, J.-E. (2019). Electronic referral systems in health care: A scoping review. *ClinicoEconomics and Outcomes Research, 11*, 325–333. https://doi.org/10.2147/CEOR.S195597

Barsky, A. E. (2017). Social work practice and technology: Ethical issues and policy responses. *Journal of Technology in Human Services, 35*, 8–19.

Berryhill, M. B., Culmer, N., Williams, N., Halli-Tierney, A., Betancourt, A., Roberts, H., & King, M. (2018). Videoconferencing psychotherapy and depression: A systematic review. *Telemedicine and e-Health, 25*, 435–446. https://doi.org/10.1089/tmj.2018.0058

Braidotti, R. (2003). Cyberfeminism with a difference. In M. Peters, M. Olssen, & C. Lankshear (Eds.), *Futures of critical theory: Dreams of difference* (pp. 239–259). Rowman & Littlefield.

Bunger, A. C., Chuang, E., Girth, A., Lancaster, K. E., Gadel, F., Himmeger, M., Saldana, L., Powell, B. J., & Aarons, G. A. (2020). Establishing cross-systems collaborations for implementation: Protocol for a longitudinal mixed methods study. *Implementation Science, 15*, Article 55. https://doi.org/10.1186/s13012-020-01016-9

Castillo de Mesa, J., de las Olas Palma García, M., & Gómez Jacinto, L. (2018). Analysis of social innovation on social networking services. *European Journal of Social Work, 21*, 902–915. https://doi.org/10.1080/13691457.2018.1461067

Chan, S., Li, L., Torous, J., Gratzer, D., & Yellowlees, P. M. (2018). Review of use of asynchronous technologies incorporated in mental health care. *Current Psychiatry Reports, 20*, Article 85. https://doi.org/10.1007/s11920-018-0954-3

Chatterjee, B. B. (2002). Razorgirls and cyberdykes: Tracing cyberfeminism and thoughts on its use in a legal context. *International Journal of Sexuality and Gender Studies, 7*, 197–213.

Clegg, C., Ellis, B., Wyatt, J., Elliott, B., Sinclair, M., & Wastell, D. (2011). *A manifesto for a socio-technical approach to NHS and social care IT–enabled business change—To deliver effective high quality health and social care for all.* University of Central Lancashire. http://clok.uclan.ac.uk/2239/1/Ellis_B_ST_Manifesto_26_08_10.pdf

Cooper, Z., & Zerden, L. de S. (2021). How COVID-19 has impacted integrated care practice: Lessons from the frontlines. *Social Work in Health Care, 60*, 146–156. https://doi.org/10.1080/00981389.2021.1904316

Cornell, P. Y., Celardo, C., Chmelka, G., Giles, A. J., Halladay, C. W., Halaszynski, J., Montano, A.-R., Rudolph, J. L., & Silva, J. W. (2021). Social work and telehealth: How Patient Aligned Care Team (PACT) social workers in the Veterans Health Administration responded to COVID-19. *Social Work in Health Care, 60*, 131–145.

Cristofalo, M. A. (2021). Telehealth, friend and foe for health care social work. *Qualitative Social Work, 20,* 399–403.

Darracott, R., Lonne, B., Cheers, B., & Wagner, I. (2019). The influences on practice in social care: An Australian study. *Human Service Organizations: Management, Leadership & Governance, 43,* 16–40. https://doi.org/10.1080/23303131.2018.1564713

Davey, J.-B., Collingwood, H., Croaker, S., Grentell, M., Rytkonen, F., & Zuchowski, I. (2021). Using a community development approach to reimagine field education during COVID-19. *Advances in Social Work and Welfare Education, 22,* 56–68.

Dearinger, A. T. (2020). COVID-19 reveals emerging opportunities for rural public health. *American Journal of Public Health, 110,* 1277–1278. https://doi.org/10.2105/AJPH.2020.305864

Dellor, E., Lovato-Hermann, K., Wolf, J. P., Curry, S. R., & Freisthler, B. (2015). Introducing technology in child welfare referrals: A case study. *Journal of Technology in Human Services, 33,* 330–344. https://doi.org/10.1080/15228835.2015.1107520

Diagram/schematic of theory. (2016, March 20). In *Wikipedia.* https://is.theorizeit.org/wiki/Socio-technical_theory

Dunst, C. J., & Bruder, M. B. (2002). Valued outcomes of service coordination, early intervention, and natural environments. *Exceptional Children, 68,* 361–375.

Fernandez, E., Woldgabreal, Y., Day, A., Pham, T., Gleich, B., & Aboujaoude, E. (2021). Live psychotherapy by video versus in-person: A meta-analysis of efficacy and its relationship to types and targets of treatment. *Clinical Psychology & Psychotherapy, 28,* 1535–1549. https://doi.org/10.1002/cpp.2594

Fish, J. N., McInroy, L. B., Paceley, M. S., Williams, N. D., Henderson, S., Levine, D. S., & Edsall, R. N. (2020). "I'm kinda stuck at home with unsupportive parents right now": LGBTQ youths' experiences with COVID-19 and the importance of online support. *Journal of Adolescent Health, 67,* 450–452. https://doi.org/10.1016/j.jadohealth.2020.06.002

Fitch, D. (2009). A shared point of access to facilitate interagency collaboration. *Administration in Social Work, 33,* 186–201.

Fitzmaurice, J. M. (1998). Telehealth research and evaluation: Implications for decision makers. *Proceedings Pacific Medical Technology Symposium-PACMEDTek. Transcending Time, Distance and Structural Barriers* (Cat. No.98EX211), 344–352. https://doi.org/10.1109/PACMED.1998.769954

Franceschini, D., Grabowski, J., Sefilyan, E., Moro, T. T., & Ewald, B. (2021). Covid-19: A critical time for cross-sector social work care management. *Social Work in Health Care, 60,* 197–207. https://doi.org/10.1080/00981389.2021.1904319

Fung, H. W., Chan, C., & Ross, C. A. (2020). A Web-based psychoeducation program for people with pathological dissociation: Development and pilot testing. *Journal of Evidence-Based Social Work, 17*, 427–442. https://doi.org/10.1080/26408066.2020.1760990

Gellis, Z. D., Kenaley, B. L., & Have, T. T. (2014). Integrated telehealth care for chronic illness and depression in geriatric home care patients: The Integrated Telehealth Education and Activation of Mood (I-TEAM) study. *Journal of the American Geriatrics Society, 62*, 889–895.

Glenn, L. (2020, August–September). *Telecounseling turns a corner: What COVID shutdowns have wrought for remote practice.* https://www.socialworkers.org/News/Social-Work-Advocates/2020-August-September/Telecounseling-Turns-a-Corner

Goldkind, L., Wolf, L., & Freddolino, P. P. (2018). *Digital social work: Tools for practice with individuals, organizations, and communities.* Oxford University Press.

Hall, K. (1996). Cyberfeminism. In S. C. Herring (Ed.), *Computer-mediated communication: Linguistic, social and cross-cultural perspectives* (pp. 147–172). John Benjamins Publishing Company.

Haraway, D. (1990). A manifesto for cyborgs: Science, technology, and socialist feminism in the 1980s. In L. Nicholson (Ed.), *Feminism/postmodernism* (pp. 190–233). Routledge.

Harris, B., Dragiewicz, M., & Woodlock, D. (2020). Technology, domestic violence advocacy and the sustainable development goals. In J. Blaustein, K. Fitz-Gibbon, N. W. Pino, & R. White (Eds.), *The Emerald handbook of crime, justice and sustainable development* (pp. 295–313). Emerald Publishing.

Health Insurance Portability and Accountability Act of 1996, Pub. L. 104-191, 42 U.S.C. § 300gg, 29 U.S.C. §§ 1181–1183, and 42 U.S.C. §§ 1320d–1320d9.

Hernandez, R., Burrows, B., Wilund, K., Cohn, M., Xu, S., & Moskowitz, J. T. (2018). Feasibility of an internet-based positive psychological intervention for hemodialysis patients with symptoms of depression. *Social Work in Health Care, 57*, 864–879. https://doi.org/10.1080/00981389.2018.1523268

Hitchcock, L. I., Sage, M., & Smyth, N. J. (2019). *Teaching social work with digital technology.* Council on Social Work Education Press.

Hysong, S. J., Esquivel, A., Sittig, D. F., Paul, L. A., Espadas, D., Singh, S., & Singh, H. (2011). Towards successful coordination of electronic health record based-referrals: A qualitative analysis. *Implementation Science, 6*, Article 84. https://doi.org/10.1186/1748-5908-6-84

Internet for All Now Act, no. SB 156, California State Legislature (2021). https://leginfo.legislature.ca.gov/faces/billNavClient.xhtml?bill_id=202120220SB156

Ip, P., Chim, D., Chan, K. L., Li, T. M. H., Ho, F. K. W., Voorhees, B. W. V., Tiwari, A., Tsang, A., Chan, C. W. L., Ho, M., Tso, W., & Wong, W. H. S. (2016). Effectiveness of a culturally attuned Internet-based depression prevention program for Chinese adolescents: A randomized controlled trial. *Depression and Anxiety, 33*, 1123–1131. https://doi.org/10.1002/da.22554

Jaffe, D. H., Lee, L., Huynh, S., & Haskell, T. P. (2020). Health inequalities in the use of telehealth in the United States in the lens of COVID-19. *Population Health Management, 23*, 368–377. https://doi.org/10.1089/pop.2020.0186

Kegler, M. C., Bundy, L., Haardörfer, R., Escoffery, C., Berg, C., Yembra, D., Kreuter, M., Hovell, M., Williams, R., Mullen, P. D., Ribisl, K., & Burnham, D. (2015). A minimal intervention to promote smoke-free homes among 2-1-1 callers: A randomized controlled trial. *American Journal of Public Health, 105*, 530–537. https://doi.org/10.2105/AJPH.2014.302260

LaMendola, W. (1985). The future of human service information technology: An essay on the number 42. *Computers in Human Services, 1*, 35–49.

LaMendola, W. (2010). Social work and social presence in an online world. *Journal of Technology in Human Services, 28*, 108–119. https://doi.org/10.1080/1522883 1003759562

LaMendola, W. (2019). Social work, social technologies, and sustainable community development. *Journal of Technology in Human Services, 37*, 79–92. https://doi.org /10.1080/15228835.2018.1552905

Larsen, K. R., & Eargle, D. (Eds.). (n.d.). *Theories used in IS Research Wiki*. Retrieved August 15, 2022, from http://IS.TheorizeIt.org

Lee, S. C. (2020). Social work and social media: Organizing in the digital age. *Journal of Public Health Issues and Practices, 4*, Article JPHIP-158. https://doi.org/10.33790/ jphip1100158

List, R., Compton, M., Soper, M., Bruschwein, H., Gettle, L., Bailey, M., Starheim, E., Kalmanek, J., Somerville, L., & Albon, D. (2021). Preserving multidisciplinary care model and patient safety during reopening of ambulatory cystic fibrosis clinic for nonurgent care: A hybrid telehealth model. *Telemedicine and e-Health, 27*, 193–199.

Longstreth, M., McKibbin, C., Steinman, B., Slosser Worth, A., & Carrico, C. (2020). Exploring information and referral needs of individuals with dementias and informal caregivers in rural and remote areas. *Clinical Gerontologist, 45*, 808–820. https://doi.org/10.1080/07317115.2019.1710735

López Peláez, A., Pérez García, R., & Aguilar-Tablada Massó, M. V. (2018). e-Social work: Building a new field of specialization in social work? *European Journal of Social Work, 21*, 804–823.

Marmo, S., Pardasani, M., & Vincent, D. (2021). Senior centers and LGBTQ participants: Engaging older adults virtually in a pandemic. *Journal of Gerontological Social Work, 64*, 864–884. https://doi.org/10.1080/01634372.2021.1937431

McNutt, J. (1996). National information infrastructure policy and the future of the American welfare state: Implications for the social welfare policy curriculum. *Journal of Social Work Education, 32*, 375–388.

McNutt, J. (1998). Ensuring social justice for the new underclass: Community interventions to meet the needs of the new poor. In B. Ebo (Ed.), *Cyberghetto or cybertopia: Race, class, gender and marginalization in cyberspace* (pp. 33–44). Praeger.

McNutt, J. (2018). *Technology, activism, and social justice in a digital age.* Oxford University Press.

Mullen, P. D., Savas, L. S., Bundy, L. T., Haardörfer, R., Hovell, M., Fernández, M. E., Monroy, J. A. A., Williams, R. S., Kreuter, M. W., Jobe, D., & Kegler, M. C. (2016). Minimal intervention delivered by 2-1-1 information and referral specialists promotes smoke-free homes among 2-1-1 callers: A Texas generalisation trial. *Tobacco Control, 25*, i10–i18.

Mumford, E. (2000). A socio-technical approach to systems design. *Requirements Engineering, 5*, 125–133. https://doi.org/10.1007/PL00010345

Pasmore, W. A. (1995). Social science transformed: The socio-technical perspective. *Human Relations, 48*, 1–21. https://doi.org/10.1177/001872679504800101

Ramanadhan, S., Daly, J., Lee, R. M., Kruse, G. R., & Deutsch, C. (2020). Network-based delivery and sustainment of evidence-based prevention in community-clinical partnerships addressing health equity: A qualitative exploration. *Frontiers in Public Health, 8*, Article 213. https://doi.org/10.3389/fpubh.2020.00213

Resnick, B. (2020, September 18). *How the pandemic forced mental health care to change for the better.* Vox. https://www.vox.com/science-and-health/21427156/what-is-teletherapy-mental-health-online-pandemic

Rushovich, B. R., Murray, K. W., Woodruff, K., & Freeman, P. C. (2017). A kinship navigator program: A comprehensive approach to support private and voluntary kinship caregivers. *Child Welfare, 95*, 111–131.

Sanders, C. K., & Scanlon, E. (2021). The digital divide is a human rights issue: Advancing social inclusion through social work advocacy. *Journal of Human Rights and Social Work, 6*, 130–143. https://doi.org/10.1007/s41134-020-00147-9

Sieck, C. J., Sheon, A., Ancker, J. S., Castek, J., Callahan, B., & Siefer, A. (2021). Digital inclusion as a social determinant of health. *npj Digital Medicine, 4*, Article 52. https://doi.org/10.1038/s41746-021-00413-8

Sklar, M., Reeder, K., Carandang, K., Ehrhart, M. G., & Aarons, G. A. (2020). *An observational study of the impact of COVID-19 and the transition to telehealth on community mental health center providers.* Research Square. https://doi .org/10.21203/rs.3.rs-48767/v1

Stamm, B. H. (1998). Clinical applications of telehealth in mental health care. *Professional Psychology: Research and Practice, 29,* 536–542. https://doi.org/10 .1037/0735-7028.29.6.536

Sweetman, A., Knieriemen, A., Hoon, E., Frank, O., Stocks, N., Natsky, A., Kaambwa, B., Vakulin, A., Lovato, N., Adams, R., Lack, L., Miller, C. B., Espie, C. A., & McEvoy, R. D. (2021). Implementation of a digital cognitive behavioral therapy for insomnia pathway in primary care. *Contemporary Clinical Trials, 107,* Article 106484.

Tomczyk, Ł., Eliseo, M. A., Costas, V., Sánchez, G., Silveira, I. F., Barros, M.-J., Amado-Salvatierra, H. R., & Oyelere, S. S. (2019). Digital divide in Latin America and Europe: Main characteristics in selected countries. *2019 14th Iberian Conference on Information Systems and Technologies (CISTI),* 1–6. https://doi.org/10.23919/CISTI.2019.8760821

VanDeMark, N. R., Burrell, N. R., LaMendola, W. F., Hoich, C. A., Berg, N. P., & Medina, E. (2010). An exploratory study of engagement in a technology-supported substance abuse intervention. *Substance Abuse Treatment, Prevention, and Policy, 5,* Article 10.

Warren, J., White, S., Day, K., Gu, Y., & Pollock, M. (2011). Introduction of electronic referral from community associated with more timely review by secondary services. *Applied Clinical Informatics, 2,* 546–564. https://doi.org/10.4338/ACI-2 011-06-RA-0039

Wilkerson, D. A., Gregory, V. L., & Kim, H. (2020). Online psychoeducation with parent management training: Examining the contribution of peer support. *Child & Family Social Work, 25,* 448–459. https://doi.org/10.1111/cfs.12701

Williams, K., Fildes, D., Kobel, C., Grootemaat, P., Bradford, S., & Gordon, R. (2021). Evaluation of outcomes for help seekers accessing a pilot SMS-based crisis intervention service in Australia. *Crisis, 42,* 32–39. https://doi.org/10.1027/0227-5910/a000681

Williams, R. S., Stollings, J. H., Bundy, L., Haardörfer, R., Kreuter, M. W., Mullen, P. D., Hovell, M., Morris, M., & Kegler, M. C. (2016). A minimal intervention to promote smoke-free homes among 2-1-1 callers: North Carolina randomized effectiveness trial. *PLOS One, 11,* Article e0165086.

Yellowlees, P. M., Parish, M. B., Gonzalez, A. D., Chan, S. R., Hilty, D. M., Yoo, B.-K., Leigh, P., McCarron, R. M., Scher, L. M., Sciolla, A. F., Shore, J., Xiong, G., Soltero, K. M., Fisher, A., Fine, J. R., Bannister, J., & Iosif, A.-M. (2021). Clinical outcomes of asynchronous versus synchronous telepsychiatry in primary care: A randomized controlled trial. *Journal of Medical Internet Research, 23,* Article e24047. https://doi.org/10.2196/24047

CHAPTER 2

A Team-Based Approach to Moderating Online Support Groups

Liam O'Sullivan and David A. Wilkerson

It was March 18, 2020, Dublin, Ireland, and Charlotte wondered if her struggles with caring for her aging mother were getting to be too much. St. Patrick's Day this year was a bit of a damp squib—a dud. No parade. Public health restrictions. No crowds. COVID-19 had arrived, and a countrywide lockdown had been mandated. The dementia day care center that Charlotte relied on was closed. Those few hours of respite three days a week were going to be hard to lose! She would also lose the two hours of home care her mother was due to get later that week.

Charlotte used social media too much, she thought, but it kept her connected while at home with her mom. She used to work in accountancy, leading a team of male accountants that she considered to be undermotivated and entitled. That was before her mom needed her. Right after the lockdown, she saw a post about a new group on Facebook: the Online Family Caregiver Support Group. "Join Now," it said. The group asked three questions. She applied. Her application was accepted within three hours. She posted a question. She waited to see if it would be approved by the moderators:

> Hi everyone—thanks for accepting me into the group. I care for my mom who has multiple health conditions including vascular dementia. I'm scared that she will get COVID. I've also been struggling for a while now with my own mental health. Sometimes, I feel like just staying in bed all day and leaving mom there too. Just for a day or two—until I get my energy back. My two brothers don't get it. They think I just sit with mom and drink tea all day. If they only knew. Sorry about the rant.

Mary, a moderator for the Online Family Caregiver Support Group, had been a family caregiver in the past and done some advocacy work for a nonprofit. She jumped at the chance to volunteer when invited. She'd been part of online communities for several years and was an active contributor in several. However, when she read Charlotte's post, she felt uncomfortable approving it. How would the other caregivers respond? Mary posted on the "mods and vols" (moderators and volunteers) private Facebook group: "Should we approve this post, guys? This lady seems quite distressed!" She thought John would know. He was on the volunteer roster today and was a professional social worker.

John led a team of social workers in intellectual disability services. He was a huge fan of social work's growing use of information and communication technology (ICT). However, his team at work was reluctant to embrace technology. So, like Mary, he joined the Online Family Caregiver Support Group's mods and vols private Facebook group when invited. He knew about the power of online communities and why people with chronic health conditions used them. He knew that some of his own family members used them, too. John wasn't sure about Charlotte's post, either. But he knew people were scared, and her post reflected growing COVID-19 fears—not just online and not just in the family caregiver community. He wasn't sleeping well. He wondered:

> Would approving the post add to other members' anxiety? Should one of the volunteers send a private message to Charlotte? What about confidentiality? Should we put in a call to the local mental health services after hours team? Where does Charlotte live? Do we have her address? Maybe I'm not cut out for this type of thing—is it really social work?

AN IRISH ONLINE FAMILY CAREGIVER
SUPPORT PROGRAM

Charlotte, Mary, and John represent the voices of a user, a nonprofessional caregiver moderator, and a professional moderator, respectively, in an online family caregiver support program that was created almost overnight by a small nonprofit Irish social services organization. The program was initiated in March 2020, following the Republic of Ireland's nationwide COVID-19 lockdown that abruptly halted the delivery of many traditional social services that family caregivers depended on. This chapter describes the development, delivery, and management of this program. The program illustrates the impact that online communities of interest can have for those who are underserved and/or marginalized. Its suite of support activities and team-based approach to moderation illustrate an important opportunity for social work and other helping professions to improve outcomes for those populations through the cost-effective use of technology.

At the time of this writing, operations of the group continue, and the program has proven to be sustainable. I (L. O'S.) led the development of the online family caregiver support program, so discussion is situated by my leadership role within the program's founding nonprofit social services organization.

Emergence of Online Support

To support is defined as "(1) to promote the interests or cause of; (2) to uphold or defend as valid or right" (Merriam-Webster, n.d.). The delivery of support has a long and proud history of usage within the field of social work to advocate for marginalized, oppressed, and underserved populations. More recently, harnessing technology for social good through online communities has resulted in the delivery of new forms of support and participatory action, as in the example of crowdsourcing:

> Virtual communities and social media platforms provide new opportunities to engage wider networks of support and the "crowd" role in problem-solving. Having ready access to the lived experiences of consumers relocates the center of authority from social work professionals to people who are the traditional consumers of social services. The availability of such stories paves the way for new approaches to collaborative problem-solving. (Berzin et al., 2015, p. 12)

These new forms of support began early in the history of the internet, when online forums established themselves as a new method to bring together those with a common interest. However, their original reach was modest (Morzy, 2013). Fast forward to the early 2020s: Now an abundance of online platforms are available that offer the potential to deliver impactful and positive outcomes for those who use them.

The language describing support programs has also evolved over the years, and now the term "communities" is most widely used where the program's main purpose is online support. Online support communities use custom or commercial ICT platforms with varying degrees of functionality. Some have apps that improve task performance with a smartphone. Some have been specifically established to provide private, professionally moderated support. Some have significant subscription costs, usually borne by the provider. Some, such as Facebook, are free, with advertising providing the income stream. Where online support exists as an adjunct to other activities, like psychoeducation, it is often referred to as a "forum."

Overall, the most robust ICT platforms can integrate synchronous (same time) and asynchronous (any time) technologies for interaction. They can include live video inputs, sharing of informational and emotional resources, scheduled virtual drop-ins, and opportunities to post questions that seek the expertise of members' shared experience. Many platforms also enable the grouping of similar posts into "topics," which can reduce repetition. The platforms can be public, private, or secret. Access and membership may be managed by a moderator and include clear membership criteria.

Beginning in October 2008, Facebook grew into the largest and most influential online communities medium (Iqbal, 2021). In October 2020, Facebook reported that 1.8 billion people used their "groups" platform every month and that there were tens of millions of "active communities" (Omnicore, 2021; see also Facebook, 2021). The same report (Omnicore, 2021) stated that 46 percent of Americans identified their most important group as being online. This represents considerable reach, and similar impact has also been reported at a global level with 2.8 billion Facebook users in 2020 (Iqbal, 2021).

While there is growing research on the use of Facebook group communities by family caregivers as well as by persons experiencing disabilities, medical conditions, mental health disorders, and social marginalization (Athanasiadis et al., 2021; Bender et al., 2011; Frost & Rickwood, 2017; Parker Oliver et al., 2014; Pendry & Salvatore, 2015; Stetten et al., 2019; Zhang, 2018), research or gray literature on the development, delivery, and management of Facebook communities is limited.

Backdrop to Creation of the Online Family Caregiver Support Program

Formal and long-term government policy in Ireland supports a large array of nonprofit organizations that deliver services with a focus on addressing poverty, preventing social exclusion, and promoting equality. The impact of Ireland's countrywide COVID-19 lockdown on family caregivers included the loss of critical social services, such as respite care, day care, special educational support, and— most relevant for some—caregiver support groups (Family Carers Ireland, 2020).

Following the COVID lockdown, as an activist and as a leader of a small not-for-profit whose business was to support family caregivers, I (L. O'S.) could not stand by and watch Ireland's family caregivers' house of cards fall. Literally, over a weekend, with the fulsome support and commitment of my colleague, and with oversight by my board of directors, we bit the bullet and decided to set up a private group using the Facebook platform.

Concern for the welfare of family caregivers initiated the decision to develop the online family caregiver support program almost immediately following the onset of COVID-19. What was remarkable about the decision to create an online family caregiver support program was that, historically, the agency was not a direct service provider, nor did it have a dedicated social work practitioner workforce. However, it did have two staff members with social work backgrounds and training as well as relationships with a network of social service providers, many of whom were collaborators in caregiver advocacy.

In addition, both agency staff members had significant experience with social media, particularly the use of Facebook for caregiver advocacy (O'Sullivan & Hughes, 2019). Beginning in 2012, they worked within their organization to coordinate Ireland's yearly online National Carers Week campaign and create a Facebook page to focus awareness on the event and the work of Irish family caregivers. Their online work was also guided by their nonprofit organization's strategic plan, which included the delivery of innovative online interventions to support family caregivers.

BUILDING THE PROGRAM

Based on their experience with social media, the program developers chose Facebook as the online platform for communications partly because of its widespread use by adults in Ireland, particularly those within the family caregiver demographic (Leonard, 2018). In addition, the program developers identified the number of online caregiver support groups operating within the Facebook platform in Ireland at the time. Only a few private groups were discovered (i.e., access was limited to current family caregivers). This limited the program developers' ability to assess the groups' operations. However, they did find that the groups served a limited population that addressed a specific demographic and health condition, and none appeared to include a team-based moderation approach.

Moderation

In more fluid online communities, as opposed to formal traditional groups, members can seek immediate support for a specific issue by posting a question for other members to offer guidance, validate experiences, or provide solace. Online support communities can be professionally moderated or entirely self-moderated. While many online support communities opt to self-moderate, a system of rules and approval processes for members' posts are often established. Nonprofit organizations appear to be the lead agencies for many of these more structured online communities and often focus on specific health conditions like smoking cessation or diabetes management. These agency-sponsored interventions implement their organizations' overall mission and seek to set the group's tone and, to a lesser degree, content focus. They also help members develop social media literacy and provide a level of individual protection from third parties that seek to obtain private information without an individual's knowledge. The moderation team, which often includes volunteers, also generally clarifies health misinformation and informs members of other reputable organizations and resources.

The program developers determined that team-based moderation, which included a mix of professional (unpaid social workers) and nonprofessional (family caregivers) volunteers, was essential for a sustainable online support program. In part, this was because the developers and their nonprofit did not have a workforce dedicated to direct service delivery and because daily and weekend moderation would be needed to adequately support these caregivers. The importance of moderation is informed by Cohen and McKay's (1984) seminal work on the four mechanisms of social support: (1) informational support, (2) emotional support, (3) tangible support, and (4) appraisal.

Mechanisms of Social Support

Informational support includes more than educational content. Moderators assess the appropriateness of posted content and delete content that may exploit group members or that is clearly outside the group's purpose.

Moderators can strengthen *emotional support*, which includes self-esteem and belonging, by welcoming and connecting new members with the group. Moderators can also participate in the development and maintenance of activities like book clubs, topic discussions, and other structured activities that help build group identity. Moderation can also temper the potential adverse effects of sharing feelings (Helgeson & Gottlieb, 2000). Moderators can assess and intervene when negative feelings create contagions that increase stress or interfere with solution-focused coping.

Moderators can improve *tangible support* by identifying new resources or providing referrals for services, such as mental health consultations. Other examples of tangible support include providing items or products to facilitate participation in supplemental activities (e.g., providing books for a book club).

Appraisal is the fourth social support mechanism and refers to self-appraisal. Essential to this mechanism is the observance of "similar others" or "coping models" (Bandura, 1997) who demonstrate the importance of persistence and effort when facing setbacks. Online group membership provides opportunities for interacting with coping models through open forum discussions and structured group activities. Nonprofessional volunteer moderators can become important coping models since they participate at a peer-to-peer level; by sharing their experiences, models provide a relational element to other users. Group participants can vicariously experience a sense of control when volunteers discuss their own mistakes, setbacks, and eventual successes. The program developers first observed the impact of peer coping models during yearly, online National Carers Week campaigns, when nonprofessional volunteers discussed their experiences at events and with the national and local media. Family caregivers highly rated these presentations and noted their appreciation for presenters' relational qualities, such as sincerity, shared experience, and optimism.

A TEAM-BASED MODERATION APPROACH

The program developers initially recruited a group of six professional social work volunteers to moderate the program. These volunteers were selected based on their knowledge of caring across the life course of four groups: (1) older adults, (2) people with dementia, (3) people with mental health support needs, and (4) children with special needs. Some of them had become limited in their ability to deliver services through their employment due to the COVID-19 lockdown, making them available to volunteer for this project.

Following a two-month observation period and based on the demands of daily group moderation and the need for additional mechanisms of social support, the program developers recruited six nonprofessional moderators. Nonprofessional moderators were members of the family caregiver program who were chosen based on their participation, interaction, and ability to serve as coping models for other caregiver group members.

The impact of nonprofessional volunteers was identified by Metz and colleagues (2017) in their comparison of the differences between paid professionals and unpaid volunteers for recipients of social services. They defined *unpaid volunteers* as "individuals who donate their time, skills, or services to an agency or organization without obligation and without receiving direct financial compensation for their work" (p. 155). Nonprofessional volunteers were found to surpass paid professionals in their ability to form meaningful relationships with social services recipients. Meaningful relationships included the qualities of sincerity, flexibility, equality, and affective trust such that recipients did not feel judged.

Metz and colleagues' (2017) research aligned with the online family caregiver support program's mix of nonprofessional and professional volunteers in its team-based moderation approach. While nonprofessionals excelled at the development of meaningful relationships, paid professionals excelled in evoking cognitive trust in which recipients found informational content to be of greater value. For this reason, the program developers determined that including nonprofessional and professional volunteers in a team-based moderation approach was the most effective way to deliver informational support, emotional support, tangible support, and appraisal. Over time, program developers recruited additional professional and nonprofessional volunteers.

Program Operations

Clear roles and responsibilities were established for program developers and volunteer moderators (see Table 2.1). Program developers were responsible for creating the program's basic architecture; managing ongoing program development; and approving, editing, or closing member posts. Moderators responded to member posts and shared resources, flagged posts that had content of concern, welcomed new members, and contributed mindfulness or wellness posts. The moderator's mods and vols private Facebook space facilitated collaboration and cloud storage of useful documents, such as suggested templates for responses, moderator meeting minutes, and moderation timetables.

Moderator Team Communications

The moderator team's communications occurred in asynchronous and synchronous online spaces. Moderators used a private Facebook group (mods and vols) for daily, asynchronous communications and the Zoom teleconferencing platform for biweekly, synchronous meetings. These meetings were recorded for those who could not attend.

Asynchronous Communications

The moderator team's mods and vols group provided a persistent space for daily communication. Professional and nonprofessional moderators exhibited no significant differences in their posting activity after the first few months: Frequency was similar, averaging two to three posts per day and six comments per post. All moderators regularly engaged, and humor was often used to build relationships and deal with challenging situations that occurred within the Online Family Caregiver Support Group.

Table 2.1: Joint Display of Program Developer and Moderator Activities

ROLES AND RESPONSIBILITIES	
Staff (1 Full-Time, 3 Part-Time)	Volunteers (*n* = 12)
• Consider/approve/negotiate membership requests. • Approve new posts. • Close comments on posts. • Negotiate editing of comments or remove comments. • Remove members. • Recruit, manage, and support volunteers. • Send individual one-on-one online private messaging to family caregivers who are exhibiting significant distress. • Arrange monthly online meetings and prepare agenda. • Be a signpost to other supports and collaboration with nonprofits. • Update template responses for various volunteer–caregiver communications. • Organize external expert video inputs/Q&As. • Liaise with academics, prepare journal articles, fundraise for the project. • Arrange quizzes, book club, competitions, and other engagement activities.	• Welcome new members. • Review comments in posts or flag for moderators. • Highlight issues of concern. • Develop and deliver regular mindfulness, wellness, cookery posts. • Comment on posts (in light of personal experience). • Share resources and information in the mods and vols group relevant to their areas of expertise. • Participate in regular online meetings. • Support with delivery of regular events (e.g., gardening club, coffee mornings). • Provide specific information (e.g., income support, condition-specific).

Notes: Q&As = question-and-answer sessions; mod and vols = moderators and volunteers.

The moderator team's private Facebook group was also used for informational, planning, and practice communications. *Informational communications* included caregiving updates (e.g., COVID-19 health guidelines); operational infographics; and moderation resources, such as how to share a video in a Zoom call and how to livestream into Facebook from Zoom. Other informational communications included suggested response templates (updated regularly) for frequently asked questions within the family caregiver group and Zoom meeting agendas and meeting minutes.

Planning communications included rotation schedules for moderators, which were pinned at the top of the moderator team's private Facebook group.

Each moderator committed to perform activities on a given day like reviewing suggested posts, welcoming new members, and observing or leading support group activities. Ideas for new structured group activities were also shared and resulted in a series of weekly and monthly events that family caregivers could participate in.

Practice communications included sharing participant feedback from the family caregiver group. That feedback was used to modify or improve moderation; determine team decision-making processes for whether to approve a post (this was initially a responsibility of program developers, but moderators began fulfilling this responsibility as the program grew); and identify strategies for removing potentially offensive posts or other rule breaches. This ongoing activity was applied for every new family caregiver post, and moderators were encouraged to ask four questions about each post in their decision-making process:

1. Is the post relevant to the group's purpose?
2. Will the post add value to this group?
3. How will the post be received by other group members?
4. Will the post violate anyone's privacy?

The moderator team also developed a plan for improving family caregivers' access to topics that they were interested in viewing or contributing to. As a part of the moderator team's decision making, approved posts were categorized according to topic, such as income support or dementia. This allowed family caregivers to search using key terms and find information most relevant to their concerns. This also reduced the repetition of similar posts.

The Facebook platform has a special "announcements feature" that prevents potentially controversial topics from dominating the Facebook group. Program developers used this feature to direct and keep comments and discussions on these various topics to one specific announcement post, rather than dominating the group's activity with multiple posts on the same topic. It includes themes, such as petitions or campaigns, research requests, and vaccination information. Other examples of announcements include posts for family caregivers to honor loved ones who have passed away. Death is a frequent part of the online family caregiver community's experience and was somewhat elevated during the COVID-19 pandemic. Postcaring can be a particularly challenging period (for a review of the research on postcaring challenges and opportunities, see Care Alliance Ireland, 2020), and those who had lost relatives were encouraged to remain in the group.

Synchronous Communications

The moderator team met online for one hour every two weeks using the Zoom tele-conferencing platform. Meetings were conducted with an agenda that included an ongoing schedule of regular topics. Although many of these topics were discussed in the mods and vols space, the increased interactive bandwidth of synchronous teleconferencing allowed moderators to engage in more nuanced discussions that provided immediate feedback, humor, and greater personalization. Regular topics included updates on weekly, monthly, and bimonthly structured support group activities; membership updates; informal support group competitions; moderator training; updates on external contacts that supported the program; and updates on moderating practices. Updates on moderating practices included refinements for "responses to suggested posts" and other templates as well as discussion tips to facilitate venting and expressions of heightened anxiety, while discouraging oversharing or excessively negative tones. Moderators also met synchronously through Zoom to participate in virtual celebrations and get-togethers.

Acknowledgment of Volunteers

Program developers thanked and acknowledged volunteer moderators with occasional small gifts. They offered funds to subsidize volunteers' internet costs, which was particularly important in the case of those family caregivers who relied on limited state income support due to their caring roles. Program developers also provided volunteer moderators with webcams and earphones or microphones, as needed.

FAMILY CAREGIVER MEMBERSHIP AND ENGAGEMENT

The program developers' goal was to create an online support program for family caregivers to ask questions and receive informational support, seek emotional support and reassurance with peers, experience a safe virtual space for self-appraisal with peer coping models, and receive limited tangible support. In the early weeks of April 2020, membership in the online family caregiver support program's discussion forum grew rapidly. Membership continued to grow, reaching more than 2,000 participants within nine months and approximately 4,500 participants after 32 months of the program's establishment.

Figure 2.1 provides a snapshot of activity in the family caregivers' discussion forum over a period of 60 days between April and June 2022. The figure illustrates a high level of participation, with 182 posts that received 8,927 comments and 20,321 reactions. The number of comments and reactions is especially noteworthy

Figure 2.1: 60-Day Display of Discussion Forum Activity (April 19–June 17, 2022)

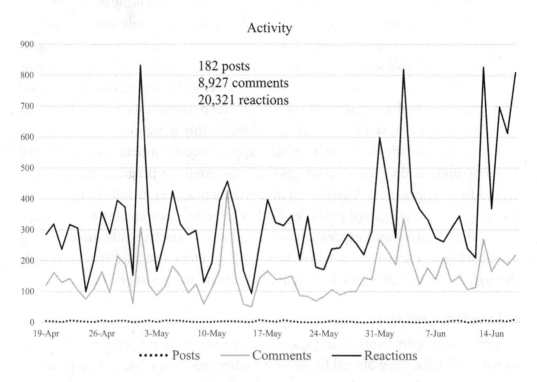

since research indicates that significantly lower levels of contributions are made by social media participants in North America, including those using online peer support and psychoeducation platforms (van Mierlo, 2014). This phenomenon has been so consistently observed that it has been tagged the 90-9-1 rule: According to the rule, 90 percent of social media participants lurk, 9 percent contribute intermittently, and only 1 percent account for most contributions (van Mierlo, 2014). Notably, more than 95 percent of caregivers participating in the program were deemed active by Facebook's metrics over the 12-month period measured, with *active* being defined as those who viewed, posted, commented, or reacted to (e.g., "liked") group content (Databox, 2022).

Membership Criteria and Group Rules

Membership criteria were devised in consultation with others who had extensive experience establishing and moderating online support groups. Inclusion criteria for membership approval included the following: (a) applicants were unpaid family caregivers, (b) applicants lived in the Republic of Ireland, and (c) applicants agreed to the rules of the group. Rules were established based on generally accepted forum norms, with a particular emphasis on respecting the confidentiality of the person being cared for.

The following rules were pinned at the front of the family caregivers' discussion forum (presented verbatim):

- Any personal comments posted in this group, which is set to private, are confidential and are not to be shared either verbally or by taking screenshots of comments. We remind people of the need to respect the privacy of others.

- Respect the opinions and privacy of others. *Please respect other posters' opinions. Do not send unsolicited private messages to other members.*

- Please ensure you do not use offensive language. *Sexist, ageist, ableist, homophobic, transphobic, and other offensive statements will be removed. Bullying or personal insults will not be tolerated & moderators reserve the right to remove offending posts, comments and remove members from the group.*

- Please ensure you do not post defamatory comments. *Comments should never be defamatory. See https://www.lawyer.ie/defamation/. Comments should not be made about cases currently before the courts.*

- No advertising or spam posting allowed. *Ads or promoting of products or personal businesses are not permitted in the group. Neither are "like and share" posts or running comps which promote products.*

- All new posts will be screened by moderators. *All new posts (not replies to existing threads) will be pre-moderated, and so there may be a slight delay in your post appearing. Please be patient with the moderation team in these instances.*

- Do not post rumors or hearsay. *All health-related posts will be reviewed by the moderation team and unless they can be verified, they will be removed without explanation or debate.*

- Respect the moderation team. *Please always remember that the moderation team are primarily volunteers, and that we all have our own caring responsibilities and families who will need support. If a post violates the rules, please report it and a moderator will review it ASAP.*

- Petitions and sharing research are permitted only in their specific threads— see in "Announcements."

- Be aware of personal information being shared. *Respect the privacy of health information for the person/s you care for. Do not post identifying information like addresses, emails, phone numbers etc.*

The activities (Care Alliance Ireland, n.d.) that made up the online family caregiver support program evolved over time (see Table 2.2). Activity development was based on an ongoing assessment of need and interest, available resources, and suggestions from moderators and caregiver group members. In addition, the four mechanisms of social support—(1) informational support, (2) emotional support, (3) tangible support, and (4) appraisal—provided further guidance for program developers in their ongoing assessment of family caregiver needs. The core activity was the open discussion forum, which moderators screened for purpose, relevance, value, and adherence to privacy considerations. The program developers soon recognized that individuals experiencing greater distress and reduced coping capacity would benefit from referral for other services. As such, limited individual case management was provided, which began with personal messages and moved to emails, phone calls, and then escalated to referral for individual services available through other family caregiver support organizations or mental health agencies.

Monthly quizzes, prepped by the program developers and moderators and delivered via Zoom, were next added. These informal, fun activities were seen to apply the mechanism of emotional support with a focus on belonging. Participation was generally limited to no more than 25 participants because greater numbers could be unwieldy to manage within the Zoom teleconferencing program.

A bimonthly book club was soon added. Interested participants received copies of one of the books chosen under discussion. Now, approximately 100 books are mailed to participants bimonthly. Book club discussions, including the use of virtual breakout rooms, have broadened participants' common connection of caring. In this way, the book club has become a vehicle for enhancing emotional support through coping mechanisms of belonging and self-esteem.

A bimonthly gardening club was also added to the suite of available program activities. The club offered a venue in which members highlighted their gardening skills, and it provided them with the opportunity to contribute pictures to its annual calendar. Now, the club is popular, with approximately 120 participants to date, and members have developed their own committee to further its engagement and support. Both the book and gardening clubs also provided limited tangible support: Moderators mailed more than 1,500 care packages, hampers, garden seeds or bulbs, and books to family caregivers over a period of 24 months.

Other member activities added to the program (and delivered synchronously via Zoom teleconferencing) included weekly coffee mornings, chair yoga sessions, art classes, and monthly caregiver workshops. Coffee mornings have had fewer participants than other activities, although those who do attend do so consistently. Approximately 20 participants attended chair yoga each week; however, members

Caregiver Support Group Activities

Table 2.2: Project Activities

Activity	Description
• Posting messages (core activity), approximately four per day	• Comments/discussion (approximately 137 per day, 335 reactions) facilitated anonymous posts to support compliance with European Union GDPR • Peer support: "I am not alone" • Information • Dilemmas • Top tips • Positivity posts • Cooking posts
• Pinned posts/threads	• Remembrances • Petitions • Research • Accessible travel/activities/ entertainment • Product recommendations • Money-saving tips • Welcome to new members
• One-on-one input/casework (core activity) for approximately 125 clients	• Private messages, phone calls, emails • Referral to family caregiver support organizations/social work mental health services
• Educative inputs	• Prerecorded videos • Subject matter experts • Live Q&As
• Zoom quizzes	• Monthly, informal fun
• Book club	• Bimonthly • Distribution of books • Breakout rooms
• Other activities	• Weekly online drop-in • Art classes • Informal competitions • Regular books/gifts/care packages • "Caregivers in Bloom" gardening club • Chair yoga • "Crafty Caregivers" group

Notes: GDPR = General Data Protection Regulation; Q&As = question-and-answer sessions.

were required to complete a health screen before participating, which may have reduced participation. Caregiver workshops focused on health-related educational presentations (either live or prerecorded), followed by question-and-answer sessions. Each of these synchronous activities was observed to enable mechanisms of emotional support like belonging and self-esteem. The caregiver workshops also provided informational support.

Family Caregiver Engagement

Facebook analytics demonstrated that 94 percent of family caregivers who joined the program over its initial 12-month period remained in the program after 18 months (Facebook analytics taken from Family Carer Support Group [Republic of Ireland]). An explanation for this high level of retention may be the high level of engagement observed in the caregiver discussion forum and in the other group activities. For instance, a significant number of caregivers routinely engaged with the discussion forum through posting, reactions, and content contributions (see Figure 2.1). This high level of engagement was also routinely demonstrated by dozens of responses from caregiver community members to caregiver posts when they included a question for the community. Further explanation may come from a larger survey of caregiver program members conducted by a PhD student to support a better understanding of the meaning participation in the group had for members. A Care Alliance Ireland internal poll of group members found that 91 percent of the respondents had never participated in a traditional, face-to-face caregiver support group.* This could suggest that as Facebook and social media usage grew over time in Ireland, the online family caregiver support program, while developed in response to COVID-19, also met a previously unmet need within the community of family caregivers. A significant number of the Irish population aged 35 to 54 years (Leonard, 2018) spends time online daily, and online support is now a "real thing."

Caregivers routinely thanked program developers and moderators for the opportunity to participate in the program. The following are exemplar posts of caregivers' overall experiences:

- "Thank you so much for setting up this group. I've searched for one for years."

- "Many, many thanks for creating this support group. I, like many family carers, can feel rather invisible and isolated. I care 24/7 for my beautiful 86-year-old little Mam."

---

* Of 480 members responding to an online poll, 44 indicated that they have been part of face-to-face caregiver support groups before COVID-19.

- "It's a lifeline for so many of us. I don't post much but I do read often and there's so much helpful advice and support, which is what we all need right now when we feel forgotten and lost."

- "You guys sure know how to cheer us all up running little raffles like this, without you all I'd be lost. It's great knowing that we are not alone."

- "Thank you all for just being there for all of us. You have helped to keep us going in a difficult year."

Moderators' Experiences

Moderating an online support group can be emotionally challenging, especially in a time of crisis. In late 2020, 11 moderators participated in a survey that asked questions about their experiences with the team. Moderators reported being highly satisfied with the communication platforms to help support their role. One volunteer nonprofessional moderator noted communications were "very positive, supportive, open to everyone's views, inclusive, respectful, at times humorous, professional, decisive, responsive, and welcoming." A nonprofessional moderator's response regarding team resources illustrates Metz and colleagues' (2017) findings that unpaid volunteers excelled in the development of meaningful relationships: "It's great to have the documents to use as a resource, as caring is emotive and I feel it's important that I don't upset anyone or cause anyone any emotional distress."

Nonprofessional volunteers' capacity for empathy (Metz et al., 2017) can also be observed in a response to a question about the moderator team's influence on their role in the Online Family Caregiver Support Group:

> Even if the original post seems to not be something I can help with, by also reading the comments, I come across people/issues that I can contribute to, even if just to sympathize with what someone is going through. I also make a point now of liking posts, commenting, etc.

Another moderator also reported on the value of their team's discussion forum and its influence on moderation: "It offers reassurance to me in my role as a volunteer. It provides a forum for discussing complex issues, getting different perspectives, and arriving at a consensus about what response to take or decision to make."

Limitations

While the online family caregiver support program has been effective from the perspective of its continued growth and the high level of active participation, sustainability requires adequate funding for ongoing operations. The Facebook groups platform and volunteer moderators provided a significant cost-benefit for start-up, and 10 months into the project, the nonprofit secured once-off limited funding to appoint a new part-time staff member to manage administrative tasks required for program operations. Thankfully, ongoing government funding was secured to ensure the full costs of the project are born from recurring funding rather than from internal organizational subsidies. Such long-term public funding is enabling comprehensive volunteer training, program development, and the capacity to support more caregivers.

As we have described, there are also limitations for participants in online support programs. Participants seek to gain control over life challenges, and the process of self-appraisal uses peer comparisons to discover how others have managed, coped, overcome, or failed at similar life challenges. While this can increase motivation and coping in the face of obstacles, it can also result in comparisons that increase anxiety, depression, or demoralization. Effective moderation and the inclusion of various activities alongside forum discussion may help mitigate this downside of self-appraisal. Volunteers with caregiving experience also mitigate this downside in their own presentation as peer coping models by emphasizing the importance of persisting in the face of obstacles.

Other limitations include accessibility and privacy concerns. Those with low levels of digital skills, literacy, or poor internet adequacy will be unable to participate effectively. More recent interventions by the lead agency and others to support with digital literacy attempt to address these obstacles to participation. Regarding privacy concerns, members can observe group rules, and moderators can be trained to prevent privacy violations, as in the use of an approval process for new posts. However, the virtual storage of online discussions or content can also pose privacy threats. There remains some debate as to who owns the data, who is responsible for it, who stores it, and who can delete it. In the European Union, the 2018 General Data Protection Regulation (Data Protection Commission, n.d.) is significant, and across many U.S. states and in other jurisdictions, similar data protection legislation emphasizes the need for practitioners to be mindful of possible data breaches and to take specific actions to minimize such risks.

CONCLUSION

Online platforms, such as Facebook groups and others, have quietly revolutionized how support is experienced by many people with health conditions or caring roles. This chapter described the development, delivery, and management of an online caregiver support program and its power to reach large numbers, address geographical isolation, and extend the vision and footprint of online social work practice. We believe that the program also provides a useful model for the role of team-based moderation in the operation of online support programs. This example illustrates the value of a mixed team of professional and nonprofessional volunteers, their overlapping roles, and their distinct contributions to the mechanisms of social support. Historically, volunteerism has played an important role in the development of social work practice (Brozmanová & Stachoň, 2014). Online family caregiver support programs, like the one we have described, extend the role of volunteerism into the online world of social work practice.

REFERENCES

Athanasiadis, D. I., Roper, A., Hilgendorf, W., Voss, A., Zike, T., Embry, M., Banerjee, A., Selzer, D., & Stefanidis, D. (2021). Facebook groups provide effective social support to patients after bariatric surgery. *Surgical Endoscopy*, *35*, 4595–4601. https://doi.org/10.1007/s00464-020-07884-y

Bandura, A. (1997). *Self-efficacy: The exercise of control*. Freedom and Company.

Bender, J. L., Jimenez-Marroquin, M.-C., & Jadad, A. R. (2011). Seeking support on Facebook: A content analysis of breast cancer groups. *Journal of Medical Internet Research*, *13*, e1560. https://doi.org/10.2196/jmir.1560

Berzin, S. C., Singer, J., & Chan, C. (2015, October). *Practice innovation through technology in the digital age: A Grand Challenge for Social Work* (Working Paper No. 12). https://grandchallengesforsocialwork.org/wp-content/uploads/2015/12/WP12-with-cover.pdf

Brozmanová, A., & Stachoň, M. (2014). Volunteering in the context of social work—Historical connection and perspectives. *Historia i Polityka*, *12*, 97–110. https://doi.org/10.12775/HiP.2014.022

Care Alliance Ireland. (n.d.). *Online family carer support group*. https://www.carealliance.ie/OnlineFamilyCarerSupportGroup

Care Alliance Ireland. (2020). *The way ahead*. https://www.carealliance.ie/userfiles/files/The%20Way%20Ahead%202020%20SP.pdf

Cohen, S., & McKay, G. (1984). Social support, stress and the buffering hypothesis: A theoretical analysis. In A. Baum, S. E. Taylor, & J. E. Singer (Eds.), *Handbook of psychology and health* (pp. 253–267). Lawrence Erlbaum.

Data Protection Commission. (n.d.). *Data protection legislation*. Retrieved November 16, 2022, from https://www.dataprotection.ie/en/dpc-guidance/law/data-protection-legislation

Databox. (2022, September 2). *Facebook engagement: What is it & how do you measure it?* https://databox.com/facebook-engagement-tips

Facebook. (2021, February 23). *The power of virtual communities.* https://www.facebook.com/community/whats-new/power-virtual-communities

Family Carers Ireland. (2020). *Caring through COVID: Life in lockdown.* https://familycarers.ie/media/1394/caring-through-covid-life-in-lockdown.pdf

Frost, R. L., & Rickwood, D. J. (2017). A systematic review of the mental health outcomes associated with Facebook use. *Computers in Human Behavior, 76,* 576–600. https://doi.org/10.1016/j.chb.2017.08.001

Helgeson, V. S., & Gottlieb, B. H. (2000). Support groups. In S. Cohen, L. G. Underwood, & B. H. Gottlieb (Eds.), *Social support measurement and intervention: A guide for health and social scientists* (pp. 221–245). Oxford University Press.

Iqbal, M. (2021, May 24). *Facebook revenue and usage (2021).* Business of Apps. https://www.businessofapps.com/data/facebook-statistics/

Leonard, R. (2018, June 29). *71% of Irish adults enjoy using Facebook and Instagram.* https://irishtechnews.ie/71-of-irish-adults-enjoy-using-facebook-and-instagram/

Merriam-Webster. (n.d.). Support. In *Merriam-Webster.com dictionary.* Retrieved October 21, 2022, from https://www.merriam-webster.com/dictionary/support

Metz, J., Roza, L., Miejs, L., Baren van, E., & Hoogervorst, N. (2017). Differences between paid and unpaid social services for beneficiaries. *European Journal of Social Work, 20,* 153–166. https://doi.org/10.1080/13691457.2016.1188772

Morzy, M. (2013). Evolution of online forum communities. In T. Özyer, J. Rokne, G. Wagner, & A. Reuser (Eds.), *The influence of technology on social network analysis and mining* (Vol. 6, pp. 615–630). Springer. https://doi.org/10.1007/978-3-7091-1346-2_27

Omnicore. (2021, July 1). *Facebook by the numbers: Stats, demographics & fun facts.* https://www.omnicoreagency.com/facebook-statistics/

O'Sullivan, L., & Hughes, Z. (2019). Incorporating Facebook into nonprofit supports for family caregivers: Reflections on its value and relevance. *Journal of Technology in Human Services, 37,* 129–141. https://doi.org/10.1080/15228835.2019.1620669

Parker Oliver, D., Washington, K., Gage, L. A., & Demiris, G. (2014). The promise of secret Facebook groups for active family caregivers of hospice patients. *Journal of Palliative Medicine, 17,* 1199–1200. https://doi.org/10.1089/jpm.2014.0311

Pendry, L. F., & Salvatore, J. (2015). Individual and social benefits of online discussion forums. *Computers in Human Behavior, 50,* 211–220. https://doi.org/10.1016/j.chb.2015.03.067

Stetten, N. E., LeBeau, K., Aguirre, M. A., Vogt, A. B., Quintana, J. R., Jennings, A. R., & Hart, M. (2019). Analyzing the communication interchange of individuals with disabilities utilizing Facebook, discussion forums, and chat rooms: Qualitative content analysis of online disabilities support groups. *JMIR Rehabilitation and Assistive Technologies, 6,* Article e12667. https://doi.org/10.2196/12667

van Mierlo, T. (2014). The 1% rule in four digital health social networks: An observational study. *Journal of Medical Internet Research, 16,* Article e33. https://doi.org/10.2196/jmir.2966

Zhang, S. (2018, October 26). Facebook groups as therapy. *The Atlantic.* https://www.theatlantic.com/technology/archive/2018/10/facebook-emotional-support-groups/572941/

CHAPTER 3

Best Practices in Technology-Based Supports in Working with Children, Adolescents, and Families

Susan Elswick, Christy Peterson, Gregory Washington, and Ebony Barnes

This chapter covers recommended practices in technology-based supports for working with children, adolescents, and families. These recommendations follow our work with communities in the southwestern portion of the U.S. state of Tennessee. Due to the COVID-19 pandemic, the 2020–2021 year witnessed a sweeping migration of educational and clinical supports to technology-based and virtual programs. Aside from increased morbidity and mortality the pandemic brought on vulnerable populations, the mitigation response of social distancing and restricted movements placed great emotional, mental, and educational hardship on many, especially at-risk populations. Many mental health practitioners were thrust into navigating therapeutic and educational programming in a virtual space, which was foreign to them because their training and expertise had not prepared them for this challenge. In response to this change in programming, therapeutic practitioners, specialized advocacy program teams, and mental health professionals needed to be knowledgeable about how virtual environments might impact the children, adolescents, and families they serve and their outcomes.

Although the initial impact of COVID-19 has subsided, virtual service delivery is here to stay. Due to unknown future variants of the virus and other unexpected pandemic-driven global changes, consumers' utilization of virtual service modalities has continually increased. Clinical practitioners face a growing need to be educated regarding the best practices for technology-based supports. The purpose of this chapter is to illustrate effective practices in supporting children, adolescents, and families in a virtual service format.

INJUSTICE AROUND DIGITAL ACCESS

Preparing families for digital behavioral health work requires an appreciation of the historical marginalization that many populations have experienced throughout the world. Oppression and racism have contributed to families of color being locked out of systems and mechanisms that could facilitate their economic mobility, growth, and full participation in society (Hamilton, 2020; Pittman, 2010). In today's public education curriculum, 21st century skills (i.e., skills, abilities, and learning dispositions critical for success in 21st century society) are embedded into the fiber of public education (Beers, 2011; Jacobson-Lundeberg, 2016); however, many families were never exposed to this type of education, training, or skills development. Individuals who have been provided access to and have been immersed in technology-rich environments are known as *digital natives* (Prensky, 2001a), whereas those who have had little to no exposure to technology-based skills are often referred to as *digital immigrants* (Hoffman & Novak, 1999; Prensky, 2001b).

Historically, families of color have experienced inadequate or no education regarding 21st century skills, and this form of social injustice has contributed to poverty and poor health outcomes (Beers, 2011; Hoffman & Novak, 1999; Pittman, 2010). Access to digital resources available via the internet and other electronic platforms is increasingly important to nurture healthy child development, support family needs, and reduce risk for poor health outcomes (Sieck et al., 2021). However, for many communities of color, both hard capital and soft capital investments have been sparse or nonexistent; this social-injustice phenomenon has been termed the *digital divide* (Cullen, 2001; Hoffman & Novak, 1999; Ramsetty & Adams, 2020; Sieck et al., 2021; Van Dijk, 2020). This digital divide refers to the gap between individuals, households, businesses, and geographic areas at different socioeconomic levels regarding both their opportunities to access information and communication technologies and their use of the internet for a wide variety of activities (Organisation for Economic Co-operation and Development, 2001). The digital divide has always been in existence, but during the COVID-19 pandemic, the digital divide for people of color and marginalized groups was exposed in the United States on a national level (Sieck et al., 2021).

NEED ACROSS COMMUNITIES IN THE UNITED STATES

Over the past 20 years, there has been growth in the U.S. infrastructure needed to give families access to technology, and households' access to and use of broadband internet services increased from 48 percent to 85 percent (U.S. Census Bureau,

2018). In urban areas, such as Memphis, Tennessee, approximately 69 percent of households have broadband access; however, in some of the city's poorest zip codes, the access rate is 30 percent or less (American Community Survey, 2018; U.S. Census Bureau, 2020). This lack of access contributes to what has been called "the homework gap," and it is estimated 45 percent of youth in the United States are unable to complete homework due to lack of computer or internet access (Pew Research Center, 2021). Approximately 35 percent of youth use cell phones as a substitute for internet access at home via a computer (Pew Research Center, 2021).

The families, and their children, in these communities that experience this digital divide are at a significant disadvantage in completing high school, college educational requirements, and job applications (Moore et al., 2018). The digital divide also further contributes to poor health outcomes experienced by communities of color at disproportionate rates. Many families in these communities lack internet access, consistent internet speed, and the digital literacy skills necessary to be successful consumers of technology (Moore et al., 2018). These aforementioned factors contributed to the underutilization of technology-mediated services, such as telehealth, when they became more available to the community in response to COVID-19 lockdowns.

Digital Needs of Youth and Adolescents

While families have been impacted by the digital divide, it is important to acknowledge the far-reaching impact specific to adolescents in the United States. Historically, youth and adolescents have not been the specific intended beneficiaries of public and private sector investments in digital infrastructure, programs, and other resources. Underfunding of school systems has been a public crisis since before the Great Recession of 2008. The 2007–2009 recession led to state funding cuts for K–12 education as well as higher education, healthcare, and human services. At least 31 states provided less state funding per student in the 2014 school year (i.e., the school year ending in 2014) than in the 2008 school year. In at least 15 states, the cuts exceeded 10 percent (Leachman et al., 2016). Limited digital resources and connectivity in impoverished communities exacerbate disparities in digital access (Lai & Widmar, 2021).

A substantial portion of funding has recently been directed at increasing site-based internet connectivity (e.g., schools, alternative programs, after-school programs, a wide range of related activities); unfortunately, though, the divide continues to expand even as youth and adolescents from lower-income households gain increased access to technology. Nearly a quarter of adults (24 percent) with household incomes below $30,000 a year say they don't own a smartphone.

About four in 10 adults with lower incomes do not have home broadband services (43 percent) or a desktop or laptop computer (41 percent; Pew Research Center, 2021). A survey conducted by the National Center for Education Statistics found only 61 percent of school-age children had internet access at home, yet most students reported requiring the internet to complete assignments (Irwin et al., 2021).

We can conclude that, while broadband availability has continued to expand, growing disparities in place-based broadband adoption persist, adding to barriers that interfere with a client's ability to master recent technologies and mobilize information resources to meet therapeutic goals. Confronting digital inequality is a complex process that is initiated by increasing digital inclusion rates. An inclusionary framework will lead to incorporating the goals of connectivity, device access, and digital literacy using a multidimensional and multilevel approach (DiMaggio & Hargittai, 2001; DiMaggio et al., 2004). Public, private, and locally oriented initiatives must aim to increase equitable access to technology regardless of ethnicity, socioeconomic status, age, or ability. One way in which we can all address digital inequalities is by reviewing and implementing practical tips on how to promote equitable access to technology within our own communities. Here are a few suggestions that could be implemented or facilitated in conjunction with local education agencies within your region:

Develop a systematic technology plan: Build your plan on a foundation of policies that address what is required to provide equitable access to technology for students and children. At their core, these policies should outline where to go for help getting digital access, ensure individuals know how to access the technology, and be flexible enough to accommodate students' diverse instructional requirements and learning styles.

Get a support community involved: Work as a liaison between all stakeholders (e.g., school leadership, parents, leadership, students). Various stakeholders will have different perspectives on these youth, providing a thorough sense of their needs and capabilities.

Initiate and support digital literacy programs: Implement digital literacy programs that allow students to catch up on their technological skills to address factors that cause discomfort with technology among youth and adolescents.

Utilize governmental resources: Take advantage of governmental resources for digital access. Many programs are available that promote technology outside of the classroom and home, including local initiatives to provide hotspots, laptop loans, or usage programs to students.

Use partnerships to enable equitable access to technology: Equitable access to technology is a societal issue. Partnerships with schools and external organizations or other entities in the community can help providers bridge their gap in funds for technology.

Because of the ongoing barriers for marginalized populations and people of color, a more innovative approach to trainings and support is needed. Next, this chapter reviews one novel approach—a digital inclusion approach—that was developed and implemented in one large urban city in the mid-south region of the United States.

A DIGITAL INCLUSION APPROACH

Macro-Level Strategy

The need for increased access to the internet is being addressed in two ways by city, state, and federal entities in the United States. One method is a *macro-level strategy* that includes providing infrastructure solutions, such as discounted and, in some cases, free internet services by internet providers in addition to increased access to computer equipment. This is not a novel approach, and as witnessed in many communities across the nation during the pandemic, many internet providers launched innovative pilot projects designed to address the digital divide needs of families by providing reduced or free internet access and computers.

In Memphis, pilot projects are being implemented to address this divide within the West Tennessee region. The funding for these projects came from the United States COVID-19 relief resources and a combination of local philanthropic foundations.

Digital Inclusion Pilot Project

A pilot project spearheaded by the University of Memphis School of Social Work and School of Urban Affairs and Public Policy focused its efforts on improving outcomes in four areas: (1) internet and computer access and literacy, (2) digital skills, (3) environments conducive to the digital agenda, and (4) creation of a 5,000-square-foot youth technology lab in underserved areas in Memphis's impoverished zip codes. Qualifying households for this project included (a) youth in the house, (b) youth in school and out of school, (c) families receiving support from at least two support organizations, (d) homes without internet access, and (e) homes without a computer.

The Digital Inclusion Project included a number of planned outcomes. They included the following: (a) within three years, connect 8,500 households to the internet; (b) in six years, retain 90 percent of household connections; (c) collect data tracking performance achievement; and (d) connect MLK Center and Linear Park with fiber infrastructure partners (i.e., City of Memphis, Urban Strategies, University of Memphis, Shelby County Schools, and Start Co.*).

Social Envelop Strategy

A second method of increasing internet access is a *social envelop strategy*; the social envelope is a metaphor that describes the setting that surrounds a technology. This metaphor allows us to grasp the relationship between recent technology and the setting into which it is introduced.

In many ways, introducing a new technology is just like placing a letter in an envelope. A letter or card must be shaped or folded in ways that allow it to enter the shape of the envelope, or a new envelope must be provided. The metaphor aptly conveys what usually happens to a technology when it is introduced into a social setting. It either fits, or something must give—either the letter (the technological use) or the envelope (the social expectations and relations of the setting). Applying this metaphor ensures households that receive broadband service can use the technology to its fullest capacity. This is where the approach of the Digital Inclusion Project is most evident. The project being spearheaded in the Memphis region is accomplishing the social envelop strategy by linking the digital inclusion efforts to existing case management work being provided by community-based human services organizations and employing providers that are coined as "digital mentors."

Digital Mentors

Within the Digital Inclusion Project, traditional digital technology companies and universities or colleges are partnering with community-based human services organizations to identify and onboard student interns (from social work, counseling, psychology, and other human services fields) who serve the community as digital mentors. Student interns are trained to be digital mentors and are paid to work 15 hours per week for a total of 30 weeks to provide this direct service to the

---

* Start Co. is a venture architect firm that supports clients and partners with design processes for launching early stage technologies, business innovations, and economic solutions. They work with start-ups, corporations, governments, universities, and other organizations looking to build data and technology solutions, new business models, and civic innovations that leverage the power of digital cities, venture development expertise, investment, and capital connectivity.

community. Following a short training period, each intern works with one cohort of households at a time to deliver digital mentoring.

From the inception of the Digital Inclusion Project, the digital mentors have had specific roles and responsibilities necessary for project success, including the following:

- utilizing a "digital passport" platform (defined in the next section) to assess the needs and goals of youth and families

- delivering six-week digital literacy content to households

- monitoring the progress of youth and families and reporting to community agency case managers

- helping youth and families solve problems and think critically about their use of technology (the ability to decipher sources and identify correct information on the internet supports interactivity and problem solving)

- reporting issues or concerns to case managers

- ensuring youth and families have the tools and skills they need (i.e., support interactivity, critical thinking, and problem solving) to be connected digitally and that these tools are in proper working order

Households for each cohort were identified by community human services organizations. These families/households have weekly access to a digital mentor, working with case managers to manage the clients' needs and develop their digital literacy skills. The goal for this project is to have each digital mentor working with a total of 30 families, onboarded gradually, over the course of the program.

Digital Passport

The digital mentors collaborated with each cohort of households over a period of several weeks, completing a *digital passport* that includes digital skills competency assessments and reassessments. These comprise online, self-guided assessments that measure proficiency in basic skills in each of 14 areas. Lesson plans are learner centered and interactive, giving learners multiple opportunities to build digital literacy skills through practice tasks. Each lesson plan includes a detailed teacher preparation guide; it also provides remote teaching pages and a remote teaching guide to give pointers on using the curricula remotely. Lessons are structured to include warm-ups, daily objectives, practice tasks, digital literacy vocabulary work, and wrap-ups. Original online content is also provided so that learners can access independently. When learners complete an assessment or reassessment, they are automatically directed to the online content corresponding to what they still need to learn. Online learning provides individualized online instruction and practice. Users can create learner accounts, which track online work and assessments completed by the learners that can inform learning growth and development of enrolled families,

The initial phase of the digital passport process begins with a baseline assessment of the current digital skills of household members in three areas: (1) consumer basic computer skills, (2) consumer software skills, and (3) consumer-reported use of technology in their daily life. Sample assessments used to determine these three areas of strength and need are provided in Figures 3.1, 3.2, and 3.3. Once the assessment is completed, goals related to training on specific gaps in ability are identified, and the digital mentors work with the families to develop an improvement plan. As part of the digital mentor programming, all household members are provided with support. Household members routinely complete a reassessment to determine what skills have been obtained, and a continuous digital mentor feedback loop on skills and accomplishments is provided. The goal for each family is proficiency in skills needed to reach agreed on goals. Skills develop while family member use the available internet and technology.

Figure 3.1: Basic Skills Family Composite Score

Basic Computer Skills Score:		*(Add initials):*_____
Mastery:		Nonmastery
1.		1.
2.		2.
3.		3.

Skill Development Needs: _____

_____

_____

Basic Computer Skills Score (Reassessment):

Recommendations:

Figure 3.2: Software Skills Family Composite Score

Software Skills Score:		*(Add initials):*_____
Mastery:		Nonmastery
1.		1.
2.		2.
3.		3.

Skill Development Needs: _____

_____

_____

Software Skills Score (Reassessment):

Recommendations:

Figure 3.3: Using Technology in Daily Life Composite Family Score

Using Technology in Daily Life Score:		*(Add initials):*_____
Mastery:		Nonmastery
1.		1.
2.		2.
3.		3.

Skill Development Needs: _____

_____

_____

Using Technology in Daily Life Score (Reassessment):

Recommendations:

Other: _____

Project Summary, Outputs, and Impact

In 20 years, the United States expanded the number of households with broadband internet from 48 percent to somewhere between 83 percent and 89 percent; however, as mentioned earlier, the number of households with broadband internet access in Memphis is currently at 69 percent (U.S. Census Bureau, 2020). Memphis has the slowest internet of all major U.S. metropolitan cities (Catalyst 30, 2020) and lags in technology deployment by 47 percent (Catalyst 30, 2020). The Digital Inclusion Project was an opportunity for Memphis to take a deliberate, inclusive approach to building a smart, connected, and equitable city. The project aimed to close the digital divide and increase digital literacy and education.

The Digital Inclusion Project leveraged community assets to develop and launch this important work. It has demonstrated positive impact within the community. Data were collected using literacy assessments results, digital passport aggregate data, peer mentor observations, and digital usage youth survey. The small pilot evaluation data indicated success. In terms of participation, in Year 1, more than 60 percent of enrolled digital inclusion families were connected to digital resources, digital learning mediums, and a digital mentor. This prompted planned expansion for the project to continue into other low-income neighborhoods throughout the West Tennessee area and tristate regions.

The University of Memphis identified and trained 12 digital mentors. Digital mentors were allocated to serve a maximum of 10 families for the digital inclusion work. Based on the digital mentor processes, 426 family engagement contacts were made in 2021. Each digital mentor completed two digital inclusion assessment activities with each youth and family for 142 enrolled families. Both self- and peer-guided assessments were administered that measured proficiency in basic skills in specific areas. The areas assessed included information and data literacy, communication and collaboration, digital content creation, safety, basic computer literacy testing, workplace skills, internet use, office packages, education, and training. Baseline and postintervention outcomes indicated noted improvement in participants' overall skills and abilities in a range of specific domains. Survey initial assessment data from the pilot group determined that 42 percent of the participants reported confidence in their ability to navigate the digital content. This rose to 57 percent post–project completion.

During the implementation of this pilot, it became evident that the training and the preparation aspects of this work were vitally important to successful outcomes. Based on our experiences, we now provide suggestions on preparing youth and families for this work. These include assisting community practitioners with understanding the service consumer's digital literacy and being prepared to meet them at their level, assisting families in understanding their roles and responsibilities as technology consumers, and supporting families in understanding how to problem solve technology issues when they arise during service delivery.

Preparing Children, Adolescents, and Their Families for Virtual Services Delivery

Working with youth in a supportive health setting can be a unique challenge, and requesting that youth also participate in service delivery in a virtual format adds an additional layer of challenge for providers. Many service providers in a range of fields (e.g., education settings, private programs, behavioral health) have reported challenges with digital service delivery. Providers often report that they struggle with maintaining a youth's focus, active communication cycles during the session, and responsive listening during service delivery (Gloff et al., 2015; Khan et al., 2021). Virtual processes can complicate an already demanding endeavor due to many factors, such as the practitioner's minimal restorative control over services being offered in a virtual space and the absence of commanding impact of in-person presence (Khan et al., 2021; Stewart et al., 2020).

To assist the youth and technology consumer with improving their willingness and their preparedness to engage, providers should consider including processes, such as motivational interviewing, establishing compatibility (the ways in which latest ideas, behaviors, and practices diffuse through populations), and engaging the consumer with supplemental materials. *Motivational interviewing* is a directive, client-centered intervention style for eliciting behavior change that assists clients and consumers in exploring and resolving ambivalence about change (Patel et al., 2019). Establishing compatibility can be accomplished by using digital literacy assessments before the delivery of any technology-based services. The findings from these types of assessments can guide decisions related to addressing the individual consumer's needs and inform the way services are offered to the individual. Ensuring that supplemental materials are also provided to individuals during digital services delivery is vital. Supplemental materials could include simple tip sheets that cover the most salient points of service delivery (e.g., intake, therapeutic sessions, technical assistance), additional resources to assist with the need being addressed during digital services delivery, and handouts related to topics covered during service delivery.

When working with children and adolescents, high-quality engagement throughout the session is the cardinal goal and a critically necessary component with children because interest often wanes when a practitioner is simply a visual representation on the displayed screen or an audio voice on the child or adolescent's chosen electronic device (Khan et al., 2021). Understanding how to engage a client within a virtual platform can be extremely challenging (Khan et al., 2021; Stewart et al., 2020). Many practitioners and providers have learned that adaptations, modifications, and additional methods of service delivery beyond basic verbal communication are necessary to sustain the consumer's attention in a virtual session. At the same time, it's also important to note that research post-pandemic shows that virtually based services, such as telemedicine, are equally as effective as in-person treatment (Barney et al., 2020; Lindgren et al., 2020; Stewart et al., 2020). Technology-based service providers can look at telehealth literature as a guide to adapting and modifying their engagement strategies during virtual services with youth to support enhanced interactions and interests.

DIGITAL PRACTICE MODIFICATIONS

Based on the Digital Inclusion Project findings, the modifications required to work with children and families via various electronic mediums can be bisected into two encompassing areas:

1. procedural guidance for addressing technical disadvantages, issues, or limitations
2. strategies for keeping children engaged during virtual sessions

Considering the following approaches and selecting the most appropriate methodology during planning will assist in compensating for the technical limitations of some youth and families as will appreciating cultural considerations during virtual service delivery.

Cognitive Ability versus Biological Age Considerations

Most adaptations should be initiated with a determination of both cognitive "age" and disposition of the consumer whom we aim to serve. One can expect that services offered via a virtual platform with youth must be more engaging than those with older-age adults. The client will still want to explore the settings they are in and remain equally observant of the environment you are broadcasting from. Interventions that have considered the consumer's cognitive needs will be well prepared to manage disruptions that are typical of lively sessions. It is important to have age- and skill-level appropriate stimuli visible and accessible to the provider or consumer, room modifications to limit distractions, motivational spaces, established quick response practices to enact at the onset of session-breaking behaviors, and adequately displayed or discussed session duration times and the availability of break requests (e.g., visual schedule detailing session that describes ways in which breaks can be requested).

Positioning for Perspective

An often overlooked but crucial aspect of technology-based services is the angling or positioning of the camera. Just as camera angles in film affect what we can see, which, in turn, affects what we are able to feel, the orientation of the video device impacts the way consumers can interpret the shared content during the session. The film sequence from a movie can dictate what we pay attention to or what moves a person during a viewing. This same understanding can be applied to sessions with technology consumers. If a provider is engaging via electronic platforms, it is imperative to consider how much of the consumer's environment you need to see as well as how much of your own should be shared. Ask the participant at the beginning if they prefer a specific camera placement. There are always differences in environments that clients may be happy to share or may be less inclined to share. These discrepancies can be caused by differences in culture or socioeconomic status among others that can contribute barriers to successful therapy sessions. Ideally, you should be able to see as much of the area where the consumer may be interacting or playing as possible, although it is equally important to grant agency over the sharing in their digital space as much as and as safely as possible.

Consider how much of your visible space is necessary for sessions. Will the visibility cause constant distractions due to varied stimuli? Will it contribute to feelings of inadequacy due to imbalances in socioeconomic factors between provider and clients (i.e., you may have more "things" than they have access to because they may come from a disadvantaged environment)? Disconnect from a static positioning for each session (unless this is soothing for your consumer). You should also be prepared for position changes as the consumer moves around the room, be sensitive to information-sharing moments that may dictate moving closer or farther away from the device to prevent discomfort, or augment a more proximal environment during these moments.

Anticipating Client Experiences to Combat Challenges of the Unintended Consequences of Technology

Even before the onset of the pandemic, the utilization of digital and communication technologies, such as tablets, personal computers, and other devices, to gain access to the healthcare continuum via remote pathways as well as healthcare management was continually increasing (De' et al., 2020). In 2000, just half of the

U.S. population had broadband access at home. Today, that number is more than 90 percent (Pew Research Center, 2021). With the continued development of recent technologies and the fundamental shift in how we connect with one another, anticipating the unintended consequences becomes critical. Readiness should include effective communication efforts to acknowledge problems that may occur utilizing technology for each type of user ranging from novice to expert. Additionally, practitioners must commit to creating a system that is staffed with the relevant personnel to ensure the best therapeutic experience for each person, each time.

Preparedness is twofold: (1) ensuring a clear commitment to responsiveness through standardization (e.g., developing frequently asked questions or tip sheets, providing immediate access to tech assist, offering tutorials) and (2) making a commitment to adapt as part of your theoretical approach, which represents an affirmation that every client's experience is unlike any other client's experience that occurred previously. This will translate into opportunities to recognize the individuality of those in the population we aim to serve, gaining clear understanding of unique needs and differing skill levels and managing expectations of what is feasible and realistic. This is particularly important when serving youth and families from impoverished backgrounds. Of particular concern is the stigma associated with reduced capacity regarding technology use.

There is a pervasive reluctance for clients from communities of color to share the limitations they have due to digital inequality. This structural reality perpetuates social, economic, and political disparities. In some cases, those with low digital literacy may begin to gain access and enter the "haves" in technology but may demonstrate reluctance to the use of technology simply because they do not know how (Real et al., 2014). These digital behaviors (e.g., missed appointments, disengagement, hesitancy to use tech products) are heavily influenced by the responses, lack of support, and infrequent digital access they have witnessed in their lifetimes. They are much less likely to gain digital fluency because of a stigmatization of perceived lower digital literacy, creating an urgent need for providers to remain vigilant in their commitment to maintaining readiness and responsiveness to address the unique technological needs of this population. It is an integral piece of the process to ensuring these clients gain more confidence in their competence to contribute to online engagements, access trusted information online, and adapt skills to take better advantage of emerging technologies.

Defining Roles and Responsibilities

In 2014, the online data warehouse of the Health Resources & Services Administration (n.d.) identified 2,000 mental health professional shortage areas designated in U.S. nonmetropolitan counties, affecting more than 66 million residents in the country. The Memphis and mid-south region fall into one of these identified health-care shortage regions. An excerpt from "County-Level Estimates of Mental Health Professional Shortage in the United States" (Thomas et al., 2009) reported that higher levels of unmet need for mental health professionals existed for counties that were more rural and had lower income levels. These reported healthcare shortage regions have often struggled with accessing enough qualified and trained mental health and allied health service providers to meet the demand and need across the region. The most disadvantaged and under-resourced communities are often those with the greatest need for mental health and other allied healthcare providers, particularly child and adolescent specialists (American Telemedicine Association, 2017).

These deficits, together with the emergence of COVID-19, emphasize the broadening need for practitioners to be trained in the implementation and acceptance of technology-based interventions and practices. The availability and accessibility of virtual services can address the long-term and emerging needs, but it is equally important to identify and adhere to specific considerations when providing technology-based services to youth, adolescents, and families who will utilize these virtual services. It is important to understand one's role and expectations in any activity provided to a consumer. For virtual programming, it is important to define the roles of the consumer and of the practitioner.

In addition, when engaging in technology-supported services, consider virtual roles and responsibilities for youth, their families, and the supporting practitioners. Share with the consumer one or more of the lists that appear in this section, discuss the list(s), and answer any questions about roles and responsibilities before starting service delivery. In its simplest form, technology consumers should have

- knowledge of basic computer skills and vocabulary (e.g., mouse, keyboard, USB, Wi-Fi).
- ability to follow instructions as needed during troubleshooting situations.
- availability during the virtual sessions to receive tech support as needed.
- availability for training as needed to assist with therapeutic goals.

If any of these basic requirements is noted as deficient in the initial onboarding of a youth or family member, the service provider should take time to educate the consumer about it. These skills can be taught face to face or in a virtual platform, but the technology-based service provider must be prepared with a simple task analysis of these skills or step-by-step process that they can cover and share with the technology consumer. These service providers can utilize *task analysis*—the process of breaking a skill down into smaller, more manageable components (Diaper & Stanton, 2003)—to support the consumer's skill acquisition.

Additionally, consider utilizing time in the virtual space to allow the consumer to role-play these specific skills utilizing the step-by-step prompts and provide the opportunity for live coaching and feedback during the session. This will assist in building the clients' technology self-efficacy (Skinner et al., 2018). These technology prerequisite skills, just like in any other type of skill development or acquisition, are necessary and needed before more complex and detailed technology-based skills can be obtained (Resnick, 2002; Sato et al., 2017). Once these prerequisite skills are developed and successful outcomes are noted, each client should also be aware of their more specific roles and responsibilities during the service delivery. The following are additional responsibilities of youth technology consumers:

- Notify the practitioner 24 hours in advance if absent.
- Turn on the computer and launch the online therapy application.
- Reach out to tech support or the tech provider if needed during troubleshooting.
- Follow a backup plan in case technology is not working (the service provider and consumer should develop a backup or technology safety plan during the intake process).
- Request assistance (e.g., emotional, technology, physical) as needed.
- Have a basic understanding of the therapy goals.
- Be engaged in the session and inform the practitioner if you need something—in addition to what they are providing—to be successful.
- Ask for breaks if needed.

As mentioned earlier, before starting services, review, discuss, plan, and practice these roles and expectations with the youth.

General Learnings and Recommendations for Practice

Practitioners and providers also have some virtual roles and responsibilities to consider when engaging in technology-supported services with consumers.

Be prepared to be engaged as an "education conductor": Consumers should enter interventions with the willingness to share what learning styles work best, acknowledge transformative moments that may affect learning tendencies, and remain reflexive in thought challenge activities. As part of this process, the technology-based service provider should complete a learning style assessment with the technology consumer in addition to the digital literacy assessments.

Commit to device management: Remain committed to completing initial and ongoing installation of software applications used during interventions and attending to demonstrating the use via various mediums (e.g., provider instruction, automated video, peer engagement). The provider needs to be aware of software applications and installation needs to keep technology at its optimal performance. The technology-based practitioners should also assist the consumer with updating and maintaining their technology.

Be an active "tech engager": The technology provider needs to collaborate with the consumer to support them in being an active tech-engaged participant by demonstrating an openness to learning and internalizing increased understanding of technology and its benefits. The tech engager assists the consumer to remain productive and purposeful but is also forthcoming about needs, such as breaks, mood changes, and external issues. It will be helpful for the consumer to practice the processes of asking for a break (using a break card or visual sign), let the provider know how they are feeling (thumbs up, thumbs down, and other online reactions), and describe needs related to confidentiality and safety within the space where they are receiving the services.

Be a culture champion: Accept and take advantage of opportunities to share the cultural and linguistic differences of consumers. Remain open and teachable about the awareness of how these differences might influence the varying levels of participation throughout the intervention duration. Utilize opportunities to engage the consumer in conversations about their cultural and linguistic preferences and needs. This is an opportunity for the provider to learn more about the consumer and embed these cultural aspects into treatment and provided services.

Accept the necessity of new or rarely used communicative behaviors: The provider should adopt a disposition that accepts the use of more verbal or nonverbal communication and instruction than normal. During face-to-face meetings, activities give clues and indicators of feelings but are not often visible during virtual sessions. It is imperative to realize a reliance on one or more styles of therapeutic engagement may be necessary, depending on current therapy goals and progress.

Be aware of visibility variances: Discuss the length of time necessary to be on-screen, appropriate means for exiting, and established emergency accommodation for unexpected instances or discomfort due to current circumstances. It is imperative that the provider collaborate with the consumer to ensure that visual cues and other means of communicating screen use and time in sessions are clear and understood.

Take an active listener role: Everyone wants to feel heard and understood, but the practitioner must be a good listener. Listen to understand as well as listen to respond. Being a good listener includes a technique known as *active listening*: Slow down, practice patience, accept deep reflection practices, and withhold judgment. Active listening is important for building the personal and professional relationship that is the foundation of therapeutic intervention and is even more important in a virtual service delivery model.

Problem-Solving Technology Issues during Virtual Programming

Being prepared to manage potential issues with technology during service delivery is important for service success. Technology-based practitioners need to develop, practice, and plan for technology issues before and during virtual programming. Practitioners should include a guide or plan for technology failure. This plan should include tips and techniques for problem solving the technology issue, but, most importantly, it should include alternative methods of accessing services if technology is down (e.g., phone calls, text messages, face-to-face options). Additionally, the practitioner should discuss with the consumer what the provider will do or what will occur if a consumer is in crisis during an intervention or virtual session. Practitioners should work to develop resource directories and community-based supports that can be leveraged when needed during service delivery. Additional problem-solving processes should be considered and prepared for discussion and practice before services are initiated.

CONCLUSION

As practitioners and service providers continue to learn ways to traverse the world of virtual programming, we must also identify ways to better support consumers and clients within virtual spaces. Service providers must continue to adapt and hone skills and service models to address the needs of the populations they are serving. The Digital Inclusion Project resulted in an increase in confidence in using technology among 57 percent of the participants. This project demonstrates the importance of addressing digital literacy and its impact for increasing accessibility and availability of digital services for populations in a mid-south region of the United States. More work, though, needs to be done in the area of social work practice and technology as it relates to supporting clients and facilitating technology-focused research in practice. The Digital Inclusion Project is a small stepping stone toward that end goal within the field of social work.

REFERENCES

American Community Survey. (2018). *Census Bureau data.* https://www.census.gov/programs-surveys/acs/data.html

American Telemedicine Association. (2017, March). *Practical guidelines for telemental health with children and adolescents, 2017.* https://www.cdphp.com/-/media/files/providers/behavioral-health/hedis-toolkit-and-bh-guidelines/practice-guidelines-telemental-health.pdf?la=en

Barney, A., Buckelew, S., Mesheriakova, V., & Raymond-Flesch, M. (2020). The COVID-19 pandemic and rapid implementation of adolescent and young adult telemedicine: Challenges and opportunities for innovation. *Journal of Adolescent Health, 67,* 164–171.

Beers, S. (2011). *Teaching 21st century skills: An ASCD action tool.* ASCD.

Catalyst 30. (2020). [PowerPoint presentation.] https://catalyst30.com/wp-content/uploads/2020/07/Catalyst30-Deck-Long-Version.pdf

Cullen, R. (2001). Addressing the digital divide. *Online Information Review, 25,* 311–320. https://doi.org/10.1108/14684520110410517

De', R., Pandey, N., & Pal, A. (2020). Impact of digital surge during Covid-19 pandemic: A viewpoint on research and practice. *International Journal of Information Management, 55,* Article 102171. https://doi.org/10.1016/j.ijinfomgt.2020.102171

Diaper, D., & Stanton, N. (Eds.). (2003). *The handbook of task analysis for human-computer interaction.* CRC Press.

DiMaggio, P., & Hargittai, E. (2001). *From the "digital divide" to "digital inequality": Studying internet use as penetration increases* (Working Paper Series No. 15). Princeton University Center for Arts and Cultural Policy Studies.

DiMaggio, P., Hargittai, E., Celeste, C., & Shafer, S. (2004). *Digital inequality: From unequal access to differentiated use.* In K. Neckerman (Ed.), *Social inequality* (pp. 355–400). Russell Sage Foundation.

Gloff, N. E., LeNoue, S. R., Novins, D. K., & Myers, K. (2015). Telemental health for children and adolescents. *International Review of Psychiatry, 27,* 513–524.

Hamilton, A. M. (2020). A genealogy of critical race and digital studies: Past, present, and future. *Sociology of Race and Ethnicity, 6,* 292–301. https://doi.org/10.1177/2332649220922577

Health Resources & Services Administration. (n.d.). *Healthcare workforce shortage areas.* https://data.hrsa.gov/topics/health-workforce/shortage-areas

Hoffman, D. L., & Novak, T. P. (1999). *The evolution of the digital divide: Examining the relationship of race to internet access and usage over time.* https://www.academia.edu/2611297/The_evolution_of_the_digital_divide_Examining_the_relationship_of_race_to_Internet_access_and_usage_over_time

Irwin, V., Zhang, J., Wang, X., Hein, S., Wang, K., Roberts, A., York, C., Barmer, A., Bullock Mann, F., Dilig, R., & Parker, S. (2021). *Condition of education 2021.* https://nces.ed.gov/pubsearch/pubsinfo.asp?pubid=2021144#:~:text=Description%3A,the%20public%20monitor%20educational%20progress

Jacobson-Lundeberg, V. (2016). Pedagogical implementation of 21st century skills. *Educational Leadership and Administration: Teaching and Program Development, 27,* 82–100.

Khan, A. N., Bilek, E., Tomlinson, R. C., & Becker-Haimes, E. M. (2021). Treating social anxiety in an era of social distancing: Adapting exposure therapy for youth during COVID-19. *Cognitive and Behavioral Practice, 28,* 669–678.

Lai, J., & Widmar, N. O. (2021). Revisiting the digital divide in the COVID-19 era. *Applied Economic Perspectives and Policy, 43,* 458–464.

Leachman, M., Albares, N., Masterson, K., & Wallace, M. (2016, January 25). *Most states have cut school funding and some continue cutting.* Center on Budget and Policy Priorities. https://www.cbpp.org/research/state-budget-and-tax/most-states-have-cut-school-funding-and-some-continue-cutting

Lindgren, S., Wacker, D., Schieltz, K., Suess, A., Pelzel, K., Kopelman, T., & O'Brien, M. (2020). A randomized controlled trial of functional communication training via telehealth for young children with autism spectrum disorder. *Journal of Autism and Developmental Disorders, 50,* 4449–4462.

Moore, R., Vitale, D., & Stawingoa, N. (2018, August). *The digital divide and educational equity. A look at students with very limited access to electronic devices at home.* Insights in Education and Work. https://www.act.org/content/dam/act/unsecured/documents/R1698-digital-divide-2018-08.pdf

Organisation for Economic Co-operation and Development. (2001). *Understanding the digital divide.* https://www.oecd.org/digital/ieconomy/1888451.pdf

Patel, M. L., Wakayama, L. N., Bass, M. B., & Breland, J. Y. (2019). Motivational interviewing in eHealth and telehealth interventions for weight loss: A systematic review. *Preventive Medicine, 126,* Article 105738.

Pew Research Center. (2021, April 7). *Internet/broadband fact sheet.* https://www.pewresearch.org/internet/fact-sheet/internet-broadband

Pittman, C. T. (2010). Race and gender oppression in the classroom: The experiences of women faculty of color with white male students. *Teaching Sociology, 38,* 183–196.

Prensky, M. (2001a). Digital natives, digital immigrants, Part 1. *On the Horizon, 9,* 1–6. https://doi.org/10.1108/10748120110424816

Prensky, M. (2001b). Digital natives, digital immigrants, Part II: Do they really think differently? *On the Horizon, 9,* 1–9. https://doi.org/10.1108/10748120110424843

Ramsetty, A., & Adams, C. (2020). Impact of the digital divide in the age of COVID-19. *Journal of the American Medical Informatics Association, 27,* 1147–1148.

Real, B., Bertot, C., & Jaeger, P. T. (2014). Rural public libraries and digital inclusion: Issues and challenges. *Information Technology & Libraries, 33,* 6–24. https://doi .org/10.6017/ital.v33i1.5141

Resnick, M. (2002). Rethinking learning in the digital age. In G. Kirkman (Ed.), *The global information technology report: Readiness for the networked world* (pp. 32–38). Oxford University Press.

Sato, B. K., Lee, A. K., Alam, U., Dang, J. V., Dacanay, S. J., Morgado, P., Pirino, G., Brunner, J. E., Castillo, L. A., Chan, V. W., & Sandholtz, J. H. (2017). What's in a prerequisite? A mixed-methods approach to identifying the impact of a prerequisite course. *CBE Life Sciences Education, 16,* Article 16. https://doi.org/ 10.1187/cbe.16-08-0260

Sieck, C. J., Sheon, A., Ancker, J. S., Castek, J., Callahan, B., & Siefer, A. (2021). Digital inclusion as a social determinant of health. *npj Digital Medicine, 4,* Article 52. https://doi.org/10.1038/s41746-021-00413-8

Skinner, A., Diller, D., Kumar, R., Cannon-Bowers, J., Smith, R., Tanaka, A., & Perez, R. (2018). Development and application of a multi-modal task analysis to support intelligent tutoring of complex skills. *International Journal of STEM Education, 5,* 1–17.

Stewart, R. W., Orengo-Aguayo, R., Young, J., Wallace, M. M., Cohen, J. A., Mannarino, A. P., & de Arellano, M. A. (2020). Feasibility and effectiveness of a telehealth service delivery model for treating childhood posttraumatic stress: A community-based, open pilot trial of trauma-focused cognitive–behavioral therapy. *Journal of Psychotherapy Integration, 30,* 274–289.

Thomas, K., Ellis, A., Konrad, T., Holzer, C., & Morrissey, J. (2009). County-level estimates of mental health professional shortage in the United States. *Psychiatric Services, 60,* 1323–1328. https://doi.org/10.1176/appi.ps.60.10.1323

U.S. Census Bureau. (2018). *2018 ACS 1-year estimates.* https://www.census .gov/programs-surveys/acs/technical-documentation/table-and-geography-changes/2018/1-year.html

U.S. Census Bureau. (2020). *2020 census results.* https://www.census.gov/programs-surveys/decennial-census/decade/2020/2020-census-results.html

Van Dijk, J. (2020). *The digital divide.* Wiley.

CHAPTER 4
Advancing Data Justice

Neil Ballantyne

Doing social work in an online world presents many opportunities, risks, and challenges. The broader implications of the datafication of society are still emerging, but there are clear issues of human rights and social justice associated with the nascent digital welfare state (Alston, 2019; Dencik, 2022; Dencik & Kaun, 2020) and the rise of algorithmic governance (AI Now Institute, 2018; Katzenbach & Ulbricht, 2019; Yeung, 2018). A burgeoning literature in the field of critical data studies (Iliadis & Russo, 2016; Kitchin & Lauriault, 2014) has focused attention on the harms that data do (Redden, 2017, 2018; Redden et al., 2020). The term "data justice" is used to refer to these issues and to foreground the disproportional impact on historically marginalized and oppressed social groups (Dencik, 2020; Dencik et al., 2018; Dencik & Sanchez-Monedero, 2022). Calls are now being made for social and community workers to consider the implications of data justice for their practice (Goldkind et al., 2019, 2021; LaMendola, 2019; LaMendola & Ballantyne, in press).

This chapter begins with an introduction to datafication and its societal implications and then explores, using three short case studies, issues with the use of algorithms in government services. The chapter concludes by considering the strategies that social and community workers might employ to achieve data justice. But first is a short preamble on my own position in relation to datafication.

PREAMBLE ON POSITIONALITY

I write this as a Scottish immigrant, social work academic working in the settler colonial state of Aotearoa New Zealand. I have had a long-standing research interest in technology applications in human services settings (Ballantyne, 1996, 2015, 2019) and, for many years, was involved with the Human Services Information

87

Technology Association (husITa).* Aotearoa New Zealand may seem like a remote context for a researcher interested in the study of human services technology, yet it was the site of the world's first initiative to trial a predictive risk modeling (PRM) tool in the child protection system (New Zealand Government, 2012b; Vaithianathan et al., 2012). This government-led initiative tested the implementation of a machine learning algorithm—trained on linked health and social welfare databases—to calculate a risk of maltreatment score for every newborn child in the country. The announcement of this development in 2012 (New Zealand Government, 2012a, 2012b) triggered a robust debate among professionals, politicians, and researchers (Ballantyne, 2019, 2021). The PRM hit the headlines for the final time in 2016, when a new minister for social development made a dramatic announcement that a planned observational study on the use of the PRM tool had been closed because of serious ethical concerns, and the minister in question stated that "these are children, not lab-rats" (Kirk, 2016). For a more detailed account of the history and dynamics of the Aotearoa New Zealand PRM tool, see Ballantyne (2019, 2021) and Jørgensen et al. (2021).

Despite the dramatic closure† of what came to be known as "the New Zealand model," the rise of big data and the promise of predictive analytics in social welfare continued to expand across the globe. Several of these applications focus on the promise of predictive analytics in the field of child protection (Jørgensen et al., 2021; Saxena et al., 2020), and some of them, especially the Allegheny project in the United States—included as a case study later in this chapter—have been strongly influenced by key actors associated with the New Zealand model (Chouldechova et al., 2018; Cuccaro-Alamin et al., 2017; Dare & Gambrill, 2017; Vaithianathan et al., 2017).

DATAFICATION OF EVERYTHING

Datafication is about more than the digitization of information or making digital information accessible on electronic networks, although both are necessary precursors to the process of datafication (Mejias & Couldry, 2019). Kitchin (2014) described *data* as the "material produced by abstracting the world into categories, measures and other representational forms . . . that constitute the building blocks

---

* husITa, established in 1987, is an international virtual association with the mission of promoting the ethical and effective use of information technology in the human services (for more information, see Human Services Information Technology Association, n.d.).

† The shuttering of initiatives to introduce automated systems into public services is not unusual and is the subject of a study titled "Automating Public Services: Learning from Cancelled Systems" by the Data Justice Lab (n.d.).

from which information and knowledge are created" (p. 1). Although data can be derived from any entity in the universe (and need not be in digital format), the term *datafication* usually refers to human data rendered digital; the ubiquitous nature of data collection (from formal administrative data collection to the routine capture of data while using the Web, cell phones, credit cards, and so on); the rise of big data (boyd & Crawford, 2011; Cukier & Mayer-Schoenberger, 2013; Manovich, 2012; Mayer-Schoenberger & Cukier, 2013); and the ways in which databases can now be linked, analyzed, and manipulated to surveil, profile, and predict human preferences, attributes, and behaviors. This phenomenon is now so pervasive that commentators refer to "the datafication of everything" (Mayer-Schoenberger & Cukier, 2013), including data captured administratively in routine government datasets, such as those held by health, social welfare, and criminal justice services. Datafication, then, is not simply about rendering data digital but the ubiquitous capture of human attributes and activities in databases that can be linked, analyzed, and classified. It includes the use of artificial intelligence (AI)—especially machine learning algorithms trained on historical data—to predict future behaviors and recommend actions in the form of automated decision making (ADM) systems to support health, welfare, and criminal justice agencies. When understood in this way, datafication presents a "profound transformation in how society is ordered, decisions are made, and citizens are monitored through 'big data'" (Hintz et al., 2018, p. 2).

Datafication is closely associated with the disciplinary field of data science. The terminology of data science, and computer science more broadly, is an important resource for social and community workers who seek to understand the difference that datafication is making to our world. The following 10 key terms will be useful for our present purposes and will help social and community workers seeking to make sense of local datafication initiatives:

Algorithm: A set of rules a computer uses to create an output, such as detecting a pattern in a dataset. The use of algorithms is associated with the rise of big data, and they are increasingly used to support decision making and to make predictions in domains as diverse as insurance, healthcare, social welfare, and law.

Algorithmic bias: Occurs when the output of an algorithmic process, such as a risk score, systematically privileges or biases one social group over another. Such biases usually occur because the historical dataset used to "train" the algorithm includes data influenced by personal or institutional prejudices in relation to race, gender, sexuality, disability, or ethnicity.

Algorithmic governance: The intentional use of algorithms to regulate, constrain, or influence the behavior of decision makers in the treatment of citizens or the management of workers.

ADM: The use of big data, machine learning algorithms, and predictive analytics to make or support decisions (with different degrees of human oversight from none to considerable) in a growing range of contexts, including healthcare, social welfare, and law.

AI: A field concerned with the study and development of machines that can perform tasks normally requiring human intelligence. Current applications of AI are closely associated with the advent of big data and machine learning.

Big data: A field associated with the rise of massive digital datasets and the use of machine learning and algorithms to detect historical patterns and generate useful insights that cannot be detected by human observers acting alone.

Datafication: The process whereby a growing number of behaviors, processes, and practices are captured digitally and rendered in a form that make them amenable to data mining, machine learning, aggregation, calculation, classification, and prediction.

Digital welfare state: Refers to the growing use of data-driven technologies by government agencies to surveil, identify, predict, detect, target, and punish citizens. Data-driven technologies are transforming existing welfare state processes, including identity verification, eligibility assessments, benefit calculations, fraud detection, risk scoring, need classification, and information sharing among welfare authorities.

Human-in-the-loop: The process of combining machine and human intelligence to achieve the best results is often referred to as "keeping a human-in-the-loop." Human oversight of algorithmic operations is assumed to be able to verify the predictions of the AI model, overrule AI-generated predictions, or send feedback to improve the model. More recently, some researchers have used the term "algorithm-in-the-loop" to emphasize primacy of the human over AI.

Machine learning: A subfield of AI involving computer algorithms that can "learn" by finding patterns in historical datasets (usually called "training" datasets). Once "trained," the algorithms then apply these findings to new datasets to make predictions or provide other useful outputs, such as facial recognition. Problems arise when the historical datasets used to train the algorithms—usually based on subjective interpretations and judgments—are flawed, incomplete, or biased (see the earlier key term, algorithmic bias).

Predictive analytics: The use of algorithms and machine learning to analyze historical datasets to model and predict future outcomes often in the form of a risk score, such as the likelihood that a child will be maltreated or that an offender will reoffend.

Some social work and social welfare commentors on datafication are keen to harness big data for social good and, while aware of the limitations and ethical issues, foreground the benefits of harnessing big data "to inform policy and practice responses to persistent social issues such as poverty, crime, child maltreatment, and health disparities" (Coulton et al., 2015, p. 10). Other more cautious and critical scholars highlight problematic ethical and practice issues associated with big data applications in social work and social welfare (Devlieghere et al., 2022; Gillingham, 2019; Gillingham & Graham, 2016; Goldkind et al., 2019, 2021; Keddell, 2014, 2019). This chapter adopts a critical approach to datafication and the adoption of algorithmic forms of decision making in government services and is grounded in critical theory and in the field of critical data studies (Iliadis & Russo, 2016; Kitchin & Lauriault, 2014). Before considering what data justice might mean for the practice of social and community workers, the next section puts the issues into context through the use of three critical case studies illustrating the datafication of government services.

DATAFICATION OF GOVERNMENT SERVICES: THREE CASE STUDIES

This section explores three short case studies in which different degrees of ADM were introduced to assist government agencies in assessing risk and to rationalize, target, or manage resources. The first case study considers the implementation of a predictive policing system in Los Angeles. The second describes an automated fraud detection and debt recovery system in the Australian social security service. The third discusses a predictive risk modeling tool used to screen families referred to child protective services in Allegheny County, Pennsylvania. All three cases involve high-stakes decision making in which actual or potential harm may occur, and all three were deeply controversial. I describe the main features of each case before offering a critical commentary on the issues.

PredPol

The Los Angeles Police Department (LAPD) has a long-standing reputation for the use of technology in policing practices and in the development of predictive policing technologies (Bhuiyan, 2021). Indeed, the LAPD was actively involved in the development of PredPol, an algorithmic, place-based predictive policing system to forecast the times and places—mapped to a 500-foot by 500-foot grid of neighborhood cells known as "hot spots"—where certain types of crime might occur (Harris, 2017). The LAPD's eagerness to harness predictive analytics as part of its SMART Policing Initiative (Stop LAPD Spying Coalition, 2018) extended to include a person-based predictive policing system. That system allocates risk scores to persons of interest considered to be connected to gun and gang violence within targeted neighborhoods—known as "hot people"—in the community.* The hope was—and the claims of the commercial developers were—that the use of these systems would support objective, data-driven, evidence-based decisions to target the distribution of limited policing resources to protect communities and reduce crime. Despite developers' claims, the algorithm used by PredPol was not especially sophisticated (Haskins, 2019a, 2019b). It used historical crime data that captured three key attributes: (1) crime type, (2) crime location, and (3) time of crime. The data were sourced from records of citizens' calls for a police service and the observed crime reports of patrol officers. As Ensign et al. (2018) highlighted, "PredPol, in essence, is predicting where incidents will be reported or discovered (since that's all it sees), not where crime will happen" (p. 3). At the beginning of each shift, officers would use the current crime rate predictions, or "hot spots," to guide their patrols, and the database was continually updated as new crime reports came in and made predictions based on historical averages combined with recent activity.

However, the result, over several years, was an intensification of police patrol presence in low-income communities of color that were already overpoliced, the collapse of community trust in the police service, and a rise in community resistance to overpolicing and data injustice. The campaigning activity and community-based research reports produced by the Stop LAPD Spying Coalition[†] (Stop LAPD Spying Coalition, 2018, 2021), in combination with the wider media and academic

---

* This short case study focuses on PredPol, but additional information about Operation Laser's person-based predictive policing system can be found in Stop LAPD Spying Coalition (2018).
† Stop LAPD Spying describes itself as a grassroots community organization founded in 2011. It works to build community power toward abolishing police surveillance and is based in the Skid Row neighborhood of downtown Los Angeles, working as part of the Los Angeles Community Action Network (see https://stoplapdspying.org).

outcry against predictive policing (Lindner, 2020), made a significant contribution to the eventual shuttering of PredPol in 2020, although not an end to all forms of predictive policing by the LAPD (Bhuiyan, 2021).

Robodebt

> In the weeks leading up to Christmas 2016, Australians were checking their letterboxes—for Christmas cards, an aunty's annual Christmas newsletter, and last-minute online gift purchases. Some Australians checking their letterbox found an unwanted surprise waiting for them—a letter from Centrelink advising they owed hundreds or thousands of dollars in Centrelink overpayments made as far back as 2010. (Miller, 2017, p. 50)

In 2001 the Australian national government amended its Social Security [Administration] Act to allow government agencies to use ADM by computer programs (Elvery, 2017). In 2016, the Australia Department of Human Services used this power to introduce an online compliance intervention (OCI) system into its Centrelink program for the administration of social security, family assistance, and other support payments (Glenn, 2017). The OCI used a data cross-matching algorithm to compare earnings recorded on a customer's Centrelink record with historical employer-reported income data from the Australian Taxation Office and issued automated debt raising and recovery notifications whenever debts were detected. The system replaced a prior process in which departmental officials evaluated discrepancies, chased down employer records, and assessed accuracy before issuing debt notifications (Braithwaite, 2020). This fully automated system became known colloquially as "Robodebt," and its error-prone nature made it so controversial that it soon became subject to a report by the Commonwealth Ombudsman (Glenn, 2017).*

The system issued millions of dollars' worth of incorrect debt recovery notices to thousands of welfare recipients (Miller, 2017) based on inaccurate personal details and mistaken employment information. Welfare recipients received debt recovery notifications that were difficult to understand and hard to contest, and they found it challenging to obtain explanations from Centrelink staff, causing many to experience anxiety, distress, and distrust of government services (Farrell & McDonald, 2019; Henriques-Gomes, 2020; Karp, 2019; Marjanovic et al., 2021).

---

* The Commonwealth Ombudsman is an independent agency established to investigate complaints about actions and decisions of Australian government agencies and acts to improve public administration.

One of the most problematic aspects of the system was that it reversed the burden of proof: It required welfare recipients to disprove the assumed debt by providing documentation of earnings going back many years. One former member of the social security Administrative Appeals Tribunal went so far as to describe the operation of Robodebt as a form of extortion (Farrell & McDonald, 2019).

In 2020, following mounting public pressure and two lost lawsuits, the Australian government declared that Robodebt was unlawful, closed the system down, and agreed to waive 470,000 debts with refunds amounting to $721 million. In June 2021, a federal court judge approved the settlement of a Robodebt class action worth more than $1.7 billion in financial benefits to approximately 430,000 individuals (Gordon Legal, n.d.).

Allegheny Family Screening Tool

In Allegheny County, Pennsylvania, workers in the county's Department of Human Services have, since 2016, been using the AI-based Allegheny Family Screening Tool (Allegheny County, n.d.) to support child welfare call screening to determine which reports of child maltreatment should qualify for investigation. Unlike our other two case studies, this algorithmic tool is still very much in use.* The AFST is a machine learning, predictive risk modeling tool trained on historical case data; it uses data held in the county's data warehouse to predict outcomes related to child maltreatment.

The AFST has not been trained to predict the likelihood of child maltreatment but uses proxy measure of the likelihood of home removal within two years of being screened in. The AFST analyzes demographic data related to children referred, their caretakers, and any alleged perpetrators, including child welfare, criminal records, and behavioral health history (Vaithianathan et al., 2017). It outputs a risk score between 1 (low risk of future placement) and 20 (high risk of future placement). A risk score of 18 or higher is considered a mandatory screen-in score, and although this recommendation can be overridden, a call screening supervisor must go through a process of completing an open-text field in the system to explain the decision to override. The AFST was not designed to replace or automate human decision making but to augment decision making about whether to investigate a call made to the child maltreatment hotline (Cherna, 2018). In this sense, it is a good example of human–AI collaboration or a system with a human-in-the-loop. Call screening workers, in consultation with their supervisors, use the risk score and a range of other data to make the final decision about whether to screen in a case.

---

* See Allegheny County (n.d.) for more information about the AFST.

There are well-established concerns about the use of algorithms in high-stakes domains, such as child protection, since social welfare workers are known to make racially disparate decisions (Dettlaff & Boyd, 2020; Roberts, 2014). Therefore, the historical data on which predictive algorithms are trained are highly likely to include such bias (Eubanks, 2018; National Coalition for Child Protection Reform, 2019; Roberts, 2019). These disparities may reflect genuinely greater risks in some population groups but may equally be influenced by personal bias and institutional racism (Dettlaff & Boyd, 2020; Roberts, 2014). In this context, there are often concerns, and some evidence, that algorithmic risk scores might amplify the bias built into training datasets, leading workers to play it safe by making biased decisions and creating a feedback loop that worsens disproportional, racially biased decision making over time (Keddell, 2014, 2019; Roberts, 2019).

Perhaps because they were mindful of these possibilities, the Allegheny County Department of Human Services has been open to external scrutiny and research (Cheng, Stapleton, et al., 2022; De-Arteaga et al., 2020; Kawakami et al., 2022). One study (De-Arteaga et al., 2020) explored how child welfare workers respond to risk scores that are erroneous (due to a technical glitch). Their findings indicated that, although workers do change their behavior as a result of the introduction of the AFST, screening in more cases with high-risk scores, "workers successfully make use of other sources of information and are more likely to override the machine when the shown score is significantly miscalculated" (De-Arteaga et al., 2020, p. 8). The findings of more recent studies (Cheng, Stapleton, et al., 2022; Kawakami et al., 2022) revealed that the AFST does indeed produce racially disproportionate scores that, if followed blindly, would have led to 20 percent more Black children than White children being screened in.* However, Cheng, Stapleton, et al. (2022) found that the intervention of workers reduced the racial disparity in screen-in rates from 20 percent to 9 percent and did so by making holistic risk assessments that put the algorithmic risk score in the context of other case information.

CRITICAL COMMENTARY ON THE CASE STUDIES

One of the fundamental issues with the datafication of society is the extent to which data science and big data applications are presented as benign, objective arbiters of ground truth. The discourse about big data includes what boyd and Crawford (2012) have described as a mythological dimension and "the widespread belief that large data

---

* Indeed, if there had been a fully automated, algorithm-only, decision-making policy with no human-in-the-loop, 71 percent of Black children referred would have been screened in (Cheng, Stapleton, et al., 2022; Kawakami et al., 2022).

sets offer a higher form of intelligence and knowledge that can generate insights that were previously impossible, with the aura of truth, objectivity, and accuracy" (p. 663). Indeed, as indicated by the preceding three case studies, and as many scholars have highlighted (boyd et al., 2014; Gitelman, 2013; Kitchin, 2014, 2021), data—especially data about human subjects—come already cooked and are shaped by many layers of prior decision making. As Kitchin (2021) put it, "Data then are not benign, neutral measures that reflect the world as it is, within technical constraints. What data are generated, and how they are produced, handled and used, is the result of choices and decisions by people" (p. 5). When data are applied by the digital welfare state to target, profile, and socially sort citizens in ways that impact their access to finances, housing, education, employment, health, and welfare services (Eubanks, 2018; O'Neil, 2016; Redden et al., 2020), it is not surprising that issues of data justice arise.

The earlier three case descriptions are necessarily short accounts of large and complex cases that continue to be debated in the literature. However, there is a reasonable degree of consensus on the main features of each case and the data harms identified. Redden et al. (2020) offer a definition of *data harm* as "the adverse effects caused by uses of data that may impair, injure, or set back a person, entity or society's interests" (para. 8). Data-driven applications that lead to the overpolicing of marginalized communities, which causes stress to vulnerable populations by making false claims of fraud or widening the net to draw too many Black families into the child protection system, are an example of data harm. While earlier conceptions of the problem of datafication tended to frame this in terms of surveillance and the loss of privacy for all citizens, more recent accounts highlight issues of social justice and the differential impacts of datafication on historically marginalized social groups. Explaining the concept of data justice, Dencik and Sanchez-Monedero (2022) contended that

> data-centric information systems are instrumental as systems of control, not just by increasing the potential for monitoring, but as sorting mechanisms. Data justice debates tend to understand how these sorting mechanisms work and what their relationship is to historical contexts, social structures and dominant agendas as not just a question of individual privacy, but one of justice. To speak of data justice is thus to recognise not only how data, its collection and use, increasingly impacts on society, but also that datafication is enabled by particular forms of political and economic organization that advance a normative vision of how social issues should be understood and resolved. (p. 3)

CASE ANALYSIS

Turning to an analysis of these three cases, the first two were closed following a sustained critique from community organizers, legal advocates, media reports, and internal auditors. The third case, the AFST, although controversial, is still in use.

In the case of PredPol, historical data were used to make predictions about where and when incidents of crime might occur, and once police were deployed to neighborhoods, any further incidents observed by police would be used to update the database on future predictions. Since it is well established that racially biased policing practices tend to focus patrols on poor and Black neighborhoods that become subject to hypersurveillance, it is highly likely that any historical dataset has racial bias baked into it (boyd et al., 2014; Crawford, 2013; Richardson et al., 2019).

In addition, since the PredPol system was updated with each new criminal incident observed, Ensign et al. (2018) argued that because "such discovered incidents only occur in neighborhoods that police have been sent to *by the predictive policing algorithm itself*, there is the potential for this sampling bias to be compounded, causing a runaway feedback loop" (p. 2). In a simulation, Lum and Isaac (2016) have shown that this feedback loop is likely to occur, causing oversurveillance of some neighborhoods and divergence from true crime rates. Such feedback loops can occur in any predictive system—"including recidivism prediction, hiring algorithms, college admissions, and the distribution of loans" (Ensign et al., 2018)—where results fed back into the system are influenced by the algorithms' own predictions.

In the case of Robodebt, the issues associated with it were not derived from training an algorithm on biased historical data but with faulty assumptions used to calculate debt and the way in which the system was operationalized. Robodebt was found to be in breach of the law* and shifted the burden of proof to welfare recipients to disprove the debt asserted. The assumed debt was calculated by the algorithm's averaging annual earnings reported to the tax office to obtain an average amount over a period of 14 days, taking no account of actual variations in earnings. Therefore,

> the apportioned data was not accurate or probative for . . . those with multiple employers, young people with varying hours, and others in casual employment. The data was not capable of reflecting the variations in loading or entitlements that increasingly occur in the modern workplace. (O'Donovan, 2020, p. 36)

---

* The outcome of a federal court case—*Amato v the Commonwealth of Australia*—supported the legal principle that "a calculation using averaged data matched from the person's pay as you go summary does not meet the standard of certainty required by the statutory provisions" (O'Donovan, 2020, p. 36).

Braithwaite (2020) highlighted that "stigma surrounding social welfare recipients and public outrage around welfare fraud have meant that the government has been able to claim social licence to run its Robodebt programme without being held accountable" (p. 244). Furthermore, Braithwaite (2020) argued that Robodebt not only inflicted harms on individual citizens, but stubborn persistence with a failing system undermined the government's integrity and threatened democracy by undermining the trust of citizens. Referring to the idea of procedural justice, Braithwaite (2020) contended:

> People expect to be treated as if their life matters and that they are no less worthy than anyone else. Procedural justice is a relational gift by government to its citizens. A substantial body of research demonstrates that treating people in a way that they perceive as being procedurally fair will increase the likelihood that they will trust and cooperate with an authority and perceive its power as legitimate. The submissions to the 2017 Senate Inquiry illustrated repeatedly that those targeted by Robodebt did not regard their treatment as procedurally fair nor respectful. (p. 253)

In the case of both PredPol and Robodebt, there was initial organizational resistance to reviewing or closing the projects. This is a phenomenon known as *project escalation* in which organizations sometimes persist with projects even in the face of feedback that strongly suggests impending project failure (Drummond, 2017).

In the case of the Allegheny AFST, concerns expressed about the tendency of algorithmic-based systems to make racially disproportionate recommendations to screen in Black children were borne out by the findings. However, in this case, keeping the child welfare call workers as humans-in-the-loop mitigated the disproportionate scores of the algorithm.* Call screening workers balanced the algorithmic risk score with other rich, qualitative, contextual data about the case and were empowered, in consultation with their supervisors, to overrule the algorithmic recommendation (Cheng, Holstein, et al., 2022; Cheng, Stapleton, et al., 2022; Kawakami et al., 2022). This evidence strongly counsels against using full ADM in high-stakes contexts and recognizes that "humans' discretionary power and ability to integrate information that is unobserved by the algorithm can have important fairness implications" (Fogliato et al., 2022, p. 25).

---

* If the AFST recommendation had been followed in all cases, 71 percent of all Black children referred would have been screened in, and only 51 percent of White children would have been screened in (Cheng, Holstein, et al., 2022).

However, a closer analysis of the rationale for workers' decision making based on qualitative data uncovered some complex issues with the nature of the human–AI partnership process and the ways in which workers took account of the AFST risk score. Significantly, although the algorithm scored risk in terms of longer-term risk of out-of-home care (within two years), workers and their supervisors were firmly focused on, and made decisions based on, immediate risk to the child's safety "or specific details about the referral that could be longer-term sources of risk, regardless of whether they would lead to removal from home" (Cheng, Stapleton, et al., 2022, p. 13). The qualitative study found that this basic value misalignment meant that "it was unclear to workers how exactly they were expected to take the AFST's assessments of long-term risk into account in ways that complemented their own judgment" (Kawakami et al., 2022, p. 15). Indeed, Kawakami et al. (2022) found that the humans in this human–AI partnership "tended to be distrustful of the tool overall" (p. 14) and Cheng, Stapleton, et al. (2022) argued that "future work is necessary in order to better evaluate how the AFST positively contributes to the decision-making process, if at all" (p. 13). The researchers also acknowledged that their focus on algorithmic fairness with respect to racially disparate decision making did not address fundamental structural inequalities or the political and economic context within which the system was deployed (Abdurahman, 2021; Roberts, 2019).

The literature includes conflicting findings on the efficacy of human-in-the-loop oversight of algorithmic systems, with two contrasting trends apparent in different decision-making contexts. On the one hand, *algorithmic aversion* refers to the tendency of human decision makers to ignore algorithmic predictions that are assumed to be mistaken even when they may be helpful; on the other hand, *automation bias* refers to the tendency of humans to comply with algorithmic recommendations even when there is conflicting information suggesting the prediction might be erroneous (De-Arteaga et al., 2020; Fogliato et al., 2022). Some studies have suggested that—contra the AFST findings—human-in-the-loop decision making can lead to an intensification of racially disparate decisions (e.g., Albright, 2019). In the context of this broader set of findings about the human oversight of government algorithms, Green (2022) has argued that "the vast majority of research suggests that people are unable to provide reliable oversight of algorithms" (p. 7) and called for a two-stage, institutional approach to the regulation of government algorithms, whereby

> first, agencies must justify that it is appropriate to incorporate an algorithm into decision-making and that any proposed forms of human oversight are supported by empirical evidence. Second,

these justifications must receive democratic review and approval before the agency can adopt the algorithm. (p. 1)

Green (2022) proposed this model of institutional oversight to avoid the dangers inherent in the flawed assumption that human oversight alone is sufficient to ensure the safety of government algorithms.

DATA JUSTICE IS A SOCIAL WORK ISSUE

One might accept that a critical approach to the social implications of datafication is an appropriate one for analysts and researchers working in the sociological subfield of science and technology studies (Ribes, 2019; Sismondo, 2010). But why should any of this be of concern to social and community workers? The *Code of Ethics of the National Association of Social Workers* (NASW, 2021) includes a definition of the mission of social work:

> The primary mission of the social work profession is to enhance human well-being and help meet the basic human needs of all people, with particular attention to the needs and empowerment of people who are vulnerable, oppressed, and living in poverty. A historic and defining feature of social work is the profession's dual focus on individual well-being in a social context and the well-being of society. Fundamental to social work is attention to the environmental forces that create, contribute to, and address problems in living. (Preamble, para. 1)

If we, as social and community workers, accept the understanding of data justice just outlined, then we must recognize that the processes of datafication impact disproportionately on historically marginalized groups, especially those "who are vulnerable, oppressed, and living in poverty" (NASW, 2021, Preamble, para. 1). This is very evident from the case study discussions and from the many instances of data harm cataloged by the Data Justice Lab (Redden et al., 2020). With regard to the NASW definition of the mission of social work, datafication is clearly a new "environmental force" that is creating "problems in living" for citizens and users of social services (Redden, 2017, 2018). Moreover, the NASW mission statement is very similar to the statement of purpose developed by the International Federation of Social Workers (2014) and by professional social work associations across the world. They all recognize the need to pay attention to the "empowerment of people who are vulnerable, oppressed, and living in poverty"

(NASW, 2021, Preamble, para. 1) and recognize the macro-level forces in societies that "create, contribute to, and address problems in living" (NASW, 2021, Preamble, para. 1). My contention here is that the datafication of our societies is an emerging macro-level force, creating harms that impact disproportionally on historically marginalized social groups. In other words, the advancement of data justice is a significant social work issue.

Advancing Data Justice

It is one thing to state that data justice is a social work issue, but what can and should social and community workers do about datafication? How can we advance data justice? There are at least three potential avenues of engagement with data justice issues, each associated with different kinds of actions. Which route to take will depend on the role, context, and remit of social workers and the particular datafication issues that emerge in their communities.

First, at a micro level, social workers act as social justice advocates for individual service users (O'Brien, 2011), and there will be many opportunities to advocate for service users experiencing data harms (Goldkind et al., 2019, 2021). However, to be effective advocates in the age of datafication, social and community workers need critical data literacy (Brand & Sander, 2020; Sander, 2020a, 2020b). Second, at a mezzo level, social and community workers can encourage citizen engagement in datafication processes, ensuring that—before implementation—the voices of those most impacted are engaged and attended to in any new development (Costanza-Chock, 2020; Data Justice Lab, 2021). Third, at a macro level, social and community workers should recognize, value, and act as allies to autonomous, community-based data activism (Dencik et al., 2019; Milan, 2019; Milan & van der Velden, 2016), including activism in relation to Indigenous data sovereignty (Kukutai & Taylor, 2016; Te Mana Raraunga, 2018; Walter et al., 2020).

Promoting Critical Data Literacy

Data literacy is a term that is in relatively common use and usually defined as the knowledge and skills citizens need to participate in the digital world.* However, in the context of data justice, the capabilities required are not simply those enabling participation; instead, citizens need to be able to understand and reflect critically on the implications of datafication. As Sander (2020a) argued, "Datafied societies need *informed public debate* about the implications of data science technologies" (p. e5-1; emphasis in the original). Yet many citizens do not have the data literacy

---

* See, for example, the European Commission's Digital Competence Framework (Carretero Gomez et al., 2017).

skills that would enable them to engage in such debate. In the context of datafication and big data, Sander (2020a) argued that *critical data literacy* is a more fitting
term, and that to be critically data literate means

> being aware of and able to critically reflect upon big data collection
> practices, data uses and the possible risks and implications that
> come with these practices, as well as being capable of implement-
> ing this knowledge for a more empowered internet usage. (p. 5)

Social and community workers may wonder how they can promote critical
data literacy when their own skills in this domain may be lacking. Clearly, there
is a role here for including critical data literacy within the social work curriculum and continuing professional development. The good news is that a growing
number of online data literacy tools are available, including workshop materials
and self-paced, interactive learning opportunities, that have been curated by data
activists and data researchers (e.g., Brand & Sander, 2020; Sander, 2019). Sander
(2020a) contended that "online data literacy tools can provide a substantial means
to work toward empowering internet users and engaging citizens in public debates
about data systems" (p. e5-1).

Advocating Citizen Engagement and Participation

Ensuring that citizens have a level of critical data literacy is, in a sense, a precon-
dition for the second avenue for advancing data justice: citizen participation in
system design (Barnett et al., n.d.; Costanza-Chock, 2018, 2020) and in reviews of
proposed plans to introduce government algorithmic systems (Data Justice Lab,
2021; Dencik, 2019; Hintz, 2020; Hintz et al., 2018; McQuillan, 2018). Arguments
for the involvement of citizens in system design, especially those citizens whose
lives are most likely to be impacted by the systems, should be familiar to most
social and community workers. Codesign and other participatory approaches
(Barnes & Cotterell, 2011) are well established as modern ways of creating responsive social services and grew out of dissatisfaction and demands of the disability
movement that there should be "nothing about us without us" (Charlton, 1998).

These same arguments have been picked up by critical data scientists and
others in the human–computer interaction community to argue for antioppres-
sive approaches to the design of digital systems (Costanza-Chock, 2020; Fox et
al., 2017; Smyth & Dimond, 2014). This perspective has crystalized into calls for
"design justice" (Costanza-Chock, 2018, 2020), now expressed in a set of 10 design
justice principles articulated by the Design Justice Network (Barnett et al., n.d.).

However, we must also be realistic and recognize that many AI system implementations are predesigned by private sector actors' adopting a technorational approach to system design with little reference to the views or perspectives of service users. Not only that, but these systems are often commercially protected and opaque. Even so, before the adoption and implementation of data-driven systems, they can still be subject to the scrutiny of community and service user organizations using a range of models of civic engagement such as mini-publics: events that bring together citizens to deliberate on issues of public concern such as citizen juries and citizen assemblies (Data Justice Lab, 2021). The idea of achieving a *social license*—gaining community acceptance and trust for the introduction of new systems or practices—is critical here, and social and community workers, in their role as advocates of social justice, have a key part to play (Dare, 2022; Data Futures Partnership, 2017; Edwards et al., 2021; Gulliver et al., 2018).

Alliances with Data Activists

Of course, not all data justice initiatives can or should be initiated by social or community workers. Indeed, some of the most significant critiques and oppositional actions emanate from community-based organizations, civil liberty organizations, and other nongovernmental actors. The very effective resistance to PredPol outlined in the earlier case study was led by the grassroots organization Stop LAPD Spying Coalition. A growing number of centers and organizations have been established to raise awareness of data justice and to challenge data harms, such as Data for Black Lives,[*] and many established nongovernmental organizations are beginning to include data justice projects[†] in their work. In these instances, social and community workers operating from a critical data perspective can, where appropriate, act as allies and supporters of community-led initiatives.

It is, however, perfectly possible that social and community workers working within agencies that are planning to introduce algorithmic systems to rationalize or target service provision might find their agency the focus of oppositional community group action. Such contradictions and tensions are not new to social work. They were described in detail many years ago in classic texts, such as *In and Against the State* (London Edinburgh Weekend Return Group, 1980) and have been recently reemphasized by Garrett (2021a, 2021b) in his call for a dissenting social work practice: one that stands "in solidarity with the exploited and dominated" (Garrett, 2021b, p. 1142). Garrett (2021b) directly addressed technological

---

[*] See https://d4bl.org/ for more information on Data for Black Lives.
[†] See, for example, the Amnesty International project that enabled citizen participation to identify and map facial recognition cameras in New York City (Amnesty International, n.d.).

developments with the statement that dissenting social work "appreciates the tremendous gains which technology brings, but is alert to the threats posed by techno-authoritarianism" (p. 1144).

CONCLUSION

The world is riding a new technological wave driven by datafication, machine learning, predictive analytics, and new forms of AI. Social services and our service users are impacted by the rise of datafication. The impact is direct—by the adoption of data-driven systems in social and community work agencies—and indirect—through other public sector and commercial actors using these systems. There is no reason to believe that datafication will slow down any time soon. Indeed, all the signs are that it will accelerate and intensify. The response of social and community workers must be grounded in our professional ethics and our commitment to human rights and social justice informed by the nascent data justice movement. Ideas like critical data literacy, design justice, citizen juries, and data activism are all relevant to social work in an online world and should become part of our professional vocabulary.

To be clear, none of the arguments made here is against the use of data systems or AI as such. Sander (2020a) contended that being critically data literate is not understood as necessarily taking a "negative" stance to all big data practices but rather involves the ability to weigh the evidence, make informed decisions, and scrutinize and respond to the sociotechnical systems of big data practices.

Nevertheless, when datafication processes are wed to oppressive political rationalities and discriminatory ways of framing social problems—even when this is unintentional—every implementation must be critically scrutinized by social and community workers, citizens, and by the historically marginalized and oppressed social groups for whom these systems can create significant problems in living. Data justice *is* a social work issue—and a very pressing one. Social and community workers cannot afford to ignore datafication or to assume that the shape data systems currently take is inevitable. Without a research-informed, critical perspective on datafication, there is a genuine risk, as Garrett (2021b) has argued, of a dystopian scenario in which practitioners "evolve into docile functionaries wholly steered by algorithms and machine learning" (p. 1145). To avoid this scenario, limit the harms that data do, and harness the empowering aspects of datafication, our profession needs to embrace critical data literacy and to champion data justice.

RECOMMENDATIONS FOR FURTHER READING

Benjamin, R. (2019). *Race after technology: Abolitionist tools for the new Jim code.* Polity Books.

Crawford, K. (2021). *The atlas of AI: Power, politics, and the planetary costs of artificial intelligence.* Yale University Press.

Eubanks, V. (2018). *Automating inequality: How high-tech tools profile, police, and punish the poor.* St. Martin's Press.

O'Neill, C. (2016). *Weapons of math destruction: How big data increases inequality and threatens democracy.* Crown.

Ullman, E. (2017). *Life in code: A personal history of technology.* Picador.

REFERENCES

Abdurahman, J. K. (2021). Calculating the souls of Black folk: Predictive analytics in the New York City Administration for Children's Services. *Columbia Journal of Race and Law Forum, 11,* 75–109. https://doi.org/10.52214/cjrl.v11i4.8741

AI Now Institute. (2018, September). *Litigating algorithms: Challenging government use of algorithmic decision systems* [Report]. https://ainowinstitute.org/litigating algorithms.pdf

Albright, A. (2019). *If you give a judge a risk score: Evidence from Kentucky bail decisions* (Harvard John M. Olin Fellow's Discussion Paper No. 85). http://www .law.harvard.edu/programs/olin_center/Prizes/2019-1.pdf

Allegheny County. (n.d.). *Allegheny Family Screening Tool.* https://www.allegheny county.us/Human-Services/News-Events/Accomplishments/Allegheny-Family-Screening-Tool.aspx

Alston, P. (2019, October 1). *Digital technology, social protection and human rights: Report of the Special Rapporteur on extreme poverty and human rights.* United Nations, Office of the High Commissioner. https://www.ohchr.org/EN/Issues/Poverty/Pages/DigitalTechnology.aspx

Amnesty International. (n.d.). *Decode surveillance NYC.* https://decoders.amnesty .org/projects/decode-surveillance

Ballantyne, N. (1996). Child care social work and the internet. *Adoption & Fostering, 20,* 50–56. https://doi.org/10.1177/030857599602000210

Ballantyne, N. (2015). Human service technology and the theory of the actor network. *Journal of Technology in Human Services, 33,* 104–117. https://doi.org/10.1080/15228835.2014.998567

Ballantyne, N. (2019). The ethics and politics of human service technology: The case of predictive risk modeling in New Zealand's child protection system. *Hong Kong Journal of Social Work, 53*, 15–27. https://doi.org/10.1142/s0219246219000044

Ballantyne, N. (2021). *"Not on my watch!": A case study in the datafication of child welfare in Aotearoa New Zealand* [Master's thesis, Massey University]. Theses and Dissertations Archive. http://hdl.handle.net/10179/16731

Barnes, M., & Cotterell, P. (Eds.). (2011). *Critical perspectives on user involvement.* Policy Press.

Barnett, V., Carter, L., Costanza-Chock, S., Hayes, R., Malivel, G., Michelson, R., Taylor, W., & Wagoner, M. (n.d.). *Zines: Issue #5: How to make a local design justice node* [*Design Justice: Local Nodes* download available]. Design Justice Network. https://designjustice.org/zines

Bhuiyan, J. (2021, November 7). LAPD ended predictive policing programs amid public outcry: A new effort shares many of their flaws. *The Guardian.* https://www.the guardian.com/us-news/2021/nov/07/lapd-predictive-policing-surveillance-reform

boyd, d., & Crawford, K. (2011, September 21). *Six provocations for big data* [Paper presentation]. Oxford Internet Institute, A Decade in Internet Time: Symposium on the Dynamics of the Internet and Society, Oxford, England. https://doi.org/10.2139/ssrn.1926431

boyd, d., & Crawford, K. (2012). Critical questions for big data: Provocations for a cultural, technological, and scholarly phenomenon. *Information, Communication & Society, 15*, 662–679. https://doi.org/10.1080/1369118X.2012.678878

boyd, d., Levy, K., & Marwick, A. (2014, October). The networked nature of algorithmic discrimination. In S. P. Gangadharan (Ed.) with V. Eubanks & S. Barocas, *Data and discrimination: Collected essays* (pp. 53–57). Open Technology Institute and New America. https://na-production.s3.amazonaws.com/documents/data-and-discrimination.pdf

Braithwaite, V. (2020). Beyond the bubble that is Robodebt: How governments that lose integrity threaten democracy. *Australian Journal of Social Issues, 55*, 242–259. https://doi.org/10.1002/ajs4.122

Brand, J., & Sander, I. (2020). *Critical data literacy tools for advancing data justice: A guidebook.* https://datajusticelab.org/wp-content/uploads/2020/06/djl-data-literacy-guidebook.pdf

Carretero Gomez, S., Vuorikari, R., & Punie, Y. (2017). *DigComp 2.1: The digital competence framework for citizens with eight proficiency levels and examples of use.* Publications Office of the European Union.

Charlton, J. I. (1998). *Nothing about us without us: Disability oppression and empowerment.* University of California Press.

Cheng, H.-F., Holstein, K., Kawakami, A., Sivaraman, V., Stapleton, L., Wu, S., & Zhu, H. (2022, May 24). *What happens when human workers oversee algorithmic tools?* [Online blog post]. Medium. https://medium.com/@kenneth.holstein/ what-happens-when-human-workers-oversee-algorithmic-tools-bbfc32e8ce61

Cheng, H.-F., Stapleton, L., Kawakami, A., Sivaraman, V., Cheng, Y., Qing, D., Perer, A., Holstein, K., Wu, Z. S., & Zhu, H. (2022). How child welfare workers reduce racial disparities in algorithmic decisions. *CHI '22: Proceedings of the 2022 CHI Conference on Human Factors in Computing Systems, 1*, Article 162. https://doi .org/10.1145/3491102.3501831

Cherna, M. (2018, March 23). We will use all resources to keep children safe. *Pittsburgh Post-Gazette.* https://www.post-gazette.com/opinion/letters/2018/03/23/We-will- use-all-resources-to-keep-children-safe/stories/201803230094

Chouldechova, A., Putnam-Hornstein, E., Benavides-Prado, D., Fialko, O., & Vaithi- anathan, R. (2018). A case study of algorithm-assisted decision making in child maltreatment hotline screening decisions. *Proceedings of Machine Learning Research, 81,* 1–15. http://proceedings.mlr.press/v81/chouldechova18a/chouldechova18a.pdf

Costanza-Chock, S. (2018, June 25–28). Design justice: Towards an intersectional feminist framework for design theory and practice [Paper presentation]. *Design as a Catalyst for Change—DRS International Conference 2018,* Limerick, Ireland. https://doi.org/10.21606/drs.2018.679

Costanza-Chock, S. (2020). *Design justice: Community-led practices to build the worlds we need.* MIT Press. https://direct.mit.edu/books/book/4605/Design -JusticeCommunity-Led-Practices-to-Build-the

Coulton, C. J., Goerge, R., Putnam-Hornstein, E., & de Haan, B. (2015). *Harnessing big data for social good: A Grand Challenge for Social Work* (Working Paper No. 11). American Academy of Social Work & Social Welfare. https://www.ncwwi.org/ files/Data-Driven_Decision_Making__CQI/Harnessing_Big_Data_for_Social_ Good_-_A_Grand_Challenge_for_Social_Work.pdf

Crawford, K. (2013, April 1). The hidden biases in big data. *Harvard Business Review.* https://hbr.org/2013/04/the-hidden-biases-in-big-data

Cuccaro-Alamin, S., Foust, R., Vaithianathan, R., & Putnam-Hornstein, E. (2017). Risk assessment and decision making in child protective services: Predictive risk modeling in context. *Children and Youth Services Review, 79,* 291–298. https:// doi.org/10.1016/j.childyouth.2017.06.027

Cukier, K. N., & Mayer-Schoenberger, V. (2013). The rise of big data. *Foreign Affairs, 92,* 28–40.

Dare, T. (2022). Social licence and norm violation. *Aotearoa New Zealand Social Work, 34,* 139–142.

Dare, T., & Gambrill, E. (2017, April). *Ethical analysis: Predictive risk models at call screening for Allegheny County.* https://www.alleghenycountyanalytics.us/wp-content/uploads/2019/05/Ethical-Analysis-16-ACDHS-26_PredictiveRisk_Package_050119_FINAL-2.pdf

Data Futures Partnership. (2017, August). *A path to social licence: Guidelines for trusted data use.* https://toi-aria.s3.amazonaws.com/documents/Summary-Guidelines.pdf

Data Justice Lab. (n.d.). *Exploring social justice in an age of datafication—Automating public services: Learning from cancelled systems.* https://datajusticelab.org/projects/automating-public-services-learning-from-cancelled-systems/

Data Justice Lab. (2021). *Advancing civic participation in algorithmic decision-making: A guidebook for the public sector.* https://datajusticelab.org/wp-content/uploads/2021/06/PublicSectorToolkit_english.pdf

De-Arteaga, M., Fogliato, R., & Chouldechova, A. (2020). A case for humans-in-the-loop: Decisions in the presence of erroneous algorithmic scores (Paper No. 509). In *CHI '20: Proceedings of the 2020 Conference on Human Factors in Computing Systems*, 1–12. https://doi.org/10.1145/3313831.3376638

Dencik, L. (2019). Situating practices in datafication—From above and below. In H. C. Stephansen & E. Treré (Eds.), *Citizen media and practice: Currents, connections and practices* (pp. 243–255). Routledge. https://doi.org/10.4324/9781351247375-18

Dencik, L. (2020). Advancing data justice in public health and beyond. *American Journal of Bioethics, 20*, 32–33. https://doi.org/10.1080/15265161.2020.1806945

Dencik, L. (2022). The datafied welfare state: A perspective from the UK. In A. Hepp, J. Jarke, & L. Kramp (Eds.), *New perspectives in critical data studies: The ambivalences of data power* (pp. 145–165). Palgrave.

Dencik, L., Hintz, A., & Cable, J. (2019). Towards data justice: Bridging anti-surveillance and social justice activism. In D. Bigo, E. Isin, & E. Ruppert (Eds.), *Data politics: Worlds, subjects, rights* (pp. 167–186). Routledge. https://doi.org/10.4324/9781315167305-9

Dencik, L., Jansen, F., & Metcalfe, P. (2018, August 30). *A conceptual framework for approaching social justice in an age of datafication.* DataJustice Project. https://datajusticeproject.net/2018/08/30/a-conceptual-framework-for-approaching-social-justice-in-an-age-of-datafication/

Dencik, L., & Kaun, A. (2020). Datafication and the welfare state. *Global Perspectives, 1*, Article 12912. https://doi.org/10.1525/gp.2020.12912

Dencik, L., & Sanchez-Monedero, J. (2022). Data justice. *Internet Policy Review, 11*, 1–16. https://doi.org/10.14763/2022.1.1615

Dettlaff, A. J., & Boyd, R. (2020). Racial disproportionality and disparities in the child welfare system: Why do they exist, and what can be done to address them?

ANNALS of the American Academy of Political and Social Science, 692, 253–274. https://doi.org/10.1177/0002716220980329

Devlieghere, J., Gillingham, P., & Roose, R. (2022). Dataism versus relationshipism: A social work perspective. *Nordic Social Work Research, 12,* 328–338. https://doi .org/10.1080/2156857X.2022.2052942

Drummond, H. (2017). Megaproject escalation of commitment: An update and appraisal. In B. Flyvbjerg (Ed.), *The Oxford handbook of megaproject management* (Vol. 1, pp. 194–216). Oxford University Press. https://doi.org/10.1093/oxfordhb/ 9780198732242.013.10

Edwards, R., Gillies, V., & Gorin, S. (2021). Data linkage for early intervention in the UK: Parental social license and social divisions. *Data & Policy, 3,* Article E34. https://doi.org/10.1017/dap.2021.34

Elvery, S. (2017, July 21). *How algorithms make important government decisions— And how that affects you.* ABC News. https://www.abc.net.au/news/2017-07-21/ algorithms-can-make-decisions-on-behalf-of-federal-ministers/8704858

Ensign, D., Friedler, S. A., Neville, S., Scheidegger, C., & Venkatasubramanian, S. (2018). Runaway feedback loops in predictive policing. In *Proceedings of the 1st Conference on Fairness, Accountability and Transparency* (Vol. 81, pp. 160–171). https://proceed ings.mlr.press/v81/ensign18a.html

Eubanks, V. (2018). *Automating inequality: How high-tech tools profile, police, and punish the poor.* St. Martin's Press.

Farrell, P., & McDonald, A. (2019, June 27). *Centrelink robo-debt system is "extortion," says former tribunal member.* ABC News. https://www.abc.net.au/news/2019-06-27/ centrelink-robo-debt-system-extortion-former-tribunal-member/11252306

Fogliato, R., De-Arteaga, M., & Chouldechova, A. (2022, March 4). A case for humans-in-the-loop: Decisions in the presence of misestimated algorithmic scores. *SSRN.* https://doi.org/10.2139/ssrn.4050125

Fox, S., Dimond, J., Irani, L., Hirsch, T., Muller, M., & Bardzell, S. (2017). Social justice and design: Power and oppression in collaborative systems. In *Proceedings of the CSCW '17 Companion: Companion of the 2017 ACM Conference on Computer Supported Cooperative Work and Social Computing* (pp. 117–122). Association for Computing Machinery. https://doi.org/10.1145/3022198.3022201

Garrett, P. M. (2021a). *Dissenting social work: Critical theory, resistance and pandemic.* Routledge.

Garrett, P. M. (2021b). "A world to win": In defence of (dissenting) social work: A response to Chris Maylea. *British Journal of Social Work, 51,* 1131–1149. https:// doi.org/10.1093/bjsw/bcab009

Gillingham, P. (2019). The development of algorithmically based decision-making systems in children's protective services: Is administrative data good enough? *British Journal of Social Work, 50*, 565–580. https://doi.org/10.1093/bjsw/bcz157

Gillingham, P., & Graham, T. (2016). Big data in social welfare: The development of a critical perspective on social work's latest "electronic turn." *Australian Social Work, 70*, 135–147. https://doi.org/10.1080/0312407X.2015.1134606

Gitelman, L. (Ed.). (2013). *"Raw data" is an oxymoron.* MIT Press.

Glenn, R. (2017, April). *Centrelink's automated debt raising and recovery system. A report about the Department of Human Services' online compliance intervention system for debt raising and recovery* (Vol. 2). Commonwealth Ombudsman. https://www.ombudsman.gov.au/__data/assets/pdf_file/0022/43528/Report-Centrelinks-automated-debt-raising-and-recovery-system-April-2017.pdf

Goldkind, L., Thinyane, M., & Choi, M. (2019). Small data, big justice: The intersection of data science, social good and social services. *Journal of Technology in Human Services, 36*, 175–178. https://doi.org/10.1080/15228835.2018.1539369

Goldkind, L., Wolf, L., & LaMendola, W. (2021). Data justice: Social work and a more just future. *Journal of Community Practice, 29*, 237–256. https://doi.org/10.1080/10705422.2021.1984354

Gordon Legal. (n.d.). *Robodebt class action: Federal court has approved Robodebt settlement.* https://www.robodebtclassaction.com.au/

Green, B. (2022). The flaws of policies requiring human oversight of government algorithms. *Computer Law & Security Review, 45*, Article 105681. https://doi.org/10.1016/J.CLSR.2022.105681

Gulliver, P., Jonas, M., Fanslow, J., McIntosh, T., & Waayer, D. (2018). Surveys, social licence and the Integrated Data Infrastructure. *Aotearoa New Zealand Social Work, 30*, 57–71. https://doi.org/10.11157/anzswj-vol30iss3id481

Harris, M. (2017, August 9). *How Peter Thiel's secretive data company pushed into policing.* Wired. https://www.wired.com/story/how-peter-thiels-secretive-data-company-pushed-into-policing/

Haskins, C. (2019a, February 14). *Academics confirm major predictive policing algorithm is fundamentally flawed.* VICE. https://www.vice.com/en/article/xwbag4/academics-confirm-major-predictive-policing-algorithm-is-fundamentally-flawed

Haskins, C. (2019b, February 6). *Dozens of cities have secretly experimented with predictive policing software.* VICE. https://www.vice.com/en/article/d3m7jq/dozens-of-cities-have-secretly-experimented-with-predictive-policing-software

Henriques-Gomes, L. (2020, February 22). "I've spent many nights crying": Welfare recipients on the true cost of Robodebt. *The Guardian.* https://www.theguardian.com/australia-news/2020/feb/23/welfare-recipients-true-cost-centrelink-robodebt

Hintz, A. (2020). Digital citizenship in the age of datafication. In S. J. Yates & R. E. Rice (Eds.), *The Oxford handbook of digital technology and society* (pp. 526–546). Oxford University Press. https://doi.org/10.1093/oxfordhb/9780190932596.013.18

Hintz, A., Dencik, L., & Wahl-Jorgensen, K. (2018). *Digital citizenship in a datafied society*. Polity Books.

Human Services Information Technology Association. (n.d.). *About*. https://www.husita.org/about-us/

Iliadis, A., & Russo, F. (2016). Critical data studies: An introduction [Commentary]. *Big Data & Society, 3*. https://doi.org/10.1177/2053951716674238

International Federation of Social Workers. (2014, July). *Global definition of social work*. https://www.ifsw.org/what-is-social-work/global-definition-of-social-work/

Jørgensen, A. M., Webb, C., Keddell, E., & Ballantyne, N. (2021). Three roads to Rome? Comparative policy analysis of predictive tools in child protection services in Aotearoa New Zealand, England, & Denmark. *Nordic Social Work Research, 12,* 379–391. https://doi.org/10.1080/2156857X.2021.1999846

Karp, P. (2019, November 28). Robodebt: The federal court ruling and what it means for targeted welfare recipients. *The Guardian*. https://www.theguardian.com/australia-news/2019/nov/28/robodebt-the-federal-court-ruling-and-what-it-means-for-targeted-welfare-recipients

Katzenbach, C., & Ulbricht, L. (2019). Algorithmic governance. *Internet Policy Review, 8*. https://doi.org/10.14763/2019.4.1424

Kawakami, A., Sivaraman, V., Cheng, H.-F., Stapleton, L., Cheng, Y., Qing, D., Perer, A., Wu, Z. S., Zhu, H., & Holstein, K. (2022). Improving human–AI partnerships in child welfare: Understanding worker practices, challenges, and desires for algorithmic decision support. In *CHI Proceedings of the 2022 CHI Conference on Human Factors in Computing Systems, 1,* Article 52. https://doi.org/10.1145/3491102.3517439

Keddell, E. (2014). The ethics of predictive risk modelling in the Aotearoa/New Zealand child welfare context: Child abuse prevention or neo-liberal tool? *Critical Social Policy, 35,* 69–88. https://doi.org/10.1177/0261018314543224

Keddell, E. (2019). Algorithmic justice in child protection: Statistical fairness, social justice and the implications for practice. *Social Sciences, 8,* Article 281. https://doi.org/10.3390/socsci8100281

Kirk, S. (2016, July 30). *Children "not lab-rats"—Anne Tolley intervenes in child abuse experiment*. Stuff. https://www.stuff.co.nz/national/health/70647353/children-not-lab-rats---anne-tolley-intervenes-in-child-abuse-experiment

Kitchin, R. (2014). *The data revolution: Big data, open data, data infrastructures & their consequences*. SAGE.

Kitchin, R. (2021). *Data lives: How data are made and shape our world*. Bristol University Press. https://doi.org/doi:10.2307/j.ctv1c9hmnq

Kitchin, R., & Lauriault, T. P. (2014). *Toward critical data studies: Charting and unpacking data assemblages and their work* (Manuscript in preparation). National Institute for Regional and Spatial Analysis, National University of Ireland Maynooth. http://mural.maynoothuniversity.ie/5683/1/KitchinLauriault_CriticalDataStudies_ProgrammableCity_WorkingPaper2_SSRN-id2474112.pdf

Kukutai, T., & Taylor, J. (Eds.). (2016). *Indigenous data sovereignty: Towards an agenda*. Australian National University Press. https://doi.org/10.22459/caepr38.11.2016.05

LaMendola, W. (2019). Social work, social technologies, and sustainable community development. *Journal of Technology in Human Services, 37*, 79–92. https://doi.org/10.1080/15228835.2018.1552905

LaMendola, W., & Ballantyne, N. (in press). Digital tools for convivial communities. In G. Kirwan & A. L. Lopez (Eds.), *Routledge handbook of digital social work*. Routledge.

Lindner, C. (2020, July 20). Why hundreds of mathematicians are boycotting predictive policing. *Popular Mechanics*. https://www.popularmechanics.com/science/math/a32957375/mathematicians-boycott-predictive-policing/

London Edinburgh Weekend Return Group. (1980). *In and against the state: Discussion notes for socialists*. Pluto Press.

Lum, K., & Isaac, W. (2016). To predict and serve? *Significance, 13*, 14–19. https://doi.org/10.1111/j.1740-9713.2016.00960.x

Manovich, L. (2012). Trending: The promises and the challenges of big social data. In M. K. Gold (Ed.), *Debates in the digital humanities* (pp. 460–475). University of Minnesota Press. http://dhdebates.gc.cuny.edu/book

Marjanovic, O., Cecez-Kecmanovic, D., & Vidgen, R. (2021). Theorising algorithmic justice. *European Journal of Information Systems, 31*, 269–287. https://doi.org/10.1080/0960085x.2021.1934130

Mayer-Schoenberger, V., & Cukier, K. (2013). *Big data: A revolution that will transform how we live, work and think*. Houghton Mifflin Harcourt.

McQuillan, D. (2018). People's councils for ethical machine learning. *Social Media and Society, 4*. https://doi.org/10.1177/2056305118768303

Mejias, U. A., & Couldry, N. (2019). Datafication. *Internet Policy Review, 8*. https://doi.org/10.14763/2019.4.1428

Milan, S. (2019). Acting on data(fication). In H. C. Stephansen & E. Treré (Eds.), *Citizen media and practice: Currents, connections and practices* (pp. 212–226). Routledge. https://doi.org/10.4324/9781351247375-16

Milan, S., & van der Velden, L. (2016). The alternative epistemologies of data activism. *Digital Culture & Society, 2*, 57–74. https://doi.org/10.14361/dcs-2016-0205

Miller, K. (2017). Connecting the dots: A case study of the Robodebt communities. *Australian Institute of Administrative Law Forum*, *89*, 50–58. http://classic.austlii .edu.au/au/journals/AIAdminLawF/2017/20.pdf

National Association of Social Workers. (2021). *Code of ethics of the National Association of Social Workers.* https://www.socialworkers.org/About/Ethics/ Code-of-Ethics/Code-of-Ethics-English

National Coalition for Child Protection Reform. (2019, June 20). *No, you can't use predictive analytics to reduce racial bias in child welfare.* NCCPR Child Welfare Blog. https://www.nccprblog.org/2019/06/no-you-cant-use-predictive-analytics-to.html

New Zealand Government. (2012a). *The white paper for vulnerable children: Volume I.* https://www.orangatamariki.govt.nz/assets/Uploads/Support-for-families/ childrens-teams/white-paper-for-vulnerable-children-volume-1.pdf

New Zealand Government. (2012b). *The white paper for vulnerable children: Volume II.* https://www.orangatamariki.govt.nz/assets/Uploads/Documents/whitepaper-volume-ii-web.pdf

O'Brien, M. (2011). Social justice: Alive and well (partly) in social work practice? *International Social Work*, *54*, 174–190. https://doi.org/10.1177/0020872810382682

O'Donovan, D. (2020). Social security appeals and access to justice: Learning from the Robodebt controversy. *PrecedentAULA*, *32*, 158 Precedent 34. http://classic .austlii.edu.au/au/journals/PrecedentAULA/2020/32.html

O'Neil, C. (2016). *Weapons of math destruction: How big data increases inequality and threatens democracy.* Crown.

Redden, J. (2017, December 7). Six ways (and counting) that big data systems are harming society. *The Conversation.* https://theconversation.com/six-ways-and-counting-that-big-data-systems-are-harming-society-88660

Redden, J. (2018, November 1). The harm that data do: Paying attention to how algorithmic systems impact marginalized people worldwide is key to a just and equitable future. *Scientific American.* https://www.scientificamerican.com/article/ the-harm-that-data-do

Redden, J., Brand, J., & Terzieva, V. (2020, August). *Data harm record (Updated).* Data Justice Lab. https://datajusticelab.org/data-harm-record/

Ribes, D. (2019). STS, meet data science, once again. *Science Technology and Human Values*, *44*, 514–539. https://doi.org/10.1177/0162243918798899

Richardson, R., Schultz, J. M., & Crawford, K. (2019). Dirty data, bad predictions: How civil rights violations impact police data, predictive policing systems, and justice. *New York University Law Review*, *94*, 192–233. https://papers.ssrn.com/ sol3/papers.cfm?abstract_id=3333423#

Roberts, D. E. (2014). Child protection as surveillance of African American families. *Journal of Social Welfare and Family Law, 36*, 426–437. https://doi.org/10.1080/09649069.2014.967991

Roberts, D. E. (2019). Digitizing the carceral state [Review of the book *Automating inequality: How high-tech tools profile, police, and punish the poor*, by V. Eubanks]. *Harvard Law Review.* https://harvardlawreview.org/wp-content/uploads/2019/04/1695-1728_Online.pdf

Sander, I. (2019, June 7). *A critically commented guide to data literacy tools.* Zenodo. https://doi.org/10.5281/zenodo.3241422

Sander, I. (2020a). Critical big data literacy tools—Engaging citizens and promoting empowered internet usage. *Data & Policy, 2*, Article E5. https://doi.org/10.1017/dap.2020.5

Sander, I. (2020b). What is critical big data literacy and how can it be implemented? *Internet Policy Review, 9.* https://doi.org/10.14763/2020.2.1479

Saxena, D., Badillo-Urquiola, K., Wisniewski, P. J., & Guha, S. (2020). A human-centered review of algorithms used within the U.S. child welfare system. In *CHI '20: Proceedings of the 2020 Conference on Human Factors in Computing Systems*, 1–15. https://doi.org/10.1145/3313831.3376229

Sismondo, S. (2010). *An introduction to science and technology studies* (2nd ed.). Wiley-Blackwell.

Smyth, T., & Dimond, J. (2014). Anti-oppressive design. *Interactions, 21*, 68–71. https://doi.org/10.1145/2668969

Stop LAPD Spying Coalition. (2018, May 8). *Before the bullet hits the body: Dismantling predictive policing in Los Angeles.* https://stoplapdspying.org/wp-content/uploads/2018/05/Before-the-Bullet-Hits-the-Body-Report-Summary.pdf

Stop LAPD Spying Coalition. (2021, November). *Automating banishment: The surveillance and policing of looted land.* https://automatingbanishment.org/

Te Mana Raraunga. (2018, October). *Principles of Māori data sovereignty* (Brief No. 1). https://static1.squarespace.com/static/58e9b10f9de4bb8d1fb5ebbc/t/5bda208b4ae237cd89ee16e9/1541021836126/TMR+Māori+Data+Sovereignty+Principles+Oct+2018.pdf

Vaithianathan, R., Maloney, T., de Haan, I., & Dare, T. (2012). *Vulnerable children: Can administrative data be used to identify children at risk of adverse outcomes?* Te Manatū Whakahiato Ora Ministry of Social Development. http://www.msd.govt.nz/about-msd-and-our-work/publications-resources/research/vulnerable-children/index.html

Vaithianathan, R., Putnam-Hornstein, E., Jiang, N., Nand, P., & Maloney, T. (2017, March). *Developing predictive risk models to support child maltreatment hotline*

screening decisions. Allegheny County Analytics. https://www.alleghenycounty
analytics.us/wp-content/uploads/2017/04/Developing-Predictive-Risk-Models-
package-with-cover-1-to-post-1.pdf

Walter, M., Kukutai, T., Carroll, S. R., & Rodriguez-Lonebear, D. (Eds.). (2020).
Indigenous data sovereignty and policy. Routledge. https://doi.org/https://doi.org/
10.4324/9780429273957

Yeung, K. (2018). Algorithmic regulation: A critical interrogation. *Regulation and
Governance, 12,* 505–523. https://doi.org/10.1111/rego.12158

CHAPTER 5

Online Opportunities for Community Action: Social Media as a Vehicle for Social Justice

Kerry Cuskelly and Imelda Ojeda

This chapter aims to be applicable to the global social work community. We understand and acknowledge, however, that across the globe, social workers live in vastly different climates and that civil liberties, such as access to the internet, freedom to engage in protest, freedom of speech, and structural support for engaging with technology as part of professional practice, may not be forthcoming in all jurisdictions. We advocate, therefore, that social workers reading this who are in the privileged position to benefit from these rights use those rights in solidarity with global colleagues through actively engaging with, and using the content of, this chapter in the fight for global social justice.

Social work has a history of engaging in community-based action (Ferguson & Woodward, 2009). Traditionally, this has taken place in person and utilized professional practice skills, such as community organization and development, social planning and social action, and social administration. As a relationship-based profession, social work has focused on in-person work, and the profession's engagement with digital technology and social media is checkered and complex (Byrne et al., 2019; Reamer, 2018). This chapter focuses on social work's attempts to move in a meaningful way toward engagement with and use of digital technology for professional practice. The specific focus of this chapter is on social work's use of social media as an organizing tool for meaningful community-based action. Traditional methods of community action in social work are outlined. Taking a realist approach, the pitfalls of social media and social work are discussed along with suggestions for how to stay safe in a professional capacity on social media. Case examples of social workers' use of social media for community action are considered, followed by practical advice for social workers thinking about using social media in their practice to support community action.

With the inception of the internet more than 30 years ago and its ensuing development from the basic connectivity phase to the most recent "internet of everything" phase, social work has had to grapple with a rapidly changing landscape for the profession, people, and communities. When considering the impact of technology on social work, typically the focus has been on the digital divide, whereby social work has been concerned with how ownership of devices, access to the internet, and digital literacy risks furthering inequality for people and communities. Other considerations relevant for social workers to consider in this space include the use of new technology, crowdsourcing of information, and the development of social networks (Steyaert & Gould, 2009). The omnipotence of the internet and technology in our daily lives has also contributed to the ability of people to communicate immediately with each other, to larger audiences, and with global reach compared with traditional forms of communication. The Pew Research Center (Beau, 2020) advises that more than half of social media users in the United States use social media platforms to engage in advocacy and activism. This is of relevance to social work, one of whose core values is a commitment to social justice and one of whose core practice skills is advocacy. In the current era, it is therefore strongly suggested that social workers should consider the use of technology as part of their "advocacy tool kit."

COMMUNITY ACTION IN SOCIAL WORK

Internationally, community social work has developed and evolved in different ways. Within these rich tapestries of social work lies the foundation for current states of community action, including those utilizing technology. Standards of practice for community social work include a long-standing commitment to upholding social justice (International Federation of Social Workers [IFSW], 2012). Ross et al. (1967), who were early proponents of community organizing as part of social work practice, suggested that through facilitation of community organizing approaches, social work could support communities to develop increased cooperative and collaborative practices. Community-based social planning is viewed as one such form of community practice (Gamble & Weil, 1995, 2009) and includes activities like neighborhood-based services, organizing for social action, and community building. Elsewhere, it is argued that community practice is core to all social work roles, whether macro or micro (Hardcastle et al., 2004).

Activist Social Work

Advocacy is also considered a core component of community social work practice at both the micro and macro levels and a foundation for activist social work. Through an explicit human rights lens, practitioners can engage in practice through a particular "moral basis," which is then filtered through to their practice on all levels, including community development, community action, policy advocacy, and activism (Ife, 2012). This chapter includes a quick guide for social activism that could be beneficial for social workers who wish to further engage in activism within their community (see the appendix at the end of the chapter).

Midgley (2001), when discussing the three main strands of international social work (i.e., activist, remedial, and development), observed that of the three, the activist strand of social work tends to be the most underdeveloped. This notion is echoed in *The Road Not Taken* (Reisch & Andrews, 2014), which traces the development of activist social work in the United States. United Kingdom–based academics Ferguson and Woodward (2009) followed this vein of thought when they discussed "rediscovering the radical kernel" (p. 16) in social work. They espoused that the activist (or radical) form of social work being in the minority is unsurprising given that the main employer of social workers is often the state. States also censor groups in their employ for focusing on the structural causes of people's distress when their analyses show a state to be a structural cause of people's personal distress. Rather, social work employers disappointingly corral the profession into focusing on people's "individual inadequacies, faulty thought patterns or stunted emotional development" (Ferguson & Woodward, 2009, p. 16). A result is the suppression of core social work approaches, such as community development, community organizing, and community practice in favor of depoliticized, technocratic approaches.

Early Examples of Community Action

Early examples of community action in social work can be seen in the development of the settlement house movement in the United Kingdom and the United States, which sought to reform society rather than the individual. In the United States, the settlement movement was actively involved in trade union development, campaigning on issues, such as child labor, and supporting labor strikes. In the United Kingdom in the 1920s, Clement Attlee wrote of the social worker as agitator in his book *The Social Worker* (Attlee, 1920). He brought this to life through examples of his own involvement in organizing soup kitchens and campaigning against the Poor Law (Ferguson & Woodward, 2009). Pethick-Lawrence, a volunteer social

worker in the 1890s, developed a cooperative dressmaker business to address people's workplace conditions as distinct from "reforming" their individual conditions
in the home.

Common Theme

A common theme running through all these approaches to community practice
and community action in social work is their alignment with the emancipatory
goals of the global definition of social work:

> Social work is a practice-based profession and an academic disci-
> pline that promotes social change and development, social cohe-
> sion, and the empowerment and liberation of people. Principles of
> social justice, human rights, collective responsibility, and respect
> for diversities are central to social work. Underpinned by theories
> of social work, social sciences, humanities and indigenous knowl-
> edges, social work engages people and structures to address life
> challenges and enhance wellbeing. The above definition may be
> amplified at national and/or regional levels. (IFSW, 2014, para. 2)

SOCIAL WORK AND ENGAGEMENT WITH TECHNOLOGY

Social work practice is still rooted in more traditional approaches in terms of
face-to-face contact, home visits, paper charts, and other documentation. The profession has thrived from that in-person interaction with clients, and a therapeutic
relationship benefits greatly from this type of engagement. However, the logistics
of travel, juggling home visits, managing documentation, and all the other tasks of
traditional service delivery can contribute to burnout. Over the past decade, there
has been an increased push for the use of technology to address these logistical
features of delivery while meeting client needs. However, some areas of the social
work field have been slow to implement technology innovations. Whether because
of budget constraints, insufficient staff training, or professional reluctance due to
lack of proven long-term efficacy of new technologies, the field has often lagged
other fields in an acceptance of technology innovation.

That all changed in 2020, when the global pandemic forced entire industries
to innovate and adapt in response to changing COVID-19 guidelines and barriers.
The use of technology in the workplace and, more specifically, within the social
service professions, rapidly evolved. The need to continue providing services to
the community while following safety guidelines, such as social distancing and

quarantine, forced and expedited technological advances and impacted our lives in ways we may have yet to realize. The pandemic changed the way we work, shop, learn, socialize, and receive healthcare and mental health services.

Clipper (2020) suggested that the need to find solutions that provide distance, safety for healthcare providers and patients, and the need for faster test results are some of the reasons why this crisis has accelerated the use of technology. Clipper also noted that the technological push is the beginning of more efficient practices that will cultivate an improvement of treatments and vaccines.

The social work profession, and the social services it delivers, is one of the industries that has experienced the benefits of technology since the outset of the pandemic. Electronic health records, mobile apps, videoconferences, and tele-health practices have assisted social workers in serving clients more effectively and efficiently. This increase in technology has also made it easier for social workers to document, organize, and access important client information and resources, which, in turn, could decrease the amount of time spent on administrative tasks and completing documents by hand. Industries that formerly operated with very little technology are now finding ways to serve people better and provide non-traditional ways of service delivery, such as videoconferencing and telehealth (de Villiers, 2020).

Barriers to Accessing Technology

Alongside the growing engagement of social work with technology is the recognition that equitable access to technology isn't a reality for a sizable portion of social workers' client populations. These accessibility gaps have been starkly highlighted by the COVID-19 pandemic. Significant barriers remain for service users and their communities' engagement with technology. It is important for social workers to acknowledge that these gaps exist and to proactively work to meaningfully address them, for example, ensuring project funding includes money for purchasing laptops for participants, making sure the budgets include allocation for digital literacy training and education, and advocating at policy level for marginalized populations' rights to be included in national digital frameworks.

Digital Equity

A key focus of community-based social work is addressing social exclusion and its impact on social determinants of health. Parrott and Madoc-Jones (2008) recommended social workers utilize new technology to address social exclusion. This should be done in the knowledge that digital exclusion functions much like social exclusion, and both reinforce each other (Steyaert & Gould, 2009). Indeed, it has been suggested that the digital divide is not so much digital in form but another facet of social exclusion (Macdonald & Clayton, 2013).

It is important for social workers to be aware that community's access to technology corresponds with several sociodemographic factors. These include income, educational level, gender, age, employment status, ethnicity, type of household, and geography. It has been observed that access to technology is greater when household income or education is higher, the household ethnicity is more Western, and the household demographic is younger (Steyaert & Gould, 2009). An essential infrastructure needed by communities is a high-speed internet connection. Without this basic and necessary infrastructure, many communities are prevented from fully functioning in today's world. However, "this structural reality effectively results in what has been called 'digital redlining' and further perpetuates social and economic disparities in society" (Sanders & Scanlon, 2021, p. 130).

Data Justice

Changes in regulations on platforms and how social media content is presented to users have influenced the rise of social movements to address the negative impact these platforms have on mental health (Pantic, 2014) and social issues (Akram & Kumar, 2017; Amedie, 2015). The *European Union Action Plan Against Disinformation* (European Commission, 2018) defined *disinformation* as "verifiably false or misleading information created, presented, and disseminated for economic gain, or to intentionally deceive the public, and may cause public harm" (p. 1). The reasons given for their action include (a) the potential for far-reaching consequences, such as public harm; (b) threats to democratic political and policy-making processes; and (c) the risks of endangering the protection of European Union citizens' health, security, and their environment.

In recent years, social media platforms have become increasingly aware of their influence and role in society, particularly to how they contribute to misinformation and the promotion of dangerous trends and topics. Mayer-Schönberger and Cukier (2013) explained that artificial intelligence facilitates real-time tracking of data that can predict and provide an insight on a person's behaviors and preferences. These data enable data owners to target specific individuals and market specific products or ideas. This big data clusters personal information into categories that will later be utilized for targeted ads for products, companies, or political candidates to reach their ideal audience.

Some of these media platforms have pledged to be better and to implement filtering systems that will protect consumers from false information or harmful content. However, it is important to remember that, as any private business, profit is also at the forefront of their decision making, and content filtering to protect the public can conflict with goals of financial gain.

A Human Right

Mossberger et al. (2003) suggested that the digital divide consists of layers of technological inclusion: (a) an access divide, (b) a skills divide, (c) an economic opportunity divide, and (d) a democratic divide. Taking a human rights approach (Ife, 2012), social workers can broaden their view from an individual response to people's needs to one in which the right to access the resources necessary to live a dignified and humane life includes access to technology. Human rights approaches in social work give social workers a framework to work from, which suggests that equitable sharing of social goods and resources is necessary for social inclusion and social development. Because of the centrality of the internet in the functioning of society today—particularly in terms of accessing vital resources, such as education, jobs, or healthcare, for example—it is reasonable for social workers to argue that universal access to internet connection is a human right (Murdach, 2011; Wronka, 2016).

SOCIAL WORK AND SOCIAL MEDIA USAGE

Evolution of Social Media Platforms in Social Work Practice

Social media has been defined as "forms of electronic communication (such as websites for social networking and microblogging) through which users create online communities to share information, ideas, personal messages, and other content (such as videos)" (Merriam-Webster, n.d.). Initially, social media existed to help end users connect digitally with friends, colleagues, family members, and like-minded individuals they might never have met in person. The invention of the smartphone along with rapid technological innovations changed the focus of social media from a desktop project to an interactive "lifestyle."

As Facebook, Reddit, Instagram, Twitter, TikTok, and others have become prolific in our personal lives, these social media platforms, by virtue of their enormous influence, have impacted social work practice within communities. Best and colleagues (2016) argued that it is relevant for social workers to be proficient in social media usage for their practice and for disseminating research. Berzin et al. (2015) suggested that through using social media platforms, social workers have a greater chance of reaching more people and impacting positively on collective social problems. Utilizing social media outlets and engaging in local grassroots efforts may look different for everyone, but even small actions can have significant impact (see the appendix at the end of the chapter). The ability to engage in *social advocacy*, the concept of empowering people to support a cause by sharing content (online) and connecting with a larger audience, has been cited by Greeson and colleagues (2018) as an important reason for social workers to utilize social media platforms.

Black Lives Matter and Social Media

Over the past decade, the growth and evolution of social movements have benefited from advances in the usage and popularity of social media technologies. A good example is the Black Lives Matter (BLM) movement, which has relied heavily on the use of social media to organize and mobilize communities and advocate for change. Moreover, the recent case of police brutality inflicted on George Floyd (Hill et al., 2020) and how his death was recorded and shared on social media created an even stronger movement that is closely tied to its digital presence. The use of the hashtag #BLM or #BlackLivesMatter has been a powerful tool for allies and supporters to express their views and stance on this issue. BLM organizers utilized this hashtag to mobilize and organize communities to protest, raise their voice, and demand racial justice. According to Reny and Newman (2021), the protests that took place immediately after the death of George Floyd were effective at decreasing positive views of police and, at the same time, increased awareness of anti-Black discrimination among left-leaning Americans.

Research conducted by Mundt et al. (2018) suggests that the BLM movement organizers utilized social media as a way of communication but not as a conscious strategy designed with the purpose of mobilizing large numbers of people. However, this tool was a key factor in the rapid growth and support the movement has had and facilitated organizing by gathering resources, building coalitions among BLM and other grassroots organizations with similar missions, and gaining oversight and influence on the overall narrative and messaging of the BLM movement.

Women's March Movement and Social Media

The Women's March movement is another example of how modern technology and digital connection have fueled social movements. The Women's March movement as an organization started in January 2017 as a protest movement following the U.S. election of President Donald J. Trump. Women around the United States and in multiple cities around the world wanted to make a powerful statement of disapproval regarding threats to reproductive rights, racism, misogyny, climate change, and immigrant rights (see https://www.womensmarch.com/ for more information about this movement).

The effectiveness of the Women's March movement has been influenced significantly by engagement with social media platforms, which has opened the door for local organizing efforts and collaboration. The Women's March movement prides itself on being intersectional and inclusive and has encouraged the unity of numerous other social causes through social media. If you have had the opportunity to attend a Women's March over the past years, you will quickly realize that it is more than just a march—it is a community connector that brings progressive individuals together.

Activist Social Worker and Social Media

For social workers, social media can be a difficult place to be. But that doesn't mean it should be avoided. There is increasing focus within social work on the use of social media as a way to promote positive interventions (Burns et al., 2021). In the age of social media and online advocacy, it is also important to recognize the difference between real impact and *keyboard activism* or *slacktivism*, which is the false sense of impact by only engaging in online efforts. Once we have been presented with the information and have formed our opinion on a particular issue, how do we get from social media to social action? Real change happens when we create a strategy and act on it.

Where can you start at the local level? Advocate in your neighborhoods! Go local, get informed on who your city council is, and get educated on the issues affecting your neighborhood (see the appendix). What are your district and your neighborhood doing? Are there local boards or commissions? If serving publicly isn't for you, who is looking to serve who supports your values and positive change? Who makes decisions about your public hospitals, how land is used, and how public housing is developed and accessed? Is there any proposed legislation in your state or country that negatively impacts women, people of color, or clients you work with? Getting informed of what is happening in your immediate community is a great place to start.

We also suggest that social workers should actively engage in digital literacy and use these skills to educate and to advocate and fight for social justice alongside communities we serve. This includes using acquired digital literacy skills to upskill communities that require them so that they can be empowered to self-organize for community-led action.

Tips for Activism

As general tips of social work involvement in activism movements, it is important to highlight good practices to ensure your advocacy effort is as successful as possible:

- Always have a call to action, and make sure you can direct individuals to a site to learn more about, or donate to, your cause.

- Listen to and identify the individuals affected by the issue as your main source of information. See what work is already being done, and "listen, listen, listen." Observe as permissible, ask what help people need, and listen some more. Remember: The movement isn't about you.

- Don't co-opt any of the movements that you find; they probably made decisions just fine before you. If they need money, supplies for a gathering, someone to answer phones, childcare providers, or help picking up trash behind the marchers, do those tasks without needing to steal the spotlight and without seeking praise. In other words, don't show up to help and make people spend emotional labor making you feel good or important.

Guidelines for Online Presence

The era of social media sharing has created the need for additional ethical guidelines for social workers and other helping professionals. Social work's *Code of Ethics* (National Association of Social Workers, 2021) increasingly references the need for social workers to be judicious in their use of social media. For any professional using social media as part of their professional identity, it is prudent to be aware of both the potential positives and negatives that can come from online activity. Some examples follow.

Own Your Opinions

Make it clear that opinions expressed are yours and not affiliated with any other entity. Twitter accounts often have messaging such as, "Views expressed are mine and not endorsements." Keep this in mind, especially if you are engaging in topics that might seem controversial for some. Your opinions are personal, but your actions might be linked to your employer or profession.

We have seen more frequently cases in the United States on how social media has made it easier to track people who post problematic content, especially racist and bigoted comments or videos. These posts eventually make it to employers, who then choose to terminate the person's employment. Remember: Your employer might have the right to terminate your employment at any time if they feel your behavior might hinder their brand or public name. Staying informed and up to date with your local employment laws is recommended. According to Corporate Compliance Insights (Spencer, 2022):

> In general, we've learned that there are repercussions for sharing posts with racist, sexist and ableist connotations, offensive opinions, and those that show illegal or risqué activity. And when people identify their employer on their social profiles (as many do), a single careless post can lead to employment consequences (for employees and employers alike). (para. 4)

When in Doubt, It Is Better Not to Post

An important component of social work is to advocate for causes you believe in and that are important to you. If you feel that the views and values of your employer are very different from your own and might create a conflict, then it may be a good idea to start looking for different employment options that will align closely with your values and work as a social worker.

Be Respectful

It can be tempting to engage in arguments online, especially if the opinions shared by others on a public forum are triggering. The reality is that nobody's opinions or point of view is going to change by reading a stranger's comment online. It is important to express our views and thoughts if you feel inclined to do so, but stay away from name-calling or insulting others online. It can backfire quickly! Remember: The internet is a public place, and anything you post, even private, is a screenshot away from being shared. Potential employers will most likely Google you and peek at your behavior online as part of their hiring process. Make sure your online presence is reflective of you and your values.

Use Your Platform for Good

Speak up and share about the issues that are important for you. Advocate for the causes you feel passionate about; invite others to support; and make a call to action for others to either donate, volunteer, and educate.

Guidelines for Working with Clients/Coworkers and Social Media

The other side of social media activity that social workers should also be aware of is the fine boundaries of engaging with clients and coworkers online. Knowing how to navigate these relationships both in person and online will save you headaches and potential issues down the road.

- Make it clear to your clients that you won't be friends with them on social media. If you notice a client following you on any social media channel, do not follow them back, and block their account from seeing your content. You can have a conversation with them—in a way they do not feel rejected—and explain how this breaks client–professional boundaries. If you have a public social work or therapy page, let your clients know that they are welcome to follow for general content, but you won't be following them back or answering direct messages with personal questions related to their treatment.

- Do not add anyone you report to or anyone who reports to you. This is an important boundary to keep, even if you have a close relationship with your supervisor and vice versa. Be cautious of venting about coworkers or clients on your social media. Your comments or sarcasm will be noticed and can potentially harm your relationship with them or even put your employment in jeopardy. Keep the venting to offline conversations.

- Another important consideration is changing your name on Facebook or creating an alternate Instagram account—for example, you could add your middle name instead of your last name or do a different spelling. This may prevent your profile from coming up in case a client is searching for you.

Guidelines for Activism

What do social workers need to be aware of when engaging in online activism? First, it is important to note that core social work skills, such as reflective practice, use of supervision, confidentiality, and boundary making, remain applicable in the digital world. Second, it is helpful to think of engaging in online practices as a social worker as an active, rather than passive, space. In this, we mean that social workers can avoid or minimize a lot of the potential pitfalls of the "dark side" of the net by being proactive in developing and maintaining their online presence.

The following tips adapted from Sowton et al. (2016) may be of use to think about when creating or reviewing your online presence:

Who Are You Now?

- What does your digital footprint look like at present? You want an accurate representation of who you are.

- Does your online profile(s) describe you in a personal or professional context? For example, do you identify with being a social worker when you post online?

- What information do you want someone to find if they search for you online?
- Is your online presence accurate and up to date?

Who Are You Going to Be in the Future?

- Do you want to keep your professional and personal identities separate or blended?
- What advantages or disadvantages might this have both in the short and long term?
- If you have multiple online identities on different platforms, is it obvious that they belong to you?
- How do your professional bodies' guidelines impact on you?
- Think ahead: How might your use of social media change if you think of yourself as a professional social worker rather than as an ordinary citizen?

Developing Your Online Presence

- Review existing privacy settings and adjust where necessary.
- Find out what (and how) information is used by the different social media sites so that you can make the best and most appropriate use of them.
- Consider who your friends and followers are and who follows you.
- Reflect on the identity you are curating online. How might your current profiles and digital footprints impact on your professional standing later?
- What do you need to be doing now to plan for, build, and develop your identity as a professional?

Downsides to Digital Intervention

At times, you as a social worker may face abuse online. In those instances, it is imperative that you seek and receive support from your line manager (and others as necessary), and that any abuse experienced online as it relates to your social work role is addressed, whether from an external source or internally from a colleague.

Burns et al. (2021) offered suggestions for organizations, managers, and practitioners when dealing with social media abuse. As well as offering practical suggestions for managing online abuse, Burns et al. also recommended the use of their reflection, assessment, and action tool within social work supervision sessions to process experience of online social media abuse, receive tangible and practical support as the recipient of such abuse, and ensure planning for mitigation against potential future abuse.

Across the globe, social workers utilize social media as a means of advocating for people's rights and showing solidarity with marginalized and oppressed populations. Through effective use of online platforms as a part of the social work advocacy tool kit, campaigns for social change can be progressed and, in many cases, be successful. The following section outlines two tangible examples of the successful use of social media in social work advocacy efforts.

Ireland

In 2018, a referendum was held to ask the public if they wished to remove the eighth amendment from the Irish constitution, which gave constitutional protection to the "unborn" equal to that of the pregnant person (Irish Council for Civil Liberties, n.d.). Social workers organized a grassroots campaign to encourage social workers to engage with the issue of reproductive justice through education of the public about social determinants of health as they pertain to reproductive justice and to campaign in support of repealing the eighth amendment. The campaign used Twitter (@SW4Choice) and Facebook (Social Workers 4 Choice) as the main tools for organizing. This was a deliberate choice. An online campaign allowed social workers to be connected and involved on a national basis.

Given the small numbers of social workers in Ireland—5,094 nationally in October 2022 (CORU, 2022)—local in-person organizing of social workers as a distinct group can be difficult due to the low density of social workers in each local area. Instead, the typical community organizing involving social workers will generally be as part of a broader group campaigning on an issue with the group makeup not being unique to social workers. While this is positive because it means collaborative and solidarity-based organizing that involves social workers and community members, the distinct voice and contribution of social workers to social issues can be lost. In the SW4Choice campaign, the social work organizers behind the campaign developed a two-pronged approach that encouraged social workers to (1) use their distinct social work voice to contribute to the repeal of the eighth movement online and (2) become involved in traditional in-person organizing as part of the broader Together4Yes (@Together4yes on Twitter) groups that developed across the country for the duration of the lead-up to the referendum.

Palestine

In 2018, a Palestinian social worker, Munther Amira, was arrested while peacefully protesting for children's rights (Amira et al., 2018). The global social work community immediately organized using online platforms (e.g., Twitter, petition websites) to call for the immediate release of Amira from prison. A social work academic based in Canada started an online petition calling for Amira's release; that petition gained around 15,000 signatures globally. Twitter was used as a means for social workers worldwide to unite under a common call for action to free Amira for upholding social work values and principles.

Sustained pressure from social workers globally and strong advocacy from the IFSW and the United Nations Special Rapporteur from the Office of the United Nations High Commissioner for Human Rights were directed to the Israeli government to release Amira. Six months after his arrest, he was released. Amira sent an open letter to the global social work community, thanking them for their efforts in assisting in his release and pledging that this support would lead to the ongoing nonviolent movement of resistance of social workers in Palestine.

CONCLUSION

Community action in social work has evolved with the profession, and it takes many forms, from community organizing to community social planning, to activist social work. These and many other forms of social work community action are contextualized through cultural, social, political, and economic spheres. As one of the many "tools" social workers have access to, online community action is a relevant practice in current social work practice and can be a valuable addition to the profession's skill base. A common theme running through traditional and current approaches to community practice and community action in social work is their alignment with the emancipatory goals of the global definition of social work. This suggests that the medium through which social work strives to achieve its goals of social justice and human rights can take many forms, up to and including technology, whereas the core values and principles of the profession remain intact.

While social work practice, by and large, remains a primarily in-person activity, the recent COVID-19 pandemic forced the global profession to rethink its traditional form of practice and engage fully with technology to continue to provide much-needed social services to communities and individuals. Incorporating technology into the fabric of the profession may be one of the "benefits" of the recent pandemic, highlighting potential for technological solutions to traditional problems in the profession—for example, making it easier for social workers to document, organize, and access information and decrease time spent on administrative tasks.

Social workers working from a human rights approach view access to technology as one of the resources necessary to live a humane and dignified life. A key focus of community social work is addressing social exclusion and its impact on social determinants of health. This includes digital exclusion and its impact on people. For social work, this typically includes addressing barriers to accessing technology, digital equity, and data justice.

Because the role of social media has changed from one of entertainment to one of connection and amplification, social workers have begun to engage with the notion of utilizing social media as an advocacy tool. They view the potential for greater positive impact on collective social problems as one reason for utilizing social media in advocacy work. To mitigate against falling into the keyboard activism trap, social workers engaging in online community action need to be aware of the limits of online activism and retain their commitment to in-person, community-based efforts alongside online ones. Social workers should actively engage in digital literacy to support upskilling communities so that they can self-organize for community action.

As with all social work–related activity, it is important to take a critical stance online and ensure boundary setting across all platforms you use. Thinking about the reasons for which platform or account will be used and how to present oneself online, in both a personal and a professional capacity, will contribute to more positive online usage.

REFERENCES

Akram, W., & Kumar, R. (2017). A study on positive and negative effects of social media on society. *International Journal of Computer Sciences and Engineering, 5,* 2347–2693. https://doi.org/10.26438/ijcse/v5i10.351354

Amedie, J. (2015). *The impact of social media on society.* Santa Clara University Scholar Commons, Advanced Writing: Pop Culture Intersections. https://scholarcommons.scu.edu/engl_176/2

Amira, R., Ballantyne, N., & Duarte, F. (2018). Promoting the empowerment and liberation of people in Palestine, 1970–75. *Critical and Radical Social Work, 6,* 119–122. https://doi.org/110.1332/204986018X15199226335088

Attlee, C. (1920). *The social worker.* G. Bell and Sons. https://ia600208.us.archive.org/4/items/cu31924013864255/cu31924013864255.pdf

Beau, P. (2020, June 17). How social media is changing our world. *Fair Observer.* https://www.fairobserver.com/business/technology/beau-peters-social-media-movements-black-lives-matter-me-too-misinformation-data-privacy-news-15251/

Berzin, S. C., Singer, J., & Chan, C. (2015, October). *Practice innovation through technology in the digital age: A Grand Challenge for Social Work* (Working Paper No. 12). https://grandchallengesforsocialwork.org/wp-content/uploads/2015/12/WP12-with-cover.pdf

Best, P., Manktelow, R., & Taylor, B. J. (2016). Social work and social media: Online help-seeking and the mental well-being of adolescent males. *British Journal of Social Work, 46*, 257–276. https://doi.org/10.1093/bjsw/bcu130

Burns, K., O'Súilleabháin, F., Cuskelly, K., & Kelleher, P. (2021). *Social media abuse, online harassment and social work* (International ed.). University College Cork, Ireland, School of Applied Social Studies. https://www.ucc.ie/en/media/academic/appliedsocialstudies/oswp/SocialMediaAbuseofSocialWorkersV1INT.pdf

Byrne, J., Kirwan, G., & McGuckin, C. (2019). Social media surveillance in social work: Practice realities and ethical implications. *Journal of Technology in Human Services, 37*, 142–158. https://doi.org/10.1080/15228835.2019.1584598

Clipper, B. (2020). The influence of the COVID-19 pandemic on technology. *Nurse Leader, 18*, 500–503. https://doi.org/10.1016/j.mnl.2020.06.008

CORU. (2022). *CORU registration statistics - October 2022.* https://www.coru.ie/news/news-for-health-social-care-professionals/coru-registration-statistics-october-2022.html

de Villiers, R. (2020). Accelerated technology adoption by consumers during the COVID-19 pandemic. *Journal of Textile Science & Fashion Technology, 6.* http://dx.doi.org/10.33552/JTSFT.2020.06.000647

European Commission. (2018). *Joint communication to the European Parliament, the European Council, the Council, the European Economic and Social Committee and the Committee of the Regions Action Plan against Disinformation.* https://www.eeas.europa.eu/sites/default/files/

Ferguson, I., & Woodward, R. (2009). *Radical social work in practice: Making a difference.* Policy Press.

Gamble, D. N., & Weil, M. O. (1995). Citizen participation. In R. L. Edwards (Ed.-in-Chief), *Encyclopedia of social work* (19th ed., Vol. 1, pp. 483–494). NASW Press.

Gamble, D. N., & Weil, M. (2009). *Community practice skills: Local to global perspectives.* Columbia University Press.

Greeson, J. K. P., An, S., Xue, J., Thompson, A. E., & Guo, C. (2018). Tweeting social justice: How social work faculty use Twitter. *British Journal of Social Work, 48*, 2038–2057. https://doi.org/10.1093/bjsw/bcx146

Hardcastle, D. A., Powers, P. R., & Wenocur, S. (2004). *Community practice theories and skills for social workers* (2nd ed.). Oxford University Press. http://ndl.ethernet.edu.et/bitstream/123456789/34740/1/6.pdf.pdf

Hill, E., Tiefenthäler, A., Triebert, C., Jordan, D., Willis, H., & Stein, R. (2020, May 31). How George Floyd was killed in police custody. *New York Times.* https://www.nytimes.com/2020/05/31/us/george-floyd-investigation.html

Ife, J. (2012). *Human rights and social work: Toward rights-based practice* (3rd ed.). Cambridge University Press.

International Federation of Social Workers. (2012, March 3). *Global standards.* https://www.ifsw.org/global-standards/

International Federation of Social Workers. (2014, July). https://www.ifsw.org/what-is-social-work/global-definition-of-social-work/

Irish Council for Civil Liberties. (n.d.). *What is the Eighth Amendment?* Retrieved February 24, 2022, from https://www.iccl.ie/her-rights/what-is-the-eighth/

Macdonald, S. J., & Clayton, J. (2013). Back to the future, disability and the digital divide. *Disability & Society, 28,* 702–718. https://doi.org/10.1080/09687599.2012.732538

Mayer-Schönberger, V., & Cukier, K. (2013). *Big data: A revolution that will transform how we live, work, and think.* Houghton Mifflin Harcourt.

Merriam-Webster. (n.d.). Social media. In *Merriam-Webster.com dictionary.* Retrieved February 24, 2022, from https://www.merriam-webster.com/dictionary/social%20media

Midgley, J. (2001). Issues in international social work: Resolving critical debates in the profession. *Journal of Social Work, 1,* 21–35.

Mossberger, K., Tolbert, C. J., & Stansbury, M. (2003). *Virtual inequality: Beyond the digital divide.* Georgetown University Press.

Mundt, M., Ross, K., & Burnett, C. M. (2018). Scaling social movements through social media: The case of Black Lives Matter. *Social Media + Society, 4.* https://doi.org/10.1177/2056305118807911

Murdach, A. D. (2011). Is social work a human rights profession? [Commentary]. *Social Work, 56,* 281–283. https://doi.org/10.1093/sw/56.3.281

National Association of Social Workers. (2021). *Code of ethics of the National Association of Social Workers.* https://www.socialworkers.org/About/Ethics/Code-of-Ethics/Code-of-Ethics-English

Pantic, I. (2014). Online social networking and mental health. *Cyberpsychology, Behavior, and Social Networking, 17,* 652–657. https://doi.org/10.1089/cyber.2014.0070

Parrott, L., & Madoc-Jones, I. (2008). Reclaiming information and communication technologies for empowering social work practice. *Journal of Social Work, 8,* 181–197.

Reamer, F. G. (2018). Ethical standards for social workers' use of technology: Emerging consensus. *Journal of Social Work Values and Ethics, 15,* 71–80. https://jswve.org/download/15-2/articles15-2/71-Use-of-technology-JSWVE-15-2-2018-Fall.pdf

Reisch, M., & Andrews, J. (2014). *The road not taken: A history of radical social work in the United States*. Routledge.

Reny, T., & Newman, B. (2021). The opinion-mobilizing effect of social protest against police violence: Evidence from the 2020 George Floyd protests. *American Political Science Review, 115*, 1499–1507. https//doi.org/10.1017/S0003055421000460

Ross, M. G., Lappin, B. W., & Lappin, X. W. (1967). *Community organization; theory, principles, and practice*. Harper & Row.

Sanders, C. K., & Scanlon, E. (2021). The digital divide is a human rights issue: Advancing social inclusion through social work advocacy. *Journal of Human Rights and Social Work, 6*, 130–143. https://doi.org/10.1007/s41134-020-00147-9

Sowton, C., Connelly, L., & Osborne, N. (2016). *e-professionalism*. University of Edinburgh. http://www.docs.hss.ed.ac.uk/iad/About_us/Digital_footprint/Student_eprofrofessionalism_guide_v1_2.pdf

Spencer, J. (2022, February 1). Can an employee be fired for sharing a questionable social media post? *Corporate Compliance Insights*. https://www.corporatecomplianceinsights.com/freedom-of-expression-fired-social-media-posts/

Steyaert, J., & Gould, N. (2009). Social work and the changing face of the digital divide. *British Journal of Social Work, 39*, 740–753. https://doi.org/10.1093/bjsw/bcp022

Wronka, J. (2016). *Human rights and social justice: Social action and service for the health and helping professions*. SAGE.

Chapter 5 Appendix

Quick Guide for Social Activism: Utilizing Social Media for Positive Change

The social work profession is evolving, growing, and reconnecting with its roots of activism and advocacy. Even in our roles as clinicians and micropractitioners, advocating for justice and equal rights for the people we serve should be at the top of our list. Words like "activism" and "advocacy" can feel overwhelming, especially when our plate is already full. The key is to find something that works for you and identify areas in which you feel your skills and knowledge can make a macro impact. The important thing is to start somewhere!

Getting involved in advocacy can look different for everyone based on your availability, proximity to resources, and interests. Running for public office is probably one of the best ways to advocate for your community, but we understand that running for office often comes with sacrifices and hard work. If you are thinking of running for office or any elected position, reach out to grassroots organizations that have been connected to the community, attend their meetings, and get familiarized with the current political landscape of your community. You will quickly find out through these conversations if there is an opportunity for you to run to either replace someone who is already in that seat or to fill a vacancy. Getting informed and gaining support from your community and constituents will be key factors to ensure a successful campaign for public office.

If you're not ready to run, you can get involved in plenty of other ways. Before you engage in extracurricular activities and hands-on activism, clarify with your employer how and when you should and can represent yourself. Some employers are fine with being named as supporting certain causes, some will only allow it with board approval, and some say never. What's often safe is using your name, the title of social worker, not identifying your employer (e.g., in name or by wearing a badge, giving out a company business card), and being careful where you identify your employer (Facebook or LinkedIn). Some may want you to put an "all opinions posted are solely my own" or something to that effect on your profile.

A QUICK GUIDE FOR ADVOCACY ENGAGEMENT

Starting an advocacy campaign or movement might feel intimidating and even overwhelming. We often think of advocacy as this massive display of activism that requires protesting, speaking in front of masses, or even going on strike. And while all those activities might be effective and inspiring, advocacy can also start at the micro and grassroots levels. One of the most useful guides to help you start your advocacy efforts is this: the "Nine Questions" by the Advocacy Institute (2002). These questions are:

1. What do we want?
2. Who can give it to us?
3. What do they need to hear?
4. Who do they need to hear it from?
5. How can we get them to hear it?
6. What do we have?

7. What do we need to develop?

8. How do we begin?

9. How do we tell if it's working?

Visit https://www.ndi.org for more information (see also The Campaign Workshop, 2015).

Advocacy comes in many shapes and forms. Another way to support causes you care about is by supporting and encouraging endorsements for candidates who align with social work values. For example, in the United States, the National Association of Social Workers (NASW) has the Political Action for Candidate Election (PACE) committee that solely focuses on endorsing and supporting candidates who can carry the social work mission. This committee works closely every election cycle with candidates who are seeking endorsement from NASW (see https://www.socialworkers.org/advocacy/political-action-for-candidate-election-pace for more information about PACE). At the national level, NASW endorses federal-level candidates, including presidential and congressional candidates, and each NASW state chapter focuses on endorsing statewide candidates (also available at https://www.socialworkers.org/advocacy/political-action-for-candidate-election-pace). Getting involved with your local social work association might be a good first step in your advocacy development.

OTHER WAYS TO GET INVOLVED IN ADVOCACY

Local City Government

City councils often have a level of influence over a city's budget. If you choose to do one thing this year, you can attend your city council budget hearings. Meeting information is usually listed on the city council website and is open to the public, unless otherwise noted. Some cities broadcast their meetings online, too, so that is a good place to start. The budget will be spent on everything from police and social services to potential new personnel additions, such as a library social worker.

If you have limited time but want to get involved, being involved in the public comments or attending the budget hearings for a city can make a yearlong impact on where your tax dollars are spent. On many occasions, a very particular grant or program has been started because one person kept showing up and demanding it. Get to know your city's process on who makes decisions about land. That process affects displacement, gentrification, resegregation, food apartheid, housing, and job access, which we all know are critical to the safety and positive development of humans.

Local Nonprofits/Special Interest Groups

One of the easiest ways you can get involved in advocacy and community work is by joining a board of directors. All nonprofits, committees, alumni chapters, and grassroots organizations have a board or council that provides oversight and informs their decision making. Most board positions have similar requirements and responsibilities, so always make sure the expectations and responsibilities are clear from the beginning so you can determine if this is something you would like to focus your energy on.

If this is your first time getting involved in a committee or board of directors, you probably will be interviewed. Ask following questions to assist you in making a decision:

- What is their application process?
- Do you need to be recommended by another board member, or can you self-nominate?
- Are there any term limits for this position?
- What is the minimum expected time commitment?
- Is there a financial commitment for this position?

Political Parties/Caucuses

If you're not ready to be directly involved, perhaps someone really great is. Again, in the United States, the NASW (2021) *Code of Ethics* calls us to be involved politically. You can volunteer through your local party office (which may be state, county, city, or districtwide) or for a cause or interest group you care about, such as caucuses for Black or Hispanic constituents, teachers, nurses, or even social workers.

You may also identify particular candidates who share your social work values and volunteer for their campaigns. Volunteering in a campaign will give you insight into the community and offer experience to both familiarize you with the community you serve and provide access to a candidate who will potentially be in public office. Making the connections with that future elected official will be useful because once they are in office, they often remember, and will feel accountable to, the ones who helped them get there.

Board of Behavioral Health, Social Work, or Other Regulatory Entities

Depending on the country in which you practice social work, you might have a regulatory board or group that oversees social workers and provides professional licenses. In the United States, each state has its own Board of Behavioral Health

Examiners in charge of issuing and managing your professional license as an LMSW or LCSW. This license might be more applicable to U.S. social workers. Boards make decisions on everything from who gets to call themselves a social worker (title protection), how much it costs to be licensed, under what circumstances a license is removed, how many days you have to document your practice, whether you can work with clients in another state, who gets to supervise, what counts toward an LCSW (or other terminal license), and so much more.

Getting involved and understanding who is on your board, who is employed by the office versus who is elected or appointed, and how much power each person has is a great place to start. You may then find in your community or state that certain things are going really well, and you want them to keep happening, or that things need to change.

CONCLUSION

It can be overwhelming to think about adding advocacy or activism to your plate. Hopefully the options we've described in this chapter provide you with a sense that participation is accessible and that the commitment can be as little as an hour a month. The important thing is to start somewhere, so we challenge you to choose one thing to get involved with and make a plan to make it happen.

APPENDIX REFERENCES

Advocacy Institute. (2002). *"Nine questions": A strategy planning tool for advocacy campaigns.* National Democratic Institute. https://www.ndi.org/sites/default/files/Handout%201%20-%20Nine%20Advocacy%20Questions.pdf

The Campaign Workshop. (2015). *The complete guide to advocacy.* https://www.thecampaignworkshop.com/sites/default/files/The-Complete-Guide-to-Advocacy.pdf

National Association of Social Workers. (2021). *Code of ethics of the National Association of Social Workers.* https://www.socialworkers.org/About/Ethics/Code-of-Ethics/Code-of-Ethics-English

CHAPTER 6

The Power of Online Synchronous Cognitive–Behavioral Group Intervention: A Get S-M-A-R-T Illustration

Virgil L. Gregory, Jr., and Lisa Werth

In September 2019, I (L.W.) was presenting at the Indiana Annual Recovery Month Symposium at the Embassy Suites in Indianapolis. The presentation focused on content from a cognitive–behavioral substance use disorders program that addressed early interventions for synthetics-marijuana-alcohol-recreational-trouble (S-M-A-R-T). I (V.L.G.), an associate professor and clinical researcher from Indiana University School of Social Work, was present in the audience given my own clinical experiences in providing similar interventions for court-ordered clients* in a community mental health center, and I recognized that S-M-A-R-T was different.

At the end of the symposium, I approached the presenter, Lisa Werth, to discuss a collaborative evaluation of the intervention's empirical outcomes. We are licensed clinical social workers and licensed clinical addiction counselors, and both of us have many years of experience working with court-mandated individuals and a mutual desire to address the rates of recidivism (Gibbs & Lytle, 2020) and the latent variables that may influence recidivism (motivation). After talking and realizing that we had overlapping practice philosophies, values, and visions regarding improving the way the criminal justice and other referral systems manage substance use charges or problems, we began meeting to collaborate on developing a study to conduct a program evaluation of the cognitive–behavioral Get S-M-A-R-T curriculum (Gregory & Werth, 2022). Over the next several months, we met via

---

* Throughout this chapter, we use the terms "participants" and "clients" interchangeably.

videoconferencing software to discuss the study's aims, research design, variables, institutional review board issues, and the Get S-M-A-R-T curriculum.

IMPETUS FOR ONLINE COGNITIVE–BEHAVIORAL INTERVENTION

The initially planned face-to-face cognitive–behavioral group intervention for S-M-A-R-T was changed to an online synchronous cognitive–behavioral group intervention (OSC-BGI) in response to the COVID-19 pandemic (Parihar et al., 2021). Yet, beyond COVID-19, several concurrent factors also have helped catalyze the expansion of online cognitive–behavioral and other interventions (Shatri et al., 2021)—for example, specific clinical populations and their respective needs.

Prior research has made a theoretical and empirical argument for the unique benefit of online cognitive–behavioral interventions in addressing social anxiety disorder (Yuen et al., 2013). Online cognitive–behavioral intervention could have a beneficial role in expanding access to, and addressing the behavioral counseling component of, low-threshold buprenorphine treatment for persons who are prescribed medications for opioid use disorder (Gregory & Ellis, 2020). Given disproportionate use of mental health services for Black individuals (Center for Behavioral Health Statistics and Quality, 2021), online cognitive–behavioral interventions could overcome some barriers that limit access (Ellis & Anderson, 2021). Others have discussed the use of online psychosocial intervention to address barriers in rural communities that limit access to mental health services (Oldham, 2016). These changes had implications for one of us (L.W.), who was facilitating the intervention; both of us, who were conducting the research; and the clients, who received the OSC-BGI for substance use.

Types of Online Cognitive–Behavioral Interventions

Given the various motivations for utilizing online cognitive–behavioral interventions, both asynchronous and synchronous options exist. *Asynchronous online cognitive–behavioral intervention* involves the communication between the provider and the client that does not occur simultaneously (Chan et al., 2018). As described by Chan and associates, asynchronous approaches have the advantages of decreased reliance on immediate online access, greater accessibility via mobile phones, fewer time restrictions for both the provider and client, and the inclusion of videos, among other factors. *Synchronous online cognitive–behavioral intervention* includes live or concurrent video or telephonic communication between the provider and the client (Chan et al., 2018).

Empirical Support for Online Cognitive–Behavioral Interventions: Mental Health

In terms of cognitive–behavioral therapy (CBT) format, the proof of concept for asynchronous online intervention and synchronous online intervention has been substantiated via meta-analyses or randomized clinical trials (RCTs) for various mental health and substance use issues. A transdiagnostic online CBT meta-analysis (Păsărelu et al., 2017) showed the intervention demonstrated large, positive effects in the treatment of anxiety and depression and a moderate positive effect in quality of life. One meta-analysis compared asynchronous, synchronous, and face-to-face methods for persons with depression (Richards & Richardson, 2012); in that meta-analysis, the asynchronous subgroup had a moderate effect size on self-reported depressive symptoms that was significantly better than its synchronous counterpart at posttreatment. Yu and colleagues (2021) conducted a meta-analysis evaluating online and face-to-face CBT for neurological insomnia and found that online CBT had significantly greater total sleep time and improved anxiety relative to the control counterparts.

Empirical Support for Online Cognitive–Behavioral Interventions: Substance Use

While we were unable to find a meta-analysis evaluating the cumulative quantitative effects of online CBT (asynchronous or synchronous), several RCTs were available and supported the efficacy of the interventions. One RCT evaluated a computer-based training for cognitive–behavioral therapy (CBT4CBT) intervention in women who were primarily African American (Kelpin et al., 2021). The CBT4CBT RCT was a hybrid of both face-to-face and asynchronous electronic CBT intervention. This study was statistically underpowered, yet it had some small effects with outcomes favoring the CBT4CBT arm: fewer relapses, longer time until relapse, and more sobriety at the follow-up period relative to the control group.

Prior RCTs that have evaluated CBT4CBT have shown significant improvement with various substances relative to treatment as usual (Carroll et al., 2008, 2014; Kiluk et al., 2016). An RCT of alcohol consumption and symptoms compared two types of synchronous online CBT to asynchronous CBT (Sundström et al., 2016). That study found superior effects in the synchronous methods, showing a significant reduction in alcohol use relative to the asynchronous arm of the study. The extant body of behavioral science literature shows promise from studies evaluating the efficacy of online CBT interventions for clients with diagnosed substance use disorders.

Synchronous Online Cognitive–Behavioral Early Interventions for Court-Ordered Clients

The empirical reports of efficacy for online CBT interventions for substance use continues to grow given the aforementioned circumstances (Parihar et al., 2021) that necessitate them. Due to the progressive nature of substance use disorders, early interventions (Fornili & Haack, 2005)—such as familial, legal, financial, occupational, marital, and many others (American Psychiatric Association, 2013)—can be used to prevent medical and psychosocial problems stemming from substance use. As previously mentioned, because of issues presented by COVID-19, we empirically evaluated an early OSC-BGI aimed at addressing motivation and hazardous substance use for persons who are court ordered or otherwise mandated for intervention (Gregory & Werth, 2022). The study was conducted online in a synchronous group format using the S-M-A-R-T cognitive–behavioral early intervention. The Get S-M-A-R-T content is different from traditional court-ordered substance use classes in that it is an experiential curriculum offering exercises developed from principles of second- (J. S. Beck, 2021) and third-wave CBT (Hayes, 2016), motivational interviewing (MI; Miller & Rollnick, 2013), and positive psychology (Lopez et al., 2019). The OSC-BGI (S-M-A-R-T) is delivered in eight-, 12-, 16-, or 20-hour doses of clinical intervention. Rather than the 30 to 50 participants in a standard substance use education classroom, Get S-M-A-R-T is designed for small groups of 15 or fewer and is facilitated by two master's-level clinicians.

The preexperimental study (Gregory & Werth, 2022) demonstrated an association between the Get S-M-A-R-T OSC-BGI and positive improvements in motivation at posttest and recidivism and self-report of DSM substance use symptoms at 12-month follow-up. It was this experience with OSC-BGI that we both began to further realize the utility and potential benefits of OSC-BGI. The purpose of this chapter is to expand social workers' use of OSC-BGI through a description of an innovative example called Get S-M-A-R-T. We articulate principles and cognitive–behavioral interventions that are used in the synchronous online group format and also discuss the implications for social work values and ethics.

OSC-BGI: GET S-M-A-R-T

Overview

The purpose of Get S-M-A-R-T is to provide clients an opportunity to further examine their relationships between their substance and their goals, values, decisions, functioning in different domains of life, and underlying mental health. Get

S-M-A-R-T is an OSC-BGI that consists of either eight-, 12-, 16-, or 20-hour dosages/groups with unique, evidence-based curricula clinical exercises and materials for substance use and mental health intervention.

Get S-M-A-R-T explores underlying causes of substance abuse. The intervention does so while respecting and empowering participants to discover the source of their behaviors that causes legal or other functional problems. These sources can often include stress, limited coping skills, inadequate social support, a skewed perspective regarding the actual consequences of substance use, trauma, and mental health issues (A. T. Beck et al., 1993). Through specialized clinical exercises and group work, Get S-M-A-R-T encourages participants to explore their personal relationship with drugs and alcohol. The OSC-BGI helps clients develop constructive patterns for wellness through which participants begin to examine problematic behaviors and gain insight regarding potential solutions.

Providers and Group Size

Get S-M-A-R-T facilitators are licensed in clinical social work (or are other master's-level, mental health–oriented professional providers) and addiction. Due to the advanced clinical exercises as well as the skills required to manage common group dynamics that emerge in the program, two social work facilitators are recommended per class.

To promote a therapeutic environment, class sizes are capped at 10 participants for the OSC-BGI format. Smaller groups are conducted to create adequate time for sharing and participation that facilitates encouragement, hope, and increased internal motivation for positive change.

Principles

Synchronous online group facilitators are trained on the following principles:

- Validate without judgment (Linehan, 1993).
- Encourage participants to challenge each other (altruism; Yalom & Leszcz, 2020).
- Reward self-responsibility (affirmation; Miller & Rollnick, 2013) and other expressions of internal locus of control.
- Practice self-awareness and mindfulness (Segal et al., 2013).

These principles, properly executed and coupled with the Get S-M-A-R-T curriculum, provide a platform that encourages substantive and positive change. As discussed in Rogers's (1957) classic article, the most essential part of the synchronous online Get S-M-A-R-T intervention is building a therapeutic alliance with the participants. Because this correlates strongly with social work values and ethics (NASW, 2021), it is also a strong foundation that allows the online intervention to be successful. You might wonder: How do you create a therapeutic alliance over an online platform? Well, much like you would do in person, you follow simple principles. These are also the principles of the Get S-M-A-R-T curriculum and certified facilitators.

Validate without Judgment

Linehan (1993) defined *validation* as communication that lets clients know both that their statements are sensible and understood given the circumstances and that the client is accepted. Each participant has a story that led them here, and, as a facilitator, it's crucial that we recognize and validate their emotions without judgment, blame, or shame. Example statements include: "It sounds like you're feeling . . ."; "Can you say more about that?"; "Help me understand . . ."; and "Thank you for sharing—I know this can be difficult to talk about." When doing this virtually, as in person, both verbal and nonverbal communication remains integral to the intervention. For example, leaning in, having eye contact, and showing interest and enthusiasm through tone of voice are important.

Encourage Participants to Challenge Each Other (Altruism)

One of the curative factors of group intervention is altruism (Yalom & Leszcz, 2020). Get S-M-A-R-T facilitates altruistic exchanges among group members that come in the form of questions, feedback, and supportive statements. These altruistic, client-to-client group behaviors are in part facilitated by the group members' modeling the facilitators' interactions with the clients. This is what Yalom and Leszcz have referred to as "imitative behavior."

In the context of the altruistic and imitative behavior curative factors, clients can identify behaviors and thought patterns in one another to help each of them recognize the flawed logic in themselves. A common example is when one client scoffs or shakes their head when another is giving excuses or rationalizing their substance use. You might gently bring attention to the scoffing client, asking why the client had that reaction to what the other said. Allow participants to hold each other accountable. Another key component is the balanced representation of principles. For example, through questions, affirmations, and feedback, the facilitators help balance the principles of validation without judgment and encourage participants to challenge each other.

Reward Self-Responsibility (Affirmation)

Affirmation has been a long-standing aspect of core skills pertaining to MI (Miller & Rollnick, 2013). Research has demonstrated the ability of affirmation to impact clinically relevant outcomes (Karpiak & Benjamin, 2004). Therefore, success of clients in Get S-M-A-R-T is conceptually and in part determined by rewarding or recognizing positive behavior. These participants might be so used to being treated like a number by "the system" that your encouragement could move mountains. Example statements include: "Everyone is on time! Thank you for that" and "I see no one has their phones out. We're off to a great start."

Practice Self-Awareness and Mindfulness

Facilitators may feel tired, distracted, or stressed outside of the virtual classroom. However, be mindful not to allow those things to be distractions once the synchronous online group begins. Similar to the CBT principle of therapeutic rapport (J. S. Beck, 2021) and Rogerian (Rogers, 1957) guidelines for establishing and maintaining therapeutic rapport, facilitators should be cognizant that they're always treating clients with respect and conveying empathy.

Segal and colleagues (2013) identified the importance of mindfulness and self-care pertaining to the group facilitators. Facilitators get themselves encouraged and excited before class about influencing positive change in clients and remain aware that everyone in the virtual room is a human deserving of an opportunity to grow and learn. Clients can tell whether the facilitators are engaged, and they will react accordingly. This is especially important online because facilitators must be the ones to keep the energy flowing in the room, which can be done by being mindful of one's own mood, emotions, and the way we approach the material and clients.

Practice Foundations

Consistent with CBT principles (J. S. Beck, 2021), the Get S-M-A-R-T curriculum is specifically designed to be educational and interactive. Therefore, the notion of and hope for change can be transformed from an elusive idea to a tangible, desirable, and attainable goal for participants. To that end, Get S-M-A-R-T has both positive psychology (Lopez et al., 2019) and MI (Miller & Rollnick, 2013) as the foundation of the curriculum. Other exercises are based in second-wave CBT (J. S. Beck, 2021) and dialectical behavior therapy (Linehan, 1993).

The OSC-BGI was innovative and was created to allow clients to create change in their lives. Furthermore, specific coping skills are taught and practiced. In the context of OSC-BGI, Get S-M-A-R-T addresses underlying mental health concerns, and participants are guided in interventions consisting of mindfulness, meditation, breathing techniques, cognitive restructuring, and the benefits of being grateful.

Clients may have dichotomous (A. T. Beck, 1976) or even attribution errors in thinking and just push it away: "It's those stupid cops" or "It's just that I was pulled over for my taillight out." Other clients may have permissive automatic thoughts (A. T. Beck et al., 1993) pertaining to their justification for using a substance in a hazardous situation. As has been indicated at various times in this chapter, the facilitators instill the CBT model and principles early on, suggesting to participants that how they think about what has happened, including having to be here, will influence their emotions and behaviors (J. S. Beck, 2021). In addition to using MI and the spirit of MI throughout, participants are presented with some cognitive–behavioral intervention skills for addressing thoughts that may contribute to risk-taking substance use behavior. We start by asking for a show of hands: "How many people are excited to be here? How many are indifferent? How many are angry or feel it is unfair?" Validate feelings and help participants understand they can take charge of their thoughts.

Get S-M-A-R-T was developed to help clients feel heard, validated, and not judged. These factors are believed to contribute to quicker establishment of rapport during a brief intervention. We have found that all the activities of the curriculum that we had done in person can be done online. Most participants need a computer or smartphone, pen, and a paper to participate. Table 6.1 provides an overview of the Get S-M-A-R-T intervention schedule for the eight-,12-, 16-, and 20-hour doses (definition of postacute withdrawal symptoms from Haskell, 2022). Each dosage of the OSC-BGI includes all of the previous sections. For example, the 20-hour dosage receives every intervention in the table, whereas the 12-hour dosage receives only the 12- and eight-hour components. For those interested in learning more about the Get S-M-A-R-T curriculum, visit the Calla Collaborative Health website (see https://callacch.com).

Monitoring Client Progress Online

Additional benefits of the synchronous online group intervention are the ease and efficiency by which technology can be used to monitor progress via online scales. Online, outcome data collection from clients can be used for visual or statistical evaluations of progress. Since the data is collected online, there is no need to manually enter data, which saves time. The online evaluation of progress can be analyzed at the individual level or group level. Facilitators can view and use the data in a feedback loop to improve services. The deidentified data can also

Table 6.1: OSC-BGI: S-M-A-R-T Program Schedule

8-Hour Intervention			
Introduction of program	State laws exercise	Biology of addiction	Brain chemistry
Impaired driving prevention	Risk reduction triggers and coping skills	Substance use spectrum exercise	Creative approach to prevention
12-Hour Intervention			
Self-assessment and mental health	Pro or con exercise	Wisdom line exercise	Substance use and families
16-Hour Intervention			
Recap of 8- and 12-hour interventions	PAWS	Coping skills explored	Addiction and change
20-Hour Intervention			
Opiates	Experiential learning	Group support	Application of CBT
DBT skills	Affirmations	Defense mechanisms	Mindfulness and meditation

Notes: Each dosage includes all of the previous dosages. CBT = cognitive–behavioral therapy; DBT = dialectical behavior therapy; OSC-BGI = online synchronous cognitive–behavioral group intervention; PAWS = postacute withdrawal symptoms, emotional and psychological symptoms that remain after the initial withdrawal symptoms have subsided and raise the risk for relapse; S-M-A-R-T = synthetics-marijuana-alcohol-recreational-trouble.

be anonymously shared with the client, referral sources, and other stakeholders provided the appropriate precautions are taken.

The Get S-M-A-R-T curriculum has used electronic scales (Gregory & Werth, 2022) with adequate psychometric statistics for clients with substance use issues to measure client-relevant outcomes. Such scales have included the measure of depressive symptoms (Patient Health Questionnaire-9; Dum et al., 2008), anxiety (Generalized Anxiety Disorder-7; Delgadillo et al., 2016), satisfaction with life (Satisfaction with Life Scale; Di Maggio, 2016; Di Maggio et al., 2021), self-esteem (Rosenberg Self-Esteem Scale; Luoma et al., 2008), and motivation (University of Rhode Island Change Assessment Scale; Field et al., 2009). Using the technological benefits provided by OSC-BGI aids in upholding the CBT principle pertaining to monitoring client progress (J. S. Beck, 2021).

Group Scheduling and Referrals

As indicated in Table 6.1, Get S-M-A-R-T is designed as either an eight-, 12-, 16-, or 20-hour intervention. In its current form, the program starts on an evening from 5:00 p.m. to 9:00 p.m. Participants meet again the next day from 9:00 a.m. to 1:00 p.m. (eight hours total) or 9:00 a.m. to 5:00 p.m. (12 hours total). The remaining eight hours of programming for the 20-hour intervention occurs in the next three consecutive weeks, with participants meeting once a week for just under three hours a week. Since Get S-M-A-R-T is developed in a way in which exercises can be utilized à la carte style, it can be broken up in many effective ways. For example, an agency has used a 10-hour junior curriculum (Get S-M-A-R-T, Jr.) for adolescents; these participants meet two hours once a week for five weeks. Because Get S-M-A-R-T is modular, it can be facilitated in several different ways to meet agency needs.

Participants are often referred to participate in Get S-M-A-R-T from many sources. Most commonly, a referral originates from an agency, such as the court, probation, university counseling or other department, or an employer. Occasionally, a participant will come voluntarily because of a personal consequence.

Most often, participants who are referred for the eight-hour intervention have been arrested for impaired driving, public intoxication, minor consumption of alcohol, or possession of marijuana or synthetics. The eight-hour intervention is typically appropriate for people experiencing their first offense but who do not meet criteria for a diagnosable substance use disorder. Participants who are referred for the 12- or 16-hour intervention may still be experiencing a first offense or work violation, but their identified risk is more severe. For example, with impaired driving, the blood alcohol concentration may be higher than .15. People experiencing multiple consequences from their substance use are generally referred for the 12- or 20-hour intervention. Clients charged with possession of controlled substance are generally referred for the 20-hour outpatient intervention.

Table 6.2 provides examples of possible referral conditions that indicate a particular Get S-M-A-R-T dosage/group. Readers should be cognizant that recommendations are only made after a thorough assessment. The items in this table are only indicators and not a substitute for comprehensive assessment and consequent considerations for appropriate level of care.

Managing Problem Situations

Through trial and error, we have also learned that some people may not be appropriate for the online platform for different reasons—for example, a participant

Table 6.2: Client Indicators for Get S-M-A-R-T Dosage

8-Hour Intervention	12-Hour Intervention	16-Hour Intervention	20-Hour Intervention
First drug or alcohol charge	First offense, BAC >.15	Second drug/alcohol charge	Multiple offenses
OWI BAC < .15	Changes in tolerance	Relationship or work issues	Other drug charges
Possession of marijuana	Some insight into choices	Blackouts	Multiple impaired driving offenses
Minor consumption < .15	Resistance or blaming	Potential mental health issues	Difficulty taking responsibility
Low-risk behaviors	Risky and dangerous behavior	Little insight into choices	Risk of substance use disorder
Demonstration of remorse	Additional consequences		

Notes: BAC = blood alcohol concentration; OWI = operating while intoxicated; S-M-A-R-T = synthetics-marijuana-alcohol-recreational-trouble.

who may be under the influence of a substance, may continue to use vape device or cigarettes despite reminders, may be disrespectful to other participants, or may allow projection of anger to spread to other members and create a bad "vibe" in the room. In extreme cases, we have removed people from the Get S-M-A-R-T program. Typically, this involves one facilitator's asking the client to step out; we then call them privately and explain that they cannot continue in the intervention due to breaking the rules. A follow-up call is scheduled to determine next steps.

Typically, coordination with the probation officer or other referral source can determine what the next steps are. For example, in one case, we had a client who was intoxicated and had to be removed; it turned out they needed a referral to a higher level of care. Another example was a client who was making sexually inappropriate comments to another participant; they were referred to an individual intervention format. This was also true for another client who was disruptive in the online platform, but when that client started doing the work individually, they seemed to get much more serious about Get S-M-A-R-T. Some individuals for several clinical reasons may have optimal outcomes in an individual setting rather than in a synchronous online group format.

Synchronous Online Group Format

As described at the beginning of this chapter, we initially planned on conducting an empirical evaluation of efficacy pertaining to the face-to-face group intervention called Get S-M-A-R-T. This was the initial plan because the Get S-M-A-R-T intervention was originally facilitated in person. The shift to an OSC-BGI came about to continue serving the increasing needs of people struggling with substance abuse and mental health concerns. Therefore, the face-to-face group intervention, like interventions facilitated by many other providers around the world in 2020 (Knechtel & Erickson, 2021), quickly transitioned to an online format; an interactive platform was created for participants to connect, learn, and engage with one another.

The synchronous online Get S-M-A-R-T includes using videoconferencing software that allows facilitators to share their screen to walk through some of the exercises because participants will also be actively engaging in the exercises at home. Participants also have access to a virtual workbook if they had not picked a workbook up at their designated location.

Unexpected Situations

Because this format was new to me (L.W.) and to my cofacilitator, the learning process included on-the-fly experiences and had some bumps along the way. For example, when the facilitators noticed a participant attending online while driving with three children in the back seat of the car, due to safety concerns, we created the rule that participants could not attend online while driving, moving around (we all get dizzy!), and at work (for privacy). We also had to remind participants that everyone on the platform could see others in their camera view, including family members' activities. It was a trial and learn for us all because we were adjusting to the COVID pandemic. Eventually, we got better at facilitating the OSC-BGI. In hybrid formats consisting of both online and face-to-face clients, the facilitators allowed one to three clients, wearing masks, to come in person to the classroom while having the others online.

Additionally, based on idiosyncratic experience, I (L.W.) found it crucial to have one face-to-face facilitator in the actual physical setting and another facilitator online. This arrangement was preferable because it enhanced active participation and group cohesion between the face-to-face and online clients. This hybrid model also came with some learning curves. Simple things, such as where to position the camera so everyone online could see the in-person participants and the facilitator and having a good microphone in the room so that online participants could hear participants sharing in the room, continued to improve from month to month.

Given the real-world events (Knechtel & Erickson, 2021; Shatri et al., 2021) that catalyzed the widespread need for synchronous online group and other online interventions, the pros and cons for both clients and providers/facilitators become more profound. The pros:

- Convenience: No travel time, parking, or commute
- Safety of participation within your own space/home
- Ease of social anxiety (participants could mute or turn off video when feeling anxious)
- Small class size
- Paperless monitoring of client progress online
- Access to people (participants attending from all over the state or country)

The cons:

- Privacy and confidentiality not guaranteed
- Internet connection a possible issue for rural participants
- Internet lags creating some delay and awkwardness in sharing
- Interruptions at home (e.g., participants' children, pets)

Strategies for Conducting Effective Synchronous Online Interventions

Based on my (L.W.'s) experience with transitioning from face-to-face to OSC-BGI, we have learned a number of strategies to accentuate the pros or benefits of synchronous online group intervention and minimize the cons. When setting up the boundaries and virtual classroom expectations for Get S-M-A-R-T, clients are informed before the first group meeting of the following basic guidelines for participation:

- Please enter the virtual room with your video "on" and your audio "muted."
- Please attend the program in a quiet area of your home. Please do not attend while driving or at work when others are present.
- Please do not use mood-altering chemicals (including smoking, vaping, and chewing tobacco) while in the program.
- We encourage participation and sharing, and to allow for a smooth transfer of communication online, please keep yourself muted unless you are talking.

- We will provide frequent breaks, and it is important to mute and turn video off when on break.

- We encourage participants to be respectful of one another by allowing each person to have their own opinions and feelings in a nonjudgmental manner.

- We review confidentiality: It is a virtual classroom, so we cannot guarantee confidentiality because we do not know each participant's personal surroundings. We review the limits of confidentiality and mandated reporting.

Group Session Structure

In accordance with the CBT principle of structured sessions (J. S. Beck, 2021), the cognitive–behavioral Get S-M-A-R-T intervention has structure. The Get S-M-A-R-T sessions, regardless of group dosage, are divided into three sections: (1) introduction, (2) intervention exercises, and (3) summary and reflection.

The introduction includes reviewing the online expectations, facilitator introductions, and client introductions that contain their reasons for coming and something novel about the client. The introduction also includes validation of the client's thoughts and emotions regarding their typically mandated referral and affirmation as well as the client's presence and participation. An important component of this introduction is initially empowering the clients to take ownership of their own path. The facilitators explain the purpose of the Get S-M-A-R-T intervention (see Table 6.1) and the importance of clients' being able to explore their ambivalence (Miller & Rollnick, 2013). The interventions exercises are determined by the day and which dosage of Get S-M-A-R-T the clients have been recommended to complete. The summary and reflection section involves a review of the session's content, feedback from the client's regarding the session, and plans for the next session.

OSC-BGI: SOCIAL WORK VALUES AND ETHICS

Thus far, we have discussed the convergence of the COVID-19 pandemic and other factors that prompted an expansion in online CBT or cognitive–behavioral interventions and the efficacy of OSC-BGI. We also provided a social work–facilitated example of an OSC-BGI with options for addressing online transitions. Another necessary component of this chapter includes the implication for social work ethical principles and standards (NASW, 2021). In prior discussions of OSC-BGI, these social work ethical principles and standards have been alluded to but not clearly discussed. This section of the chapter seeks to briefly identify several of the relevant ethical standards contained in the NASW (2021) *Code of Ethics* as it relates to OSC-BGIs.

When considering or conducting an OSC-BGI, social workers are to facilitate their interventions in a manner that is adherent to the *Code of Ethics* (NASW, 2021). As the *Code of Ethics* pertains to OSC-BGI overall, in the context of social work principles, a number of ethical standards can be used to guide social work OSC-BGI. For example, social workers in the United States providing OSC-BGI should use the NASW (2021) *Code of Ethics* Ethical Standards to guide Informed Consent (1.03), Competence (1.04), Cultural Competence (1.05), Conflicts of Interest (1.06), and Privacy and Confidentiality (1.07), among others. Likewise, social workers providing OSC-BGI outside the United States should use their analogous entities and documents to guide their ethical conduct of OSC-BGI in social work practice.

CONCLUSION

Social workers are the most abundant providers of mental health services in the United States (Heisler, 2018). The profession's mission (NASW, 2021) focuses on social workers' improving the well-being of human beings and places specific emphasis on empowering those individuals who are marginalized. Persons with substance use disorders face a wide range of familial, social, occupational, academic, legal, or medical issues (American Psychiatric Association, 2013) in addition to stigma that permeates policy and treatment (Earnshaw, 2020).

Several factors make this chapter particularly relevant: an increase in access to online communication, partly made available through smartphones; policies addressing online telehealthcare delivery (McElroy et al., 2020); the abundant empirical evidence supporting CBT (Hofmann et al., 2012); and promising research on synchronous CBT interventions (Sundström et al., 2016). With the convergence of these factors, it is anticipated that this chapter will aid social workers in considering and further expanding their OSC-BGI services in an ethical manner that fulfills the mission of the social work profession.

REFERENCES

American Psychiatric Association. (2013). *Diagnostic and statistical manual of mental disorders* (5th ed.). Author.

Beck, A. T. (1976). *Cognitive therapy and the emotional disorders.* International Universities Press.

Beck, A. T., Wright, F. D., Newman, C. F., & Liese, B. S. (1993). *Cognitive therapy of substance abuse.* Guilford Press.

Beck, J. S. (2021). *Cognitive behavior therapy: Basics and beyond* (3rd ed.). Guilford Press.

Carroll, K. M., Ball, S. A., Martino, S., Nich, C., Babuscio, T. A., Nuro, K. F., Gordon, M. A., Portnoy, G. A., & Rounsaville, B. J. (2008). Computer-assisted delivery of cognitive–behavioral therapy for addiction: A randomized trial of CBT4CBT. *American Journal of Psychiatry, 165*, 881–888. https://doi.org/10.1176/appi.ajp.2008.07111835

Carroll, K. M., Kiluk, B. D., Nich, C., Gordon, M. A., Portnoy, G. A., Marino, D. R., & Ball, S. A. (2014). Computer-assisted delivery of cognitive–behavioral therapy: Efficacy and durability of CBT4CBT among cocaine-dependent individuals maintained on methadone. *American Journal of Psychiatry, 171*, 436–444. https://doi.org/10.1176/appi.ajp.2013.13070987

Center for Behavioral Health Statistics and Quality. (2021). *Racial/ethnic differences in mental health service use among adults and adolescents (2015–2019)* (Publication No. PEP21-07-01-002). Substance Abuse and Mental Health Services Administration. https://www.samhsa.gov/data/

Chan, S., Li, L., Torous, J., Gratzer, D., & Yellowlees, P. M. (2018). Review of use of asynchronous technologies incorporated in mental health care. *Current Psychiatry Reports, 20*, Article 85. https://doi.org/10.1007/s11920-018-0954-3

Delgadillo, J., Böhnke, J. R., Hughes, E., & Gilbody, S. (2016). Disentangling psycho-pathology, substance use and dependence: A factor analysis. *BMC Psychiatry, 16*, Article 281. https://doi.org/10.1186/s12888-016-0988-1

Di Maggio, I. (2016, October 13–15). *Progettazione professionale e vulnerabilità: Il ruolo di alcune risorse di Life Design in persone con Disturbo da Uso di Sostanza* [Life design and vulnerability: The role of some life design resources in people with substance use disorder] [Paper presentation]. Conference XVI Convegno SIO-Società Italiana Orientamento, Milan, Italy.

Di Maggio, I., Montenegro, E., Little, T. D., Nota, L., & Ginevra, M. C. (2021). Career adaptability, hope, and life satisfaction: An analysis of adults with and without substance use disorder. *Journal of Happiness Studies, 23*, 439–454. https://doi.org/10.1007/s10902-021-00405-1

Dum, M., Pickren, J., Sobell, L. C., & Sobell, M. B. (2008). Comparing the BDI-II and the PHQ-9 with outpatient substance abusers. *Addictive Behaviors, 33*, 381–387. https://doi.org/10.1016/j.addbeh.2007.09.017

Earnshaw, V. A. (2020). Stigma and substance use disorders: A clinical, research, and advocacy agenda. *American Psychologist, 75*, 1300–1311. https://doi.org/10.1037/amp0000744

Ellis, D. M., & Anderson, P. L. (2021). Improving the acceptability of internet-based cognitive–behavioral therapy among Black Americans. *Technology, Mind, and Behavior, 2*. https://doi.org/10.1037/tmb0000044

Field, C. A., Adinoff, B., Harris, T. R., Ball, S. A., & Carroll, K. M. (2009). Construct, concurrent and predictive validity of the URICA: Data from two multi-site clinical trials. *Drug & Alcohol Dependence, 101,* 115–123. https://doi.org/10.1016/j.drugalcdep.2008.12.003

Fornili, K., & Haack, M. R. (2005). Policy watch. Promoting early intervention for substance use disorders through interdisciplinary education for health professionals. *Journal of Addictions Nursing, 16,* 153–160. https:// /doi/pdf/10.1080/108 84600500231946

Gibbs, B. R., & Lytle, R. (2020). Drug court participation and time to failure: An examination of recidivism across program outcome. *American Journal of Criminal Justice, 45,* 215–235. https://doi.org/10.1007/s12103-019-09498-0

Gregory, V. L., Jr., & Ellis, R. J. B. (2020). Cognitive–behavioral therapy and buprenorphine for opioid use disorder: A systematic review and meta-analysis of randomized controlled trials. *American Journal of Drug & Alcohol Abuse, 46,* 520–530. https://doi.org/10.1080/00952990.2020.1780602

Gregory, V. L., Jr., & Werth, L. (2022). Synchronous online cognitive-behavioral group intervention: 12-month evaluation for substance use mandated clients. *Research on Social Work Practice, 32,* 940–951. https://doi.org/10.1177/10497315221106785

Haskell, B. (2022). Identification and evidence-based treatment of post–acute withdrawal syndrome. *Journal for Nurse Practitioners, 18,* 272–275. https://doi.org/10.1016/j.nurpra.2021.12.021

Hayes, S. C. (2016). Acceptance and commitment therapy, relational frame theory, and the third wave of behavioral and cognitive therapies [Republished article]. *Behavior Therapy, 47,* 869–885. https://doi.org/10.1016/j.beth.2016.11.006

Heisler, E. J. (2018). *The mental health workforce: A primer* (Report No. R43255). https://fas.org/sgp/crs/misc/R43255.pdf

Hofmann, S. G., Asnaani, A., Vonk, I. J. J., Sawyer, A. T., & Fang, A. (2012). The efficacy of cognitive behavioral therapy: A review of meta-analyses. *Cognitive Therapy and Research, 36,* 427–440. https://doi.org/10.1007/s10608-012-9476-1

Karpiak, C. P., & Benjamin, L. S. (2004). Therapist affirmation and the process and outcome of psychotherapy: Two sequential analytic studies. *Journal of Clinical Psychology, 60,* 659–676. https://doi.org/10.1002/jclp.10248

Kelpin, S. S., Parlier-Ahmad, A. B., Jallo, N., Carroll, K., & Svikis, D. S. (2021). A pilot randomized trial of CBT4CBT for women in residential treatment for substance use disorders. *Journal of Substance Abuse Treatment, 132,* Article 108622. https://doi.org/10.1016/j.jsat.2021.108622

Kiluk, B. D., Devore, K. A., Buck, M. B., Nich, C., Frankforter, T. L., LaPaglia, D. M., Yates, B. T., Gordon, M. A., & Carroll, K. M. (2016). Randomized trial of computerized cognitive behavioral therapy for alcohol use disorders: Efficacy as a virtual stand-alone and treatment add-on compared with standard outpatient treatment. *Alcoholism: Clinical and Experimental Research, 40*, 1991–2000. https://doi.org/10.1111/acer.13162

Knechtel, L. M., & Erickson, C. A. (2021). Who's logging on? Differing attitudes about online therapy. *Journal of Technology in Human Services, 39*, 24–42. https://doi.org/10.1080/15228835.2020.1833810

Linehan, J. M. (1993). *Cognitive–behavioral treatment of borderline personality disorder*. Guilford Press.

Lopez, S. J., Pedrotti, J. T., & Snyder, C. R. (2019). *Positive psychology: The scientific and practical explorations of human strengths* (4th ed.). SAGE.

Luoma, J. B., Kohlenberg, B. S., Hayes, S. C., Bunting, K., & Rye, A. K. (2008). Reducing self-stigma in substance abuse through acceptance and commitment therapy: Model, manual development, and pilot outcomes. *Addiction Research & Theory, 16*, 149–165. https://doi.org/10.1080/16066350701850295

McElroy, J. A., Day, T. M., & Becevic, M. (2020). The influence of telehealth for better health across communities [Commentary]. *Preventing Chronic Disease, 17*, Article 200254. https://doi.org/10.5888/pcd17.200254

Miller, W. R., & Rollnick, S. (2013). *Motivational interviewing: Helping people change* (3rd ed.). Guilford Press.

National Association of Social Workers. (2021). *Code of ethics of the National Association of Social Workers.* https://www.socialworkers.org/About/Ethics/Code-of-Ethics/Code-of-Ethics-English

Oldham, J. M. (2016). Psychotherapy in a rapidly changing world. *Journal of Psychiatric Practice, 22.* https://doi.org/10.1097/PRA.0000000000000123

Parihar, S., Kaur, R., & Singh, S. (2021). Flashback and lessons learnt from history of pandemics before COVID-19. *Journal of Family Medicine & Primary Care, 10*, 2441–2449. https://doi.org/10.4103/jfmpc.jfmpc_2320_20

Păsărelu, C. R., Andersson, G., Nordgren, L. B., & Dobrean, A. (2017). Internet-delivered transdiagnostic and tailored cognitive behavioral therapy for anxiety and depression: A systematic review and meta-analysis of randomized controlled trials. *Cognitive Behaviour Therapy, 46*, 1–28. https://doi.org/10.1080/16506073.2016.1231219

Richards, D., & Richardson, T. (2012). Computer-based psychological treatments for depression: A systematic review and meta-analysis. *Clinical Psychology Review, 32*, 329–342. https://doi.org/10.1016/j.cpr.2012.02.004

Rogers, C. R. (1957). The necessary and sufficient conditions of therapeutic personality change. *Journal of Consulting Psychology, 21*, 95–103. https://doi.org/10.1037/h0045357

Shatri, H., Prabu, O. G., Tetrasiwi, E. N., Faisal, E., Putranto, R., & Ismail, R. I. (2021). The role of online psychotherapy in COVID-19: An evidence based clinical review. *Acta Medica Indonesiana, 53,* 352–359.

Segal, Z., Williams, M., & Teasdale, J. (2013). *Mindfulness-based cognitive therapy for depression* (2nd ed.). Guilford Press.

Sundström, C., Gajecki, M., Johansson, M., Blankers, M., Sinadinovic, K., Stenlund-Gens, E., & Berman, A. H. (2016). Guided and unguided internet-based treatment for problematic alcohol use—a randomized controlled pilot trial. *PLOS ONE, 11,* Article e0157817. https://doi.org/10.1371/journal.pone.0157817

Yalom, I. D., & Leszcz, M. (2020). *The theory and practice of group psychotherapy* (6th ed.). Basic Books.

Yu, H., Zhang, Y., Liu, Q., & Yan, R. (2021). Efficacy of online and face-to-face cognitive behavioral therapy in the treatment of neurological insomnia: A systematic review and meta-analysis. *Annals of Palliative Medicine, 10,* 10684–10696. https://doi.org/10.21037/apm-21-2387

Yuen, E. K., Herbert, J. D., Forman, E. M., Goetter, E. M., Comer, R., & Bradley, J.-C. (2013). Treatment of social anxiety disorder using online virtual environments in second life. *Behavior Therapy, 44,* 51–61. https://doi.org/10.1016/j.beth.2012.06.001

Bridging Education and Practice with e-OSCE Simulations

Samantha Wolfe-Taylor, Khadija Khaja, and Christian Deck

Advances in technology, expanding distance education course offerings, and the COVID-19 pandemic disrupted traditional teaching styles and strategies for meeting the needs of the students and social services agencies in their implementation of training for social work practice (Wolfe-Taylor et al., 2022). This has led to an increased emphasis by social work educators to explore and share the outcomes of simulation-based learning opportunities for preparing students for the field. Before the pandemic, Dodds et al. (2018) discussed the need for interactive, engaging, and immersive simulations facilitated by modern technology to bridge the gap between knowledge and skills in social work education. However, postpandemic, minimal research exists on social work students' perspectives and experiences participating in online simulation-based learning opportunities.

One form of online simulation-based learning is the e-OSCE. This chapter shares findings from a qualitative case study that was conducted with online MSW students to explore their experiences and perspectives after completing and participating in an online e-OSCE.

BACKGROUND

Definition

The *objective structured clinical examination* (OSCE) is a standardized, valid, and reliable assessment method that social work distance education programs use to ensure successful practice skills development (Bogo et al., 2014; Shaban et al., 2021). The OSCE can be used to enhance the effectiveness of social work practice courses, to improve the interactivity and engagement of online students, and to increase the rigor of practice skills assessment (Wolfe-Taylor et al., 2022).

To differentiate between the face-to-face OSCE and an online OSCE for distance education, the abbreviation "e-OSCE" is used to represent an online OSCE in distance education.

OSCE Structure

Various academic disciplines use the OSCE as a method to assess student performance in a simulated clinical environment. Within social work education, a trained examiner rates the clinical skills demonstrated by a student when they are assisting a patient or clients who need social services. Generally, four parts are involved in the design of an OSCE:

1. **Objective component:** "Skills [are] directly observed by a rater(s) who does not have a relationship with the student" (University of Toronto, 2015, p. 1).

2. **Structured component:** A "set scenario and format," and environment are developed for the OSCE to take place within.

3. **Clinical component:** "Practice skill[s]" are demonstrated and assessed.

4. **Exam component:** "Performance is evaluated on a set scale resulting in an assessment of student competence" (University of Toronto, 2015, p.1).

To illustrate, a social work student conducts a live 20-minute interview in a Zoom meeting room with an actor who portrays a client suffering from substance use. The standardized client (SC) has been trained with a detailed script to ensure realism and consistency in portrayal with other students in the class. An SC is a person who has been trained to accurately and consistently re-create the client in the case scenario during the OSCE. During the simulation, the student's application of skills is assessed by a trained rater. The rater uses a checklist to assess clinical behaviors during their observation so they can document the types and accuracy of skills that a student is demonstrating as well as key points expected to be addressed by the student. Rating includes the following elements:

- the types of questions the student asks the client
- how the student responds to answers by the client
- how well the student covers the intake assessment, psychosocial assessment, and treatment plan with the client
- the practice skills demonstrated by the student (e.g., micro-practice skills, cultural competence, collaborative goal setting, empathy, active listening, boundary setting)

Following simulation completion, students participate in a debriefing session with the instructor and the actor role-playing as the SC. The goal of the debriefing is to transform how students practice in the field. It offers students a highly interactive and engaging learning opportunity that explores lessons learned from the OSCE experience; the student's practice skills, strengths, and challenges; and an assessment of the student's practice competency.

Authenticity and reliability for the portrayal of SCs can also be increased by employing actors who are clinically trained social work practitioners and currently practicing in the community. At that time, additional questions for the student to consider and feedback on their practice skills demonstration are provided. The student also completes a written reflection on their interview with the SC. The rater provides a final assessment of the student's skill demonstration and feedback on the student's written reflection (University of Toronto, 2015).

OSCE and Virtual Simulation Research

The first face-to-face simulation in social work education was implemented nearly 20 years ago, but social work educators have been slow to adopt and adapt to simulation-based education for practice preparation (Maynard, 2021). Even though the OSCE has been identified as an effective form of simulated learning for preparing students for practice in fields, such as nursing, medicine, and dentistry (Bogo et al., 2014; Shaban et al., 2021), social work educators have only recently begun researching the effectiveness and experiences of social work students participating in an OSCE, with most of this research focusing on the use of face-to-face OSCEs in face-to-face social work programs (Fidment, 2012; Maynard, 2021).

In an OSCE study with social work students working with LGBTQ+ persons, students rated their experiences with the OSCE methodology and its reflective practices (Logie et al., 2015). Their experiences with the OSCE confirmed that the method effectively increased social work students' strengths in practicing with LGBTQ+ individuals.

Maynard (2021) conducted analysis of two face-to-face supervision practice courses that explored MSW students' perceptions on participating in standardized simulations and their beliefs about OSCE effectiveness for supervision training. All students ($N = 32$) agreed or strongly agreed that the simulation experience was an effective learning opportunity to assist in developing social work supervision competencies. Confronting competency fears and self-reflection were identified as the most valuable outcomes.

Smith et al. (2021) explored the use of virtual simulations and evaluated the initial feasibility, acceptability, usability, and effectiveness of three computerized simulations during an interpersonal social work practice course. Students stated that the simulations had strong usability and that their clinical skills improved and translated successfully to interactions with clients in the field during their practicums.

Washburn et al. (2020) conducted a mixed-methods pilot investigation that used virtual patient simulations to determine if there was an increase in MSW students' self-efficacy and diagnostic accuracy for common behavioral health concerns within an integrated care setting. They found that engagement in virtual patient simulation training increased students' self-efficacy in brief clinical assessment. Additionally, students identified the virtual simulation as a valuable adjunct to traditional classroom or field training.

Student Perspectives of the e-OSCE Pilot Study

A pilot study was conducted to address the gap in the literature regarding MSW students' experiences participating in an e-OSCE, their feedback on the experience, and their feedback on the use of an e-OSCE for practice preparation and assessment. The e-OSCE included all the procedures described for the OSCE to assess practice skills in online courses. The on-paper assessments that the students, instructor, and actors complete in a face-to-face OSCE was digitized and, most importantly, completed in real time during the debriefing period following the e-OSCE.

Given the limited research on social work students' perspectives on participating in an e-OSCE and how they might use the learning simulation experience in future practice, the following research questions were developed to explore the "how" and "what" of these causal links and to expand the knowledge base on the use of the e-OSCE in social work practice education:

- What personal practice skills strengths and challenges do first-year MSW students self-identify having during the e-OSCE experience?

- How does the e-OSCE experience impact students' level of confidence in their ability to demonstrate practice competency?

- What do students identify as lessons learned from the e-OSCE simulation?

- What are first-year MSW students' perspectives on the e-OSCE learning experience?

- What future practice considerations do first-year MSW students present at completion?

METHOD

A qualitative, exploratory embedded single-case study was selected for the study design. Qualitative methods are used to gain a deeper understanding of people's perceptions regarding a particular phenomenon (Merriam, 2009). An *embedded single-case study* focuses on a single organization, institution, or program, but the analysis might include outcomes in which logical subunits can be identified (Baxter & Jack, 2008; Yin, 2014). An *exploratory case study* is used to explore those situations in which the intervention being evaluated has no clear, single set of outcomes (Yin, 2014). Exploratory case studies allow researchers to gain further insight into the phenomenon by providing an extensive and in-depth description that answers "how" and "what" questions (Yin, 2014). Common in the social sciences, exploratory case studies are used to examine presumed causal links (Yin, 2014).

Intervention

Two MSW practice course sections were investigated. The selected course trains and assesses students in the use of micro interviewing skills and the application of practice theories throughout the planned change process. Three rehearsal interviews were created and presented throughout the semester, leading to the students' participation in the e-OSCE. Rehearsal interviews helped familiarize the students with the technology and assessment tools they would be using in their e-OSCE to minimize students' technology-related apprehension in preparation for their e-OSCE. Rehearsal interviews also provided the students with opportunities to apply what they have learned over the course of the semester, leading up to the final practice opportunity in the e-OSCE. Following the e-OSCE intervention, students completed two surveys to capture their perspectives on the effectiveness of the e-OSCE.

e-OSCE Case Scenario Design and Process

The case scenario for the e-OSCE was developed in collaboration with previous students, currently practicing social workers, and social work educators of diverse personal backgrounds; practice experiences; racial, ethnic, age, gender identity; and levels of technology experience. This diverse collaboration in the design process created space for

- student learning needs to be central.
- community partners and practitioners to share in current best practice skills for consideration as well as identification of clients' needs.

- a holistic approach to curriculum development, allowing for diverse voices to be present in the design process.
- assessment for equitable educational opportunities for students with different learning needs and accessibility needs.
- recognition and inclusion of appropriate technology tools needed for and during the e-OSCE and the impact of these technologies on the learning process.
- recognition of the different levels of technology experience that need to be considered when developing the e-OSCE and determining the most appropriate technology tools for the e-OSCE.
- evaluation of ethnic and ethical considerations in the case scenarios developed for the e-OSCE.
- evaluation of the e-OSCEs ability to meet institutional standards as a learning activity.

Case Scenario

The SC case scenario (see Appendix A) is of a veteran without housing who recently began treatment for PTSD and who needed case management services. The case scenario is provided to the students 15 minutes before the designated start time of their interview.

SCs were trained and provided a more in-depth case scenario (see Appendix B) along with a copy of the biopsychosocial-spiritual assessment students used for the e-OSCE assessment and key phrases to say during the interview. SCs were trained to identify with their own race, gender, ethnicity, or sexual orientation if asked by the student during the interview. The SCs selected were currently practicing social workers with a minimum of two years of experience post-MSW. The SCs ranged in age, ethnicity, gender identity, sexual orientation, practice experience, and race to provide a diverse pool of clients.

The reflection assignment and e-OSCE feedback forms, which were administered following the e-OSCE, were developed in collaboration with the same students, practicing social workers, and social work educators who participated in the development of the case scenario. The reflection assignment and the e-OSCE feedback form were developed electronically, and a link to these forms was embedded in the online course site for the students to access post-e-OSCE completion. A road map of the e-OSCE for students (see Figure 7.1) provides a visual demonstration of the processes leading up to, during, and after the completion of the e-OSCE simulation experience for participants.

Figure 7.1: e-OSCE Road Map to Completion

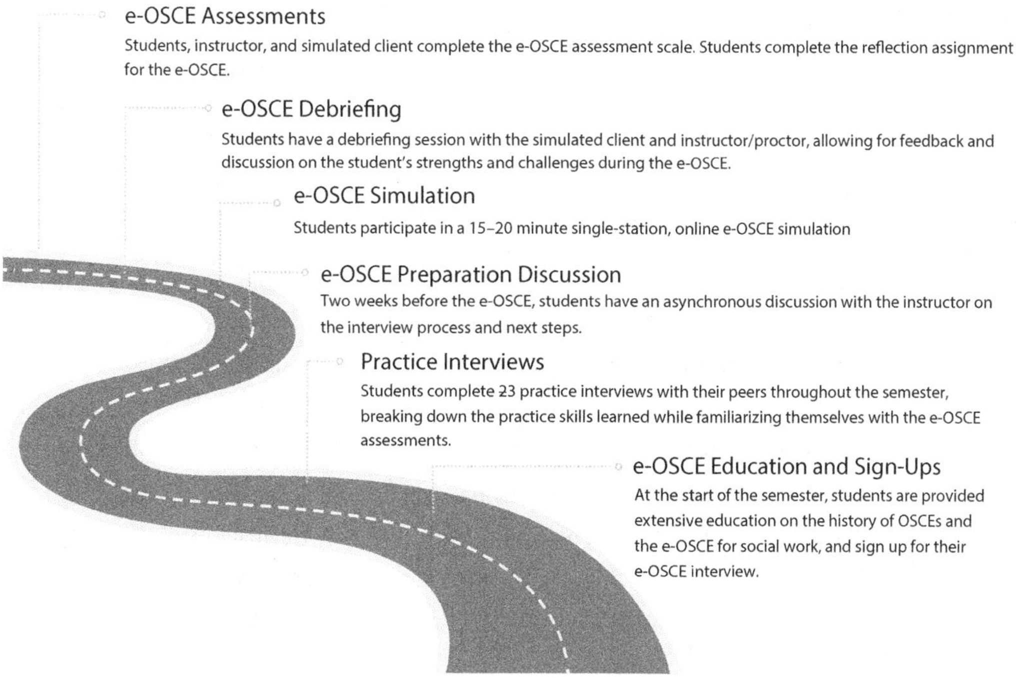

e-OSCE Assessments
Students, instructor, and simulated client complete the e-OSCE assessment scale. Students complete the reflection assignment for the e-OSCE.

e-OSCE Debriefing
Students have a debriefing session with the simulated client and instructor/proctor, allowing for feedback and discussion on the student's strengths and challenges during the e-OSCE.

e-OSCE Simulation
Students participate in a 15–20 minute single-station, online e-OSCE simulation

e-OSCE Preparation Discussion
Two weeks before the e-OSCE, students have an asynchronous discussion with the instructor on the interview process and next steps.

Practice Interviews
Students complete 23 practice interviews with their peers throughout the semester, breaking down the practice skills learned while familiarizing themselves with the e-OSCE assessments.

e-OSCE Education and Sign-Ups
At the start of the semester, students are provided extensive education on the history of OSCEs and the e-OSCE for social work, and sign up for their e-OSCE interview.

Sample and Data Collection

Participants included first-year MSW students ($N = 49$) participating in two practice course sections in their first social work practice course in a midwestern university and school of social work in the United States. Students' ages, races, ethnicities, undergraduate backgrounds, student identification numbers, previous practice experiences, or any other identifiable information were not collected during this initial study to ensure it followed the guidelines set forth by the human subjects committee and institutional review board as quality assessment/quality improvement research. Students were provided a randomized number by their instructor so that the online data collected were anonymized to the study investigators. The online data included a student e-OSCE perspectives feedback survey and reflection questions.

Qualitative data collection consisted of structured student reflections built in and stored in Qualtrics (2020) software and embedded in the last module of the course. Students wrote about their experiences participating in the e-OSCE, as guided by the following questions:

- What were your strengths and challenges in conducting the interview?

- What strategies did you use to engage the client and develop rapport?

- What is your opinion of your performance in the interview with the client?

- What do you think you have learned from the e-OSCE interview experience?

- How might this learning experience influence your approach with future clients?

- Can you describe how you feel about applying the skills you have learned in your e-OSCE to future practice?

Data Analysis

Data were analyzed using Quirkos (2022) and followed framework analysis. *Framework analysis* is a comparative form of thematic analysis that employs an organized structure of inductively and deductively derived themes to conduct cross-sectional analysis using a combination of data description and abstraction (Goldsmith, 2021). The framework method is a flexible tool that can be adapted for use with many qualitative approaches; therefore, it does not align with a particular epistemological, philosophical, or theoretical approach (Gale et al., 2013).

Researchers used a deductively driven method and built consensus on themes based on the research questions presented. On an individual basis, researchers read and coded the first reflection, then compared for categories and codes. Researchers built consensus on categories and codes to create a codebook with operational definitions. They collaboratively analyzed the second reflection to strengthen consensus and identify additional categories and codes.

Their analysis began with five initial themes developed based on the research questions:

1. practice skills demonstration
2. level of confidence
3. lessons learned from the e-OSCE experience
4. perspectives on the use of the e-OSCE for practice education
5. future practice considerations

Thirty-one main codes were identified within the five themes. The researchers then reviewed the final subcodes for definitions and exemplar quotes.

RESULTS

Research Question #1: What personal practice skills strengths and challenges do first-year MSW students self-identify having during the e-OSCE experience?

Students reported several strengths in their practice skills:

- micro-practice skills demonstration (e.g., reflecting feeling, active listening, paraphrasing, asking open-ended questions, providing good nonverbal communication, summarizing)
- intercultural competence (e.g., identifying and respecting gender pronouns and preferred names, exploring client's military service, engaging in a deeper exploration of client's lived experiences that were different than their own)
- collaborative goal setting with the client
- application of theory in practice (e.g., strengths/empowerment, systems, critical, behavioral, psychodynamic, biological)

As it pertains to the challenges or areas for improvement within their practice skills, students reported some of the following challenges or areas for growth:

- using too many closed-ended questions
- addressing or exploring cultural differences or cultural needs of the client
- gathering information as it relates to the presenting problem
- having nervousness impact engagement or depth of the conversation (see Table 7.1)

Research Question #2: How does the e-OSCE experience impact students' level of confidence in their ability to demonstrate practice competency?

Several students identified a lower level of confidence at the start of the e-OSCE session. However, they were able to recognize that as the simulation experience continued. As they began engaging with the client, their level of confidence in their practice skills and demonstration of these skills increased (see Table 7.2).

The data in Table 7.3 and Table 7.4 reveal an increase in the students' identifying an increased level of confidence in their practice skills after the e-OSCE experience ($f = 21$) versus their increased level of confidence during the e-OSCE experience ($f = 8$). We see a decrease in the students' identifying a decreased level of confidence in their practice skills after the e-OSCE experience ($f = 2$)

Table 7.1: Theme 1: Strengths/Challenges in Practice Skills Demonstration

Theme	Major Code	f	Definition	Examples
Strengths and challenges in practice skills demonstration	Strengths	226	Students self-identify the strengths they presented within their practice skills demonstration during the e-OSCE	"Engagement was informed by asking open-ended questions to gain insight based on the client's perspective on why the case scenario is what it is. I then utilize the situation being faced to empower the client; help them see their strengths, and help them see how systems, environments, and people play a role in their situation."
	Challenges	73	Students self-identify the challenges they presented within their practice skills demonstration during the e-OSCE	"I struggled to ask questions that fully covered all aspects of the biopsychosocial in a way that was in depth and allowed me to gain the big picture. At the end, I began to stumble when the client did not want to utilize a shelter. Her refusal shook me up a bit, and I felt scattered in my conversation at that point."

Note: e-OSCE = electronic objective structured clinical examination.

versus their decreased level of confidence during the e-OSCE experience ($f = 4$). Additionally, we see an increase in students' comments ($f = 28$) on their overall level of confidence after the e-OSCE than their comments ($f = 16$) regarding their level of onfidence during the e-OSCE experience. Students also identified that the feedback provided from the SC and instructor during the debriefing session helped increase their level of confidence after the e-OSCE. However, two students identified a lower level of confidence in their skills after completing the e-OSCE experience but could critically recognize their need for additional practice opportunities to improve these skills.

Table 7.2: Theme 2: Level of Confidence during the e-OSCE

Theme	Major Code	f	Definition	Example
Level of confidence during the e-OSCE interview	Increased	8	Students self-identify having an increased level of confidence in their practice skills during the interview process	"Once I began interacting with the client, I felt more confident as well."
	Decreased	4	Students identify their confidence but do not describe an increased or decreased level of confidence in their practice skills during the interviewing process	"I felt confident as the interview was progressing but lost some of my focus and confidence toward the end, when I felt that I had not helped the client identify two interventions."
	Students' general discussion of their confidence	16	Students identify their confidence but do not describe an increased or decreased level of confidence in their practice skills during the interview process	"I was nervous in the beginning but hit my stride partway through and was relaxed and confident."

Note: e-OSCE = electronic objective structured clinical examination.

Research Question #3: What do students identify as lessons learned from the e-OSCE simulation?

On multiple occasions, students spoke about their learning experiences from participating in the e-OSCE as positive and helpful to the learning process. Students identified a multitude of lessons learned from the e-OSCE experience (see Table 7.4). To provide more depth on the lessons learned, some of these lessons discussed the following:

Table 7.3: Theme 3: Level of Confidence after the e-OSCE

Theme	Major Code	f	Definition	Example
Level of confidence after completion of the e-OSCE interview	Increased level of confidence	21	Students identify having an increased level of confidence in their practice skills during the interview process	"I feel much more confident using these skills in real life than I did prior to e-OSCE."
	Decreased level of confidence	2	Students identify having a decreased level of confidence in their practice skills after completing the e-OSCE	"I have learned that I am not the best interviewer and need a lot of practice. I am not as confident as I thought I would be during this process."
	Students' general discussion on their confidence	28	Students identify their confidence but do not describe an increased or decreased level of confidence in their practice skills during the interview process	"I was timid, scared, and nervous to speak to a client when I began this course. Now I feel confident to utilize theories, set goals, and engage the client after completing the e-OSCE."

Note: e-OSCE = electronic objective structured clinical examination.

- how and what types of theories they were able to apply in practice or see as influential in the planned change process
- how to engage with a client using verbal and nonverbal cues
- how to manage their own emotions and feelings (e.g., anxiety and concern for the client's situation) during the interview
- the significance of intercultural competence in practice and rapport building by recognizing the client's gender identity, desired name, gender pronouns, and lived experiences participating in the military
- the importance of needing additional practice or practice opportunities like the e-OSCE to better prepare themselves for the field
- the value of feedback and supervision from their peers and those practicing in the field on the practice skills they demonstrated during the e-OSCE experience
- their growth and ability to demonstrate practice competence

Table 7.4: Theme 4: Lessons Learned

Theme	Major Code	f	Definition	Example
Lessons learned from the e-OSCE experience	Engaging a client	58	Students emphasize learning how to engage a client or use engagement practice skills to build rapport with the client after the e-OSCE	"To remember that you are dealing with and talking to a person, not a clock, and not system; therefore, engaging with the client is most important, and to let the other factors take a back seat."
	Practice setting can have an impact on the experience	17	Students describe the impact the practice setting or location can have on the interview process with a client	"I learned that the setting [in] which you work is also an important factor in determining your approach as well as interviewing questions and goals with your client."
	Feedback matters	9	Students emphasize the significance of feedback after the e-OSCE from the SC and professor in their learning process	"I was still excited after it was over because I was able to debrief with the professional and the professor. We discussed both strengths and weaknesses. I enjoyed it because they pulled our strengths that I didn't even recognize."
	Significance of practice in skills development	9	Students identify how continued practice can help improve their social work practice skills	"I learned that just because I already work in the field and possess certain skills that I can still learn and grow using the skills that I learned in the OSCE interview."
	How to apply theory in practice	7	Students recognize the correlation between theory and practice	"I also think I learned more about connecting theory to a person's life. Before, I was not applying theory in the right way."

Continued

Theme	Major Code	*f*	Definition	Example
	Inter-cultural competence	5	Students identify the integration of inter-cultural competence into practice as a lesson learned	"While we were both White males, I had not served in the military or lived in a military culture, so I tried to ask questions that would encourage the client to share more about their time in the military and that lifestyle."
	Man-agement of one's emotions	5	Students identify learning how to man-age their emotions during an interview with a client	"That I need to calm my nervousness to really be able to engage and assist a client."

Notes: e-OSCE = electronic objective structured clinical examination; OSCE = objective structured clinical examination; SC = standardized client.

Research Question #4: What are first-year MSW students' perspectives on the e-OSCE learning experience?

As students reflected on the e-OSCE learning opportunity, several students had positive things to say about their experience, such as (a) it was an educational experience for them by helping them identify practice areas that they still need to work on improving, (b) it provided a realistic environment in which to practice their skills, (c) it helped increase their confidence in their abilities to practice with real clients, (d) they found it to be an enjoyable learning experience, and (e) it created a positive learning environment for constructive feedback. However, some students felt that the e-OSCE experience required them to cover more than one could or should in such a short amount of time and felt overwhelmed by the requirements and expectations while having the instructor present for the interview (see Table 7.5).

Research Question #5: What future practice considerations do first-year MSW students present after completing the e-OSCE simulation?

Students were able to identify some practical and critical ways in which they could apply in their future social work practice what they had learned from the e-OSCE experience. For example, some students stated that the e-OSCE experience will

Table 7.5: Theme 5: Students' Perspectives on the e-OSCE Experience

Themes	Major Codes	f	Definition	Example
Students' perspectives on the e-OSCE experience	Educational learning experience	17	Students identify the e-OSCE simulation as a helpful and educational learning experience for them	"Because the OSCE is a part of my first experiences interviewing clients, the reflections I've done around mine and my peer performances, it has given me a foundation to further build microskills."
	Provides insight on students' level of confidence and their social work practice skills	13	Students identify the e-OSCE learning experience as an appropriate method to gain insight into their level of confidence and the strengths and challenges within their practice skills	"The OSCE has been an eye-opening experience, helping me see where I need to grow and how much I have grown already in just one semester. I have learned a lot about social work and myself and know I will continue to do so."
	Challenging learning experience	10	Students identify the e-OSCE as a challenging learning experience due to their limited experience or due to limited time to complete the e-OSCE experience	"I felt very nervous. I had not practiced before with a difficult client. I was also nervous about the time limit. There was too much to cover in a short amount of time."
	Supportive learning environment through constructive feedback	6	Students describe the e-OSCE simulation in a positive way, emphasizing how enjoyable or positive the experience was for them	"It also allowed me to have great discussion and get feedback in order to help me see things from a different perspective, as well as new ways of how to engage in the process."

Continued

Themes	Major Codes	f	Definition	Example
	Realistic simulated learning experience	4	Students identify the e-OSCE experience as a realistic simulated learning opportunity to help prepare them for the field	"I feel the OSCE gave me a realistic rehearsal to interviewing a client in practice."
	Enjoyable experience	4	Students identify the e-OSCE learning experience as an enjoyable learning opportunity to participate in	"I loved it. It was amazing."

Notes: e-OSCE = electronic objective structured clinical examination; OSCE = objective structured clinical examination.

positively influence their future work as it relates to (a) their approach in engaging a client in the planned-change process, (b) how they communicate and interact with the client as they gather information, and (c) being more aware of their own and their clients' body language and nonverbal cues. Additionally, students believed that they would feel less anxious with their future clients and more comfortable with the use of theory in practice and the interviewing process itself after participating in the e-OSCE experience (see Table 7.6).

LIMITATIONS

Although this research was carefully prepared, there were limitations that are important to discuss. Because we collected data as part of the course's assignments, we had no demographic information about the participants, limiting the ability to make comparisons across groups. Further, the smaller sample size prohibited advanced statistics. Recognition of self-selection bias needs to occur because convenience sampling was used to determine the sample for the qualitative analysis.

Due to the limited research on the use of e-OSCE in social work education, more studies are needed that compare outcomes and limitations of using e-OSCEs for social work practice preparation and skills evaluation. Further, the reflection survey and feedback survey are not validated instruments; the questions were created from the goals and objectives outlined in the practice course.

Table 7.6: Theme 6: Future Practice Considerations after the e-OSCE

Theme	Major Code	f	Definition	Example
Future practice considerations after the e-OSCE	Future use of microskills developed	30	Students provide details about using the microskills they developed and used from the e-OSCE simulation in their future practice with clients	"I feel that the skills learned are incredibly applicable. Regardless of where the interview is done, the foundational elements of interviewing are still being utilized and can be transferred to future practice whether online or in person."
	Have a more focused approach to their practice with clients	11	Students describe using the e-OSCE experience to help them recognize how to remain focused on the client while ensuring appropriate time management skills are used in their future practice	"This experience will influence my approach with future clients, as I can ask many open-ended questions with them. I will use the entire planned change process when interviewing future clients."
	Have a client-centered approach to practice	10	Students identify using the skills they gained from the e-OSCE simulation in their future practice to help them remain focused on the client and the client's needs rather than on the task at hand or a checklist of items to complete	"I will focus more on what the client feels the issue is, even if it is not the reason for the referral, and see where this takes us. It may be that there is a great deal of underlying issues to the major issue at hand that need to be addressed first."

Continued

Theme	Major Code	*f*	Definition	Example
	Will continue to evaluate one's practice skills	3	Students identify an increased awareness of their and their client's nonverbal cues and how they might use these to guide their practice skills in the future	"I will continue to be aware of my strengths and weaknesses in order to focus on improving my inter-viewing skills."
	Telehealth practices	2	After completing the e-OSCE experience, students consider the use of technology in their future practice	"I will be able to com-municate with clients using technology and know how to establish a tech failure plan in the future."

Note: e-OSCE = electronic objective structured clinical examination.

Technology can present challenges for the effectiveness of e-OSCEs. These challenges can include (a) poor internet reliability; (b) speed of internet; (c) dropped calls; (d) poor audio or video quality; (e) poor training of examiners; (f) digital repositories of exam data that are not secure; (g) financial expenditures; and (h) training needed by students, examiners, and administrative staff when more technology is being used in online teaching and learning environments (Shorbagi et al., 2022).

DISCUSSION AND IMPLICATIONS

Given the field of social work is identified as a helping profession rooted in addressing social injustices, schools of social work and social work faculty are uniquely positioned to advance the literature and explore nontraditional ways of educating students. The exploration of new technologies in training social work students via the use of e-simulations to create authentic, high-impact educational learning opportunities that prepare students for "real world" application can be at the forefront of social work education and practice innovation. Further research on the use of e-OSCEs in social work practice education is needed to identify the following:

- if there are differences in the experiences of students who participate in an e-OSCE based on their race, age, gender identification, previous educational background, technology and learning management system use experience, full-time/part-time enrollment status, accessibility needs, or practice experience
- if there are differences in the experiences of face-to-face and online students when they complete an e-OSCE
- if there are differences in students' field practicum readiness for students who participated in an e-OSCE versus students who did not participate in an e-OSCE
- if face-to-face students would have similar results on the feedback form as the online students

Additionally, if further research on the use of e-simulations in social work distance education identifies positive learning outcomes and better practice preparation for social work students, this will create additional evidence-based knowledge on whether online social work practice education is as effective as learning in face-to-face practice education.

While the first OSCE utilized in social work education and practice occurred in 2005, less research has examined "assessing social work students' ability to practice" via an anti-racist perspective (Lynch, 2022, p. 9). In what research has been done, there has been a "lack of consistency as it relates to incorporating dimensions of culture and diversity or assessing students' skills in their simulated interactions with clients" related to diversity and difference (Lynch, 2022, p.10). The profession of social work has also been critiqued for not trying to investigate the effectiveness of simulations to assess students' anti-racist practice skills, let alone assessing those skills in an online learning environment via the use of e-OSCEs (Lynch, 2022).

Social work educators have an obligation to train social work students in anti-racist practices, and simulation-based education is a potential tool for social work educators to use for such training and assessment. Social work is also called to address racist policies and actions in practice (Lynch, 2022), including social work educational policies, practices, and actions. Given the diverse demographics in the United States, it is important for the social work profession to acknowledge and understand the historical trauma and experiences of Black, Indigenous, and People of Color. To do so, we must better prepare students "to practice through an anti-racist lens to best meet" needs of diverse communities (Lynch, 2022, p. 3).

More social work research is needed on the "extent to which anti-racism is being assessed as a learning outcome" (Lynch, 2022) in social work education, which includes classes taught online. The use of e-OSCEs to address competencies that center on anti-racism practice is something the social work profession needs to consider because it can provide an innovative opportunity to address the impact of power and privilege and can provide students with real-time learning to engage in anti-racist practice.

CONCLUSION

Although technology advances for educational and practice purposes are being created at a fast pace, social work education has remained reactive rather than proactive in the development, implementation, and evaluation of distance education policies, technologies, and innovation. The desire for social work distance education is growing rapidly, and the need for authentic, high-impact practice online learning experiences are necessary in the preparation of social work students for the future. This study illustrates that social work practice skills can be enhanced by training students with e-OSCEs during their education to ensure they gain best practice skills to utilize once they are in the field. This study makes an important new contribution to the knowledge base on social work students' experiences participating in an e-OSCE and whether social work students identify the e-OSCE as an appropriate simulation-based educational experience to use for practice preparation.

Transforming OSCEs to an online environment can also reduce numerous logistical barriers that historically have limited their use by schools of social work (Lu et al., 2011). Instead of renting space and video recording equipment, schools of social work can use a free, online communication platform (e.g., Zoom, Skype, Google Meet) to create the environment necessary for interactivity. Instead of paying actors who aren't social workers to role-play as the client, schools of social work can engage clinically trained social work practitioners currently practicing in the community in the e-OSCE process, drawing on their expertise in the field to evaluate students and the e-OSCE process. This also ensures that the actor who role-plays scenarios with students is familiar with the appropriate practice skills competencies that students are being trained to master.

REFERENCES

Asakura, K., Sewell, K., Rawlings, M., Bay, U., & Kourgiantakis, T. (2022). Marion Bogo, a visionary, innovator, and leader: Reflecting on her groundbreaking work on simulation-based social work education. *Journal of Social Work Education.* https://doi.org/10.1080/10437797.2022.2069626

Baxter, P., & Jack, S. (2008). Qualitative case study methodology: Study design and implementation for novice researchers. *Qualitative Report, 13*, 544–559. https://doi.org/10.46743/2160-3715/2008.1573

Bogo, M., Rawlings, M., Katz, E., & Logie, C. (2014). *Using simulation in assessment and teaching: OSCE adapted for social work.* Council on Social Work Education.

Dodds, C., Heslop, P., & Meredith, C. (2018). Using simulation-based education to help social work students prepare for practice. *Social Work Education, 37*, 597–602. https://doi.org/10.1080/02615479.2018.1433158

Fidment, S. (2012). The objective structured clinical exam (OSCE): A qualitative study exploring the healthcare student's experience. *Student Engagement and Experience Journal, 1*, 1–18. https://doi.org/10.7190/seej.v1i1.37

Gale, N. K., Heath, G., Cameron, E., Rashid, S., & Redwood, S. (2013). Using the framework method for the analysis of qualitative data in multi-disciplinary health research. *BMC Medical Research Methodology*, 13, Article 117. https://doi.org/10.1186/1471-2288-13-117

Goldsmith, L. J. (2021). Using framework analysis in applied qualitative research. *Qualitative Report, 26*, 2061–2076. https://doi.org/10.46743/2160-3715/2021.5011

Logie, C. H., Bogo, M., & Katz, E. (2015). "I didn't feel equipped": Social work students' reflections on a simulated client "coming out." *Journal of Social Work Education, 51*, 315–328. https://doi.org/10.1080/10437797.2015.1012946

Lu, Y. E., Ain, E., Chamorro, C., Chang, C.-Y., Feng, J. Y., Fong, R., Garcia, B., Leibson Hawkins, R., & Yu, M. (2011). A new methodology for assessing social work practice: The adaptation of the objective structured clinical evaluation (SW-OSCE). *Social Work Education, 30*, 170–185. https://doi.org/10.1080/02615479.2011.540385

Lynch, B. (2022). Moving from dialogue to demonstration: Assessing anti-racist practice in social work education utilizing simulation, *Social Work Education.* https://doi.org/10.1080/02615479.2022.2098946

Maynard, S. P. (2021). Standardized simulations in social work supervision courses: MSW students' perceptions. *Journal of Social Work Education, 57*, 557–568. https://doi.org/10.1080/10437797.2019.1671274

Merriam, S. B. (2009). *Qualitative research: A guide to design and implementation.* Jossey-Bass.

Qualtrics. (2020). [Computer software]. https://www.qualtrics.com

Quirkos. (2022). Version 2.5.2 [Computer software]. https://www.quirkos.com

Shaban, S., Tariq, I., Elzubeir, M., Alsuwaidi, A. R., Basheer, A., & Magzoub, M. (2021). Conducting online OSCEs aided by a novel time management Web-based system. *BMC Medical Education, 21,* Article 508. https://doi.org/10.1186/s12909-021-02945-9

Shorbagi, S., Sulaiman, N., Hasswan, A., Kaouas, M., Al-Dijani, M. M., El-hussein, R. A., Daghistani, M. A., Nugud, S., & Guraya, S. Y. (2022). Assessing the utility and efficacy of e-OSCE among undergraduate medical students during the COVID-19 pandemic. *BMC Medical Education, 22,* Article 156. https://doi.org/10.1186/s12909-022-03218-9

Smith, M. J., Bornheimer, L. A., Li, J., Blajeski, S., Hiltz, B., Fischer, D. J., Check, K., & Ruffolo, M. (2021). Computerized clinical training simulations with virtual clients abusing alcohol: Initial feasibility, acceptability, and effectiveness. *Clinical Social Work Journal, 49,* 184–196. https://doi.org/10.1007/s10615-020-00779-4

University of Toronto, Factor-Inwentash Faculty of Social Work. (2015). *OSCE adapted for social work: Fact sheet.* https://socialwork.utoronto.ca/wp-content/uploads/2015/09/OSCE-Fact-sheet-for-Field-Instructors.pdf

Washburn, M., Parrish, D. E., & Bordnick, P. S. (2020). Virtual patient simulations for brief assessment of mental health disorders in integrated care settings. *Social Work in Mental Health, 18,* 121–148. https://doi.org/10.1080/15332985.2017.1336743

Wolfe-Taylor, S. N., Khaja, K., Wilkerson, D. A., & Deck, C. K. (2022). The future of social work education: A guide to developing, implementing, and assessing e-simulations. *Advances in Social Work.* Advance online publication. https://doi.org/10.18060/24912

Yin, R. K. (2014). *Case study research: Design and methods* (5th ed.). SAGE.

Chapter 7 Appendix A

Case Scenario: Billy Anderson (Instructions for Students)

You are a social worker for a program that provides services to veterans without housing in the community. Your agency takes self-referrals as well as referrals from healthcare professionals, the U.S. Department of Veterans Affairs (VA), and families. The goal of your agency is to provide wraparound services to improve the living situations and mental health of your clients.

Your role is to meet with the client for an initial interview to conduct a bio-psychosocial assessment, to develop an initial plan to address any identified housing needs, and to connect your client to available resources. Your agency provides ongoing case management services as needed but does not provide traditional counseling services. The first interview is conducted via videoconferencing.

In this scenario, you are meeting Billy, referred to your agency from the local VA hospital. Billy was recently released from the hospital for a minor inpatient surgery. The inpatient social worker made the referral to your agency on discovering that Billy has been without a home for the past six months. Billy was discharged to a friend's home but was only able to stay there for the one-week recovery needed for the recent surgery. The inpatient social worker states that they have completed a psych evaluation and have diagnosed Billy with PTSD. **You will have 15–20 minutes to conduct an initial assessment with the client and participate in collaborative goal setting with the client.**

Chapter 7 Appendix B
Case Scenario: Billy Anderson (Instructions for the Standardized Client)

Client Demographic Information

You are role-playing as Billy, a standardized client. If asked by the students, please use your own race, ethnicity, gender, and sexual orientation. Incorporate the following demographic characteristics for this client into your role play:

- Billy is 32 years old, lives in an urban area, and has been without housing for the past six months.

- Billy is the only child of two parents, now deceased.

- Billy is single with no children and has no family living locally to provide support.

- Billy was enlisted in the military for eight years (four years of active duty and four years in the Individual Ready Reserve [IRR]).

- Billy was deployed to Iraq for 12 months during their active duty. Billy last served for the army as an IRR roughly 11 months ago. During their time in the IRR, Billy completed course work for a bachelor's degree in criminal justice for an online program. Billy struggled through the program due to their difficulty concentrating and lack of sleep and chose to "stop-out" of the program roughly two years in.

- Billy does not have reliable transportation at this time and uses the city bus or friends for transportation.

- Billy does not currently hold any type of civilian employment.

- Billy does not wish to apply for Social Security Disability Insurance or Supplemental Security Income.

- Billy has no history or current substance abuse/use/misuse.

History of Presenting Problem

- Since Billy left the military 11 months ago, they have been couch surfing with friends from the military.

- Billy is having difficulty sleeping due to nightmares of their deployment to Iraq, is having difficulty concentrating, is startled by loud noises, is having difficulty connecting with people, is easily agitated, and has a diminished interest in activities they once enjoyed.

- Although Billy has some support in the community with their friends from the military, Billy does not have any family members living where they are currently residing.

- Billy was in a long-term relationship for nearly five years before their deployment. The relationship ended four months into their deployment to Iraq.

- Billy is currently seeing a psychiatrist for treatment of PTSD but has only been in treatment since being released from the hospital six weeks ago.

- Before their deployment, Billy had no history of any depression, anxiety, or mental health diagnoses.

- Billy has no history or current suicidal thought/ideations/actions.

Emotional State

- Billy is a soft-spoken, reserved, and a slightly guarded individual.

- Billy has difficulty maintaining eye contact and is anxious and emotionally detached.

- Billy often has flashbacks as well as nightmares, which keep them up at night.

- Billy stopped engaging in activities they liked doing before their deployment (e.g., running, playing pool with friends at a local pub, and playing baseball).

- Billy can sometimes be irritable and agitates easily.

- Billy is educated and articulate.

- Billy is eager to work and have a place of their own but has difficulty maintaining a job due to their current emotional state.

Items to be Used Verbatim as the Client

- "You know that feeling you get when someone jumps out and tries to scare you and you are on high alert for a few minutes? That alertness never goes away for me."

- "I don't really have any family here, but I do have some friends that I served with in the Army that I stay with from time to time."

- "Well, I was able to save up some money while deployed, so I have been living on that for a while now, but I know that I need to get a job or do something because the money won't always be there."

- "I don't know, I was hoping to get a criminal justice degree so I could be a probation officer, DEA [Drug Enforcement Administration] agent, or police officer. I think I would really like that and be good at it."

- "I didn't think I would stay here, so I didn't get a place or anything when I got done serving."

Social Worker's Goals for the Client

- Introduce themselves and allow the client to introduce themselves as well.

- Build rapport with the client.

- Explore the feelings and emotional experiences the client has with the PTSD diagnosis.

- Explore mental health needs or concerns.

- Explore friend or family supports.

- Determine what financial resources the client currently has or needs.

- Explore potential areas of employment or career goals the client has.

- Create a short-term goal with the client on obtaining more permanent housing.
- Create a long-term goal of employment, schooling, or both.
- Connect the client with appropriate community resources.
- Ensure there are no technology needs or concerns.

CHAPTER 8

Creating a Digital School Safety Service: A Pathway from Traditional Analog to Digital Practice

*James R. Brown and John M. Keesler**

Social workers can serve many different roles within a school community: special services evaluator, individualized education plan committee member, behavioral plan manager, social and emotional group facilitator, home visitor, school safety committee planner, conflict resolution faciliator, teacher consultant, and beyond, depending on the system's needs. As a school social worker, one of my (J.R.B.'s) responsibilities was to deliver an in-class bullying prevention program. This two-hour-long bullying prevention training provided students and their teachers with a common definition of bullying and an understanding of the various types of bullying (e.g., verbal, physical, relational). Students were given information regarding the potential effects of bullying on their well-being and strategies on how to interrupt a bullying incident. In addition, students were engaged in creating role plays using bullying situations they had encountered. Role plays helped students to integrate ways to address the bullying without harming themselves or compromising their reputations. This training occurred for the school body, classroom by classroom by classroom.

I believed that I was doing my job providing students with a face-to-face universal intervention in which everyone who was present for the intervention received the same prevention service. Looking back, I realize my service had multiple limitations:

- I had no control of those students who were absent the day that I delivered the bullying prevention training to their classroom. Although their absences could have been due to any number of reasons, what if their

---

* This chapter is informed by J.R.B.'s shift from analog school social work practitioner to digital school social work practice researcher. J.M.K. joined in the research on digital practice for school bullying.

absence was due to fear of being bullied? Invariably, a certain percentage of students never received the in-class prevention service.

- For those who received the training, their parents had no idea what their child had learned regarding bullying. As such, parents were potentially left ill equipped to engage their youth in any discussion about bullying so that a shared, cohesive narrative occurred between school and home regarding bullying. Injustice and inequity can result, particularly for those parents who suspect their child is being bullied but are not engaged by the school or have neither confidence nor a reference point to begin a discussion on such a topic.

- Due to time limitations, the training included neither a baseline/follow-up evaluation nor a basic feedback loop for students to communicate privately about bullying. While an evaluation can be critical to assessing student learning and the impact of the training, a confidential opportunity for students to communicate their concerns can be instrumental for school officials to address bullying, whether it is overt or covert.

- Shy or less-verbal students may have withheld sharing personal experiences or questions in a face-to-face class setting. As such, to reach all students, alternative strategies are likely warranted to foster student safety (particularly psychological safety) and provide students with an opportunity to have their voices heard.

THAT WAS THEN, THIS IS NOW

After 13 years, I left my job as a school social worker to pursue a doctorate in my beloved profession. As I sought to engage in translational research that had an immediate impact for social work practitioners, I allowed my practice history to guide my journey. My roots were firmly planted in school social work. After five years of being a student again and researching the issue of school safety, I graduated with my PhD and started publishing on parents' experiences with reporting school bullying to school officials. I published several more studies on bullying before I began to consider the potential for technology to help prevent and intervene with incidents of bullying from an ecological systems perspective.

DEVELOPING A DIGITAL PERSPECTIVE

Many of the challenges I encountered during my years as a school social worker could potentially be averted through technology. By having a digital bullying prevention program available for students, school social workers could decrease logistical barriers and concerns about who is absent during the face-to-face training. Similarly, the content could be shared with students' primary caregivers to reinforce what students are learning at school and to bridge school and home life. Further, if a learner were curious and wanted to revisit the training, they could. In addition, after the groundwork is laid for the training across the school (e.g., "Bullying 101"), follow-up booster dosages could be sent to students via the school digital platform, email, or text. These boosters could reinforce key points from the curriculum and serve as intermittent reminders for students to report incidents of bullying or to reflect on their own behavior within the bullying dynamic.

In this chapter, my research colleague and I share our efforts and journey to harness and use technology to address bullying and promote school safety. As a part of this journey, we discovered the potential of shifting from traditional practice to the use of technology for digital practice. We hope to inspire and encourage the reader to consider transformative ways within their agency, institution, or service circle that can address the unique needs of their clients and advance their practice into an era of technology.

BEGINNING THE DIGITAL SCHOOL SAFETY PROJECT

Ready? On Your Mark, Get Set, Go!

Sometimes, it seems like external forces encourage you to move forward on an opportunity. Case in point: A few years ago, I received a call from my university's networker who was aware of my idea to develop a digital bullying prevention program. He stated that an independent entrepreneur wanted to help make my idea become reality. I was very intrigued by the prospect!

Forming the Team

After an initial meeting with the entrepreneur, I recruited three colleagues with diverse talents to help form a team: (1) David, a longtime friend and collaborator who had a background in online learning and digital social work practice; (2) John, a newer faculty member with experience in disabilities, trauma, and organizational environment; and (3) Sheila, an expert in the implementation of classroom wellness strategies. In addition, the entrepreneur introduced the team to Sarah, an out-of-state high school counselor who later became instrumental in pilot-testing the online service.

I was strategic in who I invited to the team; I knew everyone had to play well together in the sandbox. Previously, I had been involved in various projects that seemed to grind on due to one person's continually overstepping or not caring about others. With the current project, I gave thoughtful consideration on who could contribute. I had worked with most of the team members before, so I knew their personalities and the gifts and talents that each could provide. The ability to work together was essential because the team met weekly via Zoom teleconferencing software and face-to-face for one year to develop a digital school safety service.

Developing and Refining the Script

The development of an outline for the bullying prevention school safety service was rooted in my bullying prevention work as a school social worker. In addition, my own research and evaluation of bullying prevention programs from experts like Gaffney et al. (2021) and the early pioneer of bullying prevention, Olweus et al. (2020), allowed me to understand bullying and its interconnecting characteristics. In incorporating my knowledge, skills, and practice experiences, I wrote an outline in which I envisioned a youth narrating the script with vignettes that exemplified various aspects of the digital content. The new connection with the entrepreneur afforded the opportunity and support to resurrect the outline I had already established.

The team engaged in an iterative process over the next few months to revise the original outline and to create a script. The entrepreneur provided strategies that helped translate the script into an interactive service for students. Together, we arranged the flow of the program so that learning was scaffolded, and we created various branching opportunities (i.e., when a student responds to one of several choices, they are subsequently directed to a corresponding video segment).

Once completed, the high school counselor piloted the script with her *E-team*, a group of students who had a high level of engagement and emotional intelligence. Since the so-called experts were all adults older than 40, this process provided insight regarding language and content that would better reach youth. Over the course of three weeks, the high school counselor and I met via Zoom to edit the script line by line.

Lights, Camera, Action!

Although the entrepreneur provided free consultation, money was needed to develop professionally produced video content, including professional narration. Fortunately, my university's networker who connected us with the entrepreneur alerted us to an internal seed grant for innovation. This was a small grant funded by my university to provide a foundation for subsequent external grant applications. We submitted a proposal and were subsequently awarded $25,000. The entrepreneur connected the team with a video producer who was willing to engage with us on the project. The grant covered the cost of contracting with the producer to translate the scripted outline into accessible video content.

The producer guided the team in rearranging, revising, and segmenting the scripted outline into sections of content that were video friendly. This involved another series of meetings and phone calls in which we read aloud the script and reworked any "clunky" text. In addition, the producer facilitated the recruitment of actors. As social workers, we emphasized the importance of diversity among the actors—that they would represent *some* degree of diversity in gender and race. After viewing audition content, the team identified and contracted with two male actors and two female actors to narrate the script. Both Black and White individuals were represented by each gender. Each actor used the same script to ensure the delivery of consistent content.

Online Service Development

We faced two subsequent challenges: What digital platform would house the school safety service? Who would create the infrastructure to build the content into a user-friendly service? Fortunately, the entrepreneur had previously created a platform that was currently in use with several schools. Although we were able to use the platform, the team was advised that there would be some cost associated with developing the actual program and infrastructure for the school safety service. We were judicious in our budget and had sufficient funds left from the innovation grant to cover this additional cost.

The final program wove together the video content with written text followed by knowledge-check questions to assess student learning. The program fostered students' mastery of content by preventing the learner from moving on in the service until they had correctly answered the knowledge-check questions.

Evaluation/Design and Institutional Review Board

Ensuring that the school safety service increased student knowledge was a critical component for the endeavor. Although it is best practice to always ensure that your efforts produce intended results, the effectiveness of the service was particularly important to the team given that we are both social work practitioners and researchers. Thus, we developed a pilot study using a quasi-experimental design to "test" the school safety service. Several cohorts of comparable students (e.g., same grade level) were randomly assigned to participate in either the digital service or in an online survey.

The team submitted a formal proposal to the university institutional review board (IRB) for approval. (This process is a university requirement of faculty who engage in research with human subjects to ensure their safety.) It took nearly two months to get IRB approval because the process was delayed with several revisions that we were required to make to the protocol.

Recruitment

Once we received IRB approval, we approached the schools for student participation. We created a recruitment video that was delivered at a statewide school counselor conference that Sarah had alerted us to. (Although the video was only about five minutes long, it took us about three hours to come up with a presentable final video that we were satisfied with. If nothing else, several of us had a good laugh during the process because we did not use a script!)

The counselors were instructed to express their interest via email with the research team, and these counselors became the "gateway" for their schools to access the service. The recruited school counselors subsequently participated in a two-hour training with the entrepreneur, focusing on how to gain access to the service. After the training, they rolled out the project: first to parents for their consent and then to students who provided their assent before completing the school safety service.

Focus Group

After everyone who wanted to participate in the school safety service had the opportunity to do so, we circled back to conduct focus groups with students as a follow-up evaluative component. The team encountered several obstacles (e.g., school exams, holidays, competing demands) and was able to only conduct one focus group about two months later with 10 students from one school.

CONSIDERATIONS FOR DIGITAL ENTREPRENEURSHIP AND LESSONS LEARNED

In our project development, we described the process and steps we took to develop a digital school safety service. It presented the nuts and bolts of *our* experience. Given that the shift to digital practice was new to us, we wanted to share some of our learning with you. In the following sections, we strive to present some tips, reflections, and probing questions to guide your future efforts to implement the digital age in your social work practice.

Exploring Your Work

Think about your work as a social worker. What seems to resonate with your face-to-face audience? Is there a way to go beyond delivering it face-to-face with the use of technology? Consider these questions:

- What would that look like?
- Who would need to be involved?
- What resources might be available in building it?
- What obstacles must be overcome?
- Who is the target audience?

Whether you are creating something within your workplace or a private venture, answering these questions will help you see the path forward in design and development. What follows are the steps our team took to develop the online school safety service.

Mapping Out the Plan

As academics, we spend a considerable amount of time thinking, but one thing that was critical for our team was to move from thinking to creating. We needed to complement our ideas with visual aids, such as whiteboards, so that everyone on the team could work toward a common vision.

As you begin to think about your own endeavors, we encourage you to shift from thinking to creating early in the process. Making diagrams, schematics, and a map to inform what you will be doing are just a few ideas. A map can help to outline the flow of your content—from introduction to end point. A map serves as a repository for your ideas, a place to unpack your knowledge and determine where to place information; it also includes a diagram of who says or does what and when. This process can help make sense of the content and create a logical sequence for its delivery.

Here is my (J.R.B.'s) reflection from some of the work I did on the school safety service:

> I started by listing necessary content items, then created a schematic to insert that content. The schematic included branching where a person could respond with "yes" or "no" to a question or could select a particular response on a multiple-choice item to advance to the next part of the service. After I mapped it out using a schematic, I pretended I was a scriptwriter and began writing

using pencil and paper. After the schematic was done, I wrote out a script that took topics I had placed in my schematic and pretended a youth was talking to another youth to connect with on the following:

- what is and what is not bullying
- types of bullying: verbal, physical, relational/cyberbullying
- identification of school hot spots for bullying, including a menu of areas and a write-in option
- roles that happen within a bullying dynamic
- self-identification of one's own role in bullying dynamic
- menu of help-seeking options for each self-identified role
- asking to talk with a school official—hotlink appointment

Cultural Humility in Practice: "We Don't Really Use That Word, We Use . . ."

Developing a final scripted outline took a bit of time through multiple iterations. This process is not uncommon; however, the team was intentional in taking another step to engage students in the process. It was critical for us to understand what high-school youth thought about the script. The school counselor piloted the script with students whom she believed would provide a developmental lens to examine the wording. Not only were the students able to see things differently from a team of middle-aged adults, but their feedback provided some level of validity to the content and questions that were asked in the school safety service (Royce et al., 2016). During a conference call with the counselor and students, the students highlighted words that were outdated or just did not make sense to them. They identified places where the language needed to be clearer and more explicit. In many ways, this was an exercise in cultural humility.

Although members of the team had expertise in working with youth, we recognized the limitations of our knowledge and that our lens was not that of present-day youth. We needed to see the script through *their* eyes. Regardless of how much experience one has or how much one knows, as social workers, we are called to cultural humility—to take a step back and to learn from those we are striving to help. Think about what you know, maybe imagine what you do not know, and allow the intended audience of your program or intervention to inform you about their beliefs, values, language, and understanding. For many of us, this requires some degree of intentionality.

Video Development

Developing video content was central to the school safety service. Once we integrated the students' feedback into the script, we turned our attention to finding a video developer. It was important for us to work within the financial means of our grant. Without the grant funds, we would have had to take a different course of action.

As you think about your digital venture or project, consider a few things early on. Can you develop your digital service or project on your own, perhaps just by using agency or community resources, or do you need to hire someone? Is your initial effort focused on developing a prototype or a final product? How much will it cost, and where will the money come from? Fundamentally, cost is often driven by the level of sophistication you need. For example, with videography, it is important to consider the visual *and* the audio. Having a controlled environment can help to reduce background noise, and by reducing background noise, you are likely to increase your client's ability to attend to the content.

The money from the grant our team was awarded facilitated our ability to hire an external private video developer, which ultimately made the process easier for us. They refined the script, turned it into a storyboard, auditioned and found four excellent youth narrators, and collaborated on a mutually beneficial time line. The digitized videos were available to us via a link for download.

When working on your project, think early about associated costs. Familiarize yourself with what resources are available to you through your school, organization, or community. Public service organizations can sometimes provide small amounts of money (e.g., United Way, Kiwanis, Elk Club, other local clubs). For larger sums of money, community or state grant foundations may be useful. Consider the amount of time it will take to write your proposal or complete your grant application, the time it will take for the funders to review the applications, and the parameters within which funds can be used. Remember: This process often takes much longer than you might think, so plan wisely.

Diversity: Infusing the Profession's Values

The social work profession honors diversity across the human experience. As social workers, we are charged with embracing the values of our profession and the National Association of Social Workers' (2021) *Code of Ethics*. Efforts to represent diversity in your digital product will help you to reach a broader audience.

In our school safety service, our videos represented four different narrators: two males, two females, with each gender representing both Black and White individuals. While we recognize the breadth of diversity, our ability to expand who was represented in the videos was inherently limited by our budget and the nature of a pilot project. Interestingly, we found that most youth in our study selected the Black female narrator to be their training guide. Although our sample predominantly comprised White students, the small sample size and our lack of inquiry as to why students chose a particular narrator limit our ability to interpret this finding. It is possible that this could represent some degree of cultural curiosity, and it provides us with a beginning point for subsequent inquiry in future endeavors.

Empowerment and Choice: Aligning with Trauma-Informed Care

Social work emphasizes client empowerment. The use of technology to empower clients can be viewed in various ways. First, digital services, especially Web-based ones, are often available to clients around the clock compared with face-to-face services, which often are only available during regular business hours. Thus, digital services can empower clients through increasing accessibility. Second, digital services and assessments can provide clients with opportunities to exercise their voice and be empowered to make choices for themselves. For example, our school safety service not only provided students with the opportunity to select a narrator based on gender and ethnicity, but it also provided branching choices based on their decisions through the program. *Branching* allows a participant to select from a menu of options so that interventions are tailored to be more person specific. Similarly, we provided students with choices about personal help-seeking options. This technique can be useful to bolster client understanding of different options that are available to them.

In addition, approaches that emphasize empowerment and choice nicely align with *trauma-informed care*, an approach to service delivery that is rooted in an understanding and recognition of trauma and its impact on well-being. Depending on the conceptualization and model, trauma-informed care is rooted in principles of safety, trustworthiness, collaboration, empowerment, and choice (Fallot et al., 2011).

Data Capture: What Do You Want to Measure?

It was critical for us to assess the efficacy of the service to increase student knowledge and understanding of bullying. Ideally, every program or intervention should have some mechanism to measure its impact on the intended audience. That impact could be increased knowledge, changes in beliefs or attitudes, improved mood, or all of these. How will you capture the impact of your digital program or service? This is important to parse out, including familiarizing yourself with different tools and options before jumping too far ahead. Although quantitative data are excellent for gathering large amounts of information that can be analyzed with statistical software, qualitative data can get you rich, nuanced information about individuals' experiences.

The type of data you are seeking will ultimately guide your data collection strategies. For example, multiple choice or true/false questions can be built into a quiz administered at the end of various sections of your digital program. Similarly, open-ended questions can provide participants opportunities to reflect on their personal experiences and individual learning as well as the opportunity to provide additional insight. For example, after we had students use a checklist to identify places where bullying occurred in their school, we queried them about any other places they were aware of. Despite an exhaustive list, students were able to identify even more places that were prone to incidents of bullying. Likewise, you can use a pretest/posttest strategy to assess changes in participants' attitudes or knowledge before and after their engagement in your program or service. Further, data can be used to understand the demographics of who is using your service to assess for between group differences (e.g., parents versus students; men versus women), to learn about problem spots or challenges with the logistics of your service, to understand completion rates of participants (e.g., do certain participants drop off earlier than others who finish the service?), and to improve your product or identify next-steps for development.

After the team delivered the school safety service, we conducted a focus group with some students who had participated in the service. First developed in the 1920s for psychological questionnaires, focus groups have evolved into surveying groups of people, usually consumers, about their beliefs and attitudes toward products, such as a new car model or a television show pilot (Wilkinson, 2004). Although we used a semistructured guide to query students regarding their experiences with the school safety service, the focus group format allowed students to explore and describe their experiences in detail. Student were prompted to select a pseudonym based on their color preference. The following quote from a student illustrates the depth of their perspective:

> I am Red. Hey, the [service] went into more detail on what they are trying to figure out. They wanted to see our perspective . . . trying to get in to actually see what is going on . . . trying to hear about, how to help, kind of prevent not just help, to also prevent. This is something new. . . . The characters and having other people

to choose, I guess you can come off and say it was reassuring. . . . [It was] like talking to someone that wanted to hear, that you can relate to. You can choose between a boy and a girl and can get advice from someone you wanted to.

Red's statement added to our belief that the characters we provided to narrate reached the viewer personally. Additionally, the feedback students provided was essential to inform the next iteration of service ("version 2.0"). Here are more excerpts from the focus group to help illustrate additional content that they were advocating for:

> OK, this is Aqua. I think cyberbullying is a big part of bullying in general. You could get cyberbullied and then it'll get brought to school also. So, I think for the [service] there should be a bigger part for cyberbullying because it's such a big part of our community and everyone seems to get cyberbullied at some point in their life. It needs to be a bigger thing in the [service] because I'm sure more people relate to that rather than relating to say getting bullied in their school bathroom.

* * *

> **Pink:** I think just having different options. Everyone is different and have their own ways with wanting to deal with things so having different options, being anonymous, getting help right away from school, or other people [professional help], just having multiple options for anyone.

With this feedback, we could go in several directions. For example, the team has considered making a field placement with social work students to respond beyond the online module with more proximal text support for the bully, target, or witnesses. Ultimately, your service delivery and data collection can be a cycle that collects data in real time and informs subsequent revisions such that your service is constantly improving to meet the ever-evolving needs of your target population. One caveat, however, is that if you intend to publish your results in a peer-reviewed journal, proactively contact your IRB, human subjects committee or other ethics review board to approve your recruitment strategies, methodology, and efforts to safeguard participants.

Anonymity versus Participant Identity

In our data collection, we assured students that their data would remain anonymous. It is important to consider whether participants should remain anonymous or be identifiable. Anonymity may be necessary to protect the participants' identity and to create a safe space that fosters participant honesty in responding. Safety through participant anonymity can be central to collecting data that most accurately reflects your participants' experiences, beliefs, or attitudes. One limitation associated with anonymity, however, is the inability to follow up with participants. In this case, it may be important to provide participants with a mechanism or opportunity to contact someone should they have concerns. This pathway should be separate from any data that are collected, again, to ensure security and privacy associated with an individual's responses.

Having participants' identity may be in your best interest as well as in that of your participants. For example, data collection may be needed to certify completion of a module or program for an individual. It is important to alert participants up front on how their identity or responses may be used, particularly with participants who may be part of a *vulnerable* population (e.g., children and youth, people with cognitive impairments or intellectual disabilities, those who are involved in the criminal justice system). You may need to get creative to ensure that your target audience fully understands what is being asked of them before they participate in your digital service. For example, you can create narrated or animated videos (e.g., Powtoon, n.d.) to help your audience understand things like informed consent and research. Although the participation of children and youth in research requires parental consent before their assent, it is invaluable to ensure all participants the right to voice their desires and perspectives.

It is important to also remember that sometimes demographic information can compromise anonymity. For example, if you pilot your digital service with a specific organization or classroom, certain demographic data may make responses identifiable. Imagine you've collected data on gender or race; if the classroom only had a few students who were Black and one student who identified as transgender, anonymity of responses may be compromised. As such, extra care must be given in protecting such identifiable traits that could be harmful to participants' well-being.

Divergent Interests and Concerns

As academic social workers engaged in research, evaluation was a critical component for us. However, it was far less important to the entrepreneur. On more than one occasion, the entrepreneur stated that setting up the data collection for the school safety service was "a labor-intensive process" and very difficult to change once created. On reflection, we knew little about how the data capture process was done and felt we were at the mercy of the entrepreneur and his team. Although in the end we got most of what we wanted, it would have been helpful to have either had more experience and familiarity with the entrepreneur and his platform or to have had someone from the university on our team who understood digital research and had expertise with information technology.

In addition, we collectively recognized the importance of data security and privacy, but the entrepreneur desired extra levels of protection that exceeded research standards. He was convinced that only the highest security would be used for this service. However, the layers needed to access were lengthy and cumbersome for participants. Unless you were highly motivated and computer savvy, it was simply too technical and confusing to access. Although a good number of counselors had expressed initial interest, only eight committed to the project. However, given the challenges, many students whom we anticipated *would* participate did not. The complexity and challenges with accessing the service is exemplified in a correspondence from one of the counselors at a participating school: "The process was not easy to navigate—the passwords and approval codes were very cryptic and cumbersome—this may have been off-putting for parents." Even when we asked for a simple link, the entrepreneur insisted on security, often citing the IRB. Since many counselors lacked the self-efficacy to access the service, they gave up. All but one school was able to "crack the code" successfully.

Limitation in Research with Schools

The team had plenty of experience conducting research, but we lacked a relationship with the partnering schools. We leveraged their participation through Sarah (the school counselor who was introduced to the team by the entrepreneur), and technology reduced logistical barriers for communication, but the physical distance between the team and the schools (which were in another state) was a barrier to building collaboration. Further, we could have benefited from additional experience and knowledge of the schools' experience with research, their respective student body, and their communities. In some cases, the schools had internet firewalls that prevented folks from accessing the school safety service. In addition to the extra security levels created by the entrepreneur that prohibited many folks from participating, other factors challenged student participation. Here is an excerpt from communication with one of the school counselors:

The research/academic language of the letter that was sent (to parents) was difficult to understand, even though we included a summary in parent-friendly language as well. The legal language is scary to non-academics. There may have been concerns with anonymity of student data. Two students told me that their parents don't "tell the government stuff." . . . Providing the resources in multiple languages may also have increased participation.

In addition, we conducted a focus group with students to explore their experience using the online service. Because of the geographical distance (roughly 400 miles), the focus group was conducted with Zoom. The Zoom focus group meeting occurred during the students' school lunch period; however, we planned for school staff to provide pizza and beverages. We also negotiated with school staff to provide a private location where only students would be present during the focus group. We did this to maintain students' confidentiality and limit the potential of school staff presence to bias students' responses. School staff waited outside the office, and students were afforded privacy and autonomy during the focus group.

CONCLUSION

It is most likely to be advantageous to your agency, the clients, and you as a service provider to create digital practice service delivery. It is up to you to assess the risks and rewards of doing so. Hopefully, our story will help to demystify the steps needed to proceed. Creating a client-centered digital practice service delivery takes time, imagination, support, collaboration, and persistence. Service providers who are willing to contribute in such a way are a key part of building and delivering services to a wider audience and moving social work in a forward direction. As an outcome, digital programs and services can provide unique opportunities for clients to access services while also providing the opportunity for clients to review and even share content. Further, digital services, such as our school safety service, provide the same exact dosage of content with the option of selecting who delivers the message (narrators) each and every time. Now the question becomes this: What steps must you take in developing your online idea for the greater good?*

---

* Please visit https://ssw.iu.edu/community/community-outreach/preventing-school-bullying to see an example of the bullying prevention video.

REFERENCES

Fallot, R. D., McHugo, G. J., Harris, M., & Xie, H. (2011). The trauma recovery and empowerment model: A quasi-experimental effectiveness study. *Journal of Dual Diagnosis, 7,* 74–89. https://doi.org/10.1080/15504263.2011.566056

Gaffney, H., Ttofi, M. M., & Farrington, D. P. (2021). What works in anti-bullying programs? Analysis of effective intervention components. *Journal of School Psychology, 85,* 37–56. https://doi.org/10.1016/j.jsp.2020.12.002

National Association of Social Workers. (2021). *Code of ethics of the National Association of Social Workers.* https://www.socialworkers.org/About/Ethics/Code-of-Ethics/Code-of-Ethics-English

Olweus, D., Solberg, M. E., & Breivik, K. (2020). Long-term school-level effects of the Olweus Bullying Prevention Program (OBPP). *Scandinavian Journal of Psychology, 61,* 108–116. https://doi.org/10.1111/sjop.12486

Powtoon: The Visual Communication Platform. (n.d.). *Creating jaw-dropping videos and presentation.* https://www.powtoon.com/?locale=en

Royce, E., Thyer, B., & Padgett, D. (2016). *Program evaluation* (6th ed.). Cengage.

Wilkinson, S. (2004). Focus groups: A feminist method. In S. N. Hesse-Biber & M. L. Yaiser (Eds.), *Feminist perspectives on social research* (pp. 271–295). Oxford University Press.

CHAPTER 9

Digital Hybrid Psychoeducation: Model Development and Case Illustration

David A. Wilkerson

The development of a practice model for digital hybrid psychoeducation is the focus of this chapter. The term *hybrid* is used to refer to psychoeducation that includes both individual and group components. This usage of this term also differs from that in earlier chapters because it does not refer to the joining of digital and analog practice intervention components; rather, it refers to the joining of digital individual and group intervention components. The chapter demonstrates methods and opportunities for joining, synergizing, amplifying, and personalizing individual and group work with the model. It also addresses what Chan and Holosko (2016) referred to as "a type of theoretical black box" (p. 97) in the literature of digital social work interventions, which is the absence of theoretical and conceptual explanations of digital technology's contribution to intervention outcomes.

While the chapter's intervention focus is digital hybrid psychoeducation, a through line for this book is social work's move from analog to digital practice spaces. As described by Funk and Fitch in chapter 1, the term *analog* refers to on-the-ground practice, and *digital* refers to online practice. Related terms are "asynchronous" and "synchronous." *Asynchronous delivery* overcomes both time and space, as in the example of text messaging, whereas *synchronous delivery* overcomes space, as in the example of teleconferencing. Consequently, this chapter's discussion includes notes on my own move from office-based analog practice to digital practice for the delivery of psychoeducation. A case illustration continues the through line of analog to digital practice. In the example, change occurred for a family through digital hybrid psychoeducation, but it failed to do so through analog psychotherapy sessions.

DEFINING PSYCHOEDUCATION

A detailed discussion of psychoeducation, its history, uses, and evidence base is beyond the purpose of this chapter. However, readers are encouraged to review Lukens and McFarlane's (2004) description of psychoeducation as an evidence-based practice. It is available on the internet, although its focus is analog rather than digital practice. They defined *analog psychoeducation* as "a professionally delivered treatment modality that integrates and synergizes psychotherapeutic and educational interventions" (p. 206). Psychoeducation outcomes include improved communication, increased coping skills, improved problem solving, improved stress management, increased understanding of symptoms and their course, and increased knowledge of resources.

Psychoeducation is also an inclusive and flexible intervention. It has been adapted as an evidence-based practice for a wide range of health and psychosocial concerns for individuals, groups, families, children, adolescents, and adults. However, its inclusiveness and flexibility have resulted in ambiguity regarding its definition and elements of intervention. Lukens and McFarlane (2004) stated that "the term psychoeducation is used inconsistently" (p. 220), resulting in a lack of clarity on what works to produce change. For example, Tursi et al. (2013) completed a systematic literature review of the effectiveness of analog and digital psychoeducation practices for unipolar depression. Their conclusions supported the effectiveness of psychoeducation for improving major depression prognosis and outcomes; however, they also noted that "the mechanism of action of PE [psychoeducation] is unknown" (p. 11).

The Role of Groups in Psychoeducation and Identifying Mechanisms for Change

Defining an intervention and identifying its mechanisms for change are necessary steps for research, replicability, and the development of practice knowledge. *Group psychoeducation* is an evidence-based practice that is used in prevention and treatment of major psychiatric disorders ranging from schizophrenia, substance abuse, and mood disorders to major health conditions, including cancer and their psychosocial challenges. However, like psychoeducation, defining group psychoeducation and its mechanisms for change has also been inconsistent.

Unlike group psychotherapy, which embodies a significant literature regarding its mechanisms for change (e.g., therapeutic factors like installation of hope and universality; Yalom, 2020), group psychoeducation is primarily described as a delivery method for psychoeducation. Without identified mechanisms for change that are attributable to group delivery, it could be assumed practitioners' choice of group psychoeducation over individual psychoeducation would only be to achieve economies that result from the delivery of a group versus individual intervention.

Digital Practice with Psychoeducation, Definition, and Mechanisms for Change

In the case of digital practice with individual and group psychoeducation, the development of our practice knowledge has also been limited by inconsistent definitions of the interventions. A comprehensive review of online psychoeducation was unavailable at the time of this writing, although practice reviews of internet mental health delivery have included digital psychoeducation. The definitions from these reviews have been inconsistent.

For instance, Barak et al.'s (2008) meta-analysis of internet-mediated psychotherapies compared internet delivery of psychoeducation, cognitive–behavioral therapy (CBT), and behavior therapy. Their description of digital psychoeducation did not recognize digital group psychoeducation, and digital psychoeducation was described as individual delivery through static websites that "employ didactic and informatic techniques" (p. 135). Abbott and colleagues' (2008) review of best practices for internet-delivered psychotherapy included digital psychoeducation and described it as an individual, self-guided, Web-based delivery of structured treatment programs, usually CBT, without professional interaction. Barak and Grohol (2011) described digital psychoeducation to consist of self-guided, Web-based delivery of training. These definitions merge psychoeducation with bibliotherapy and contribute to further inconsistency.

Digital Group Psychoeducation

Although a definition of digital group psychoeducation was absent from the aforementioned descriptions of internet-delivered psychoeducation, there have been examples of online interventions that appear to deliver digital group psychoeducation but are identified by other names. For instance, Rains and Young's (2009) meta-analysis of computer-mediated support groups provided a definition that included (a) focus on a health problem, (b) an educational component, (c) a group communication component, and (d) closed membership enrollment. Health conditions included depression, panic disorders, chronic illnesses, and eating disorders. Their meta-analysis of 28 studies determined that participation in computer-mediated support groups produced positive health outcomes and its mechanisms for change were influenced by smaller group size, longer group duration, and the inclusion of access to both synchronous and asynchronous communication channels.

Given the inconsistent definitions and limited research of digital group psychoeducation, several key questions are addressed. What are the conceptual explanations for change that develop from integrating individual and group work within digital psychoeducation? Can integrating online group work with individual training in a hybrid format amplify practice components of intervention like Web-based individual skills training? This second question recognizes Lukens and McFarlane's (2004) definition of psychoeducation as an intervention that "integrates and synergizes" (p. 206) the elements of psychotherapy and education. In addition to these questions, a further area for exploration can be observed in chapter 1 in this book and Funk and Fitch's analysis of analog and digital practice. Being unbound from a physical location for treatment delivery potentially improves treatment access, availability, and adherence. For instance, DuPaul et al. (2020) described several uses of technology to enhance psychosocial interventions for children and adolescents with ADHD, including increased access to evidence-based treatments as well as enhanced capacity for shared decision making between families and their providers. In the case of group psychoeducation, unbounding delivery from a physical location may enable practitioners to discover new ways to enhance the capacity of the intervention for creating change.

Moving from Analog to Digital Practice

In response to COVID-19 lockdown measures, Weinberg (2020) developed a digital group psychotherapy practice review to support practitioners' move from analog to digital practice. That review is also available on the internet and summarizes research findings for online individual as well as group therapies. However, neither digital psychoeducation nor asynchronous delivery was represented in Weinberg's review, and both are the focus of my own move from analog to digital practice. Unlike with Weinberg, my move wasn't influenced by COVID-19 since my online work began more than a decade before the pandemic onset. However, it resulted from similar logistical concerns—like what do you do when your clients are unable to attend on-the-ground office sessions?

My practice focused on families and children diagnosed with disruptive disorders. I had become increasingly concerned with the pervasive practice of separately targeting client diagnostic signs and symptoms for management with multiple medications while ignoring the psychosocial aspects of a presenting problem. Consequently, I sought training and began to deliver an analog group psychoeducation program for parent management training (PMT). Following training, I delivered PMT programs for school systems in my community, which I adapted from an evidence-based Canadian model (Cunningham et al., 1995).

However, compared with Canada's greater communitarian influence on social engagement, I was surprised by the lower training participation rates I experienced in my community in the midwestern United States. An aim to understand and address low engagement and participation adherence led to an interest in the use of technology-mediated service delivery to address logistical barriers to attendance, such as time, distance, and travel.

DEVELOPING A HYBRID PSYCHOEDUCATIONAL INTERVENTION

My interest in the use of digital psychoeducation to address logistical barriers to attendance led me to the develop an internet-delivered, hybrid PMT program comprising two main practice components: (1) individual, asynchronous, Web-based parenting skills training modules and (2) group-based, synchronous discussion. The individual component of Web-based training modules was developed for delivering the principles of parent management through video examples and self-assessments of understanding. The video examples demonstrated underlying principles, and quizzes and self-assessments deepened focus and knowledge acquisition. This digital content was also readily available to participants to return to and review during the intervention.

The group component was developed to meet goals of group work in psychoeducation, which include social learning, peer support, and mutual aid (Furr, 2000; Lukens & McFarlane, 2004). Groups were structured with a problem-based learning (PBL) format (described later). Group discussions also provided a second content level of learning, whereby participants worked together to troubleshoot examples of parenting problems and discussed the application of parent management principles delivered in the individual training modules for themselves and their peers.

The program was designed for delivery to parents of adolescents, and the asynchronous, Web-based component included three skills training modules: (1) balanced parenting, (2) avoiding responsibility, and (3) noncompliance. The individual training modules were professionally developed with adherence to the principles of course design (Wiggins & McTighe, 2011), and the content was developed by subject-matter experts based on social learning and behavioral theories as well as educational models, including PBL (de Graaff & Kolmos, 2003; Hill et al., 2009); attributional processes (Harvey & Weary, 1984); and cognitive load theory (Renkl et al., 2009).

Group discussions were originally planned for synchronous, group video-conferencing delivery and later shifted to asynchronous delivery following a trial demonstration of the program. The trial demonstration was my first experience with online delivery, and it opened my thinking about mechanisms of change in digital hybrid psychoeducation.

Trial Demonstration

The purpose of the trial demonstration was to check usability of digital delivery. An abbreviated version of the full program was delivered online to 25 graduate university students. They completed two asynchronous, individual training modules and met for two synchronous, desktop videoconferencing group sessions. Overall, participant reaction to the asynchronous, individual Web-based training was more positive than was reaction to the synchronous, videoconferencing group discussion. Reese et al. (2015) also described teleconferencing difficulties in their online parent training program, which included frozen video and poor audio.

Unlike the synchronous group training, asynchronous individual training was uniformly described by the participants to be highly usable and interactive based on its practice activities, quizzes, and self-assessments. Participants described training as effective for knowledge gains, including "learning how to talk to a child," "don't get into a power struggle," and recognition of the value of balancing democratic parenting (e.g., negotiating, mutual problem solving) and behavioral parenting (e.g., redirecting behavior, remaining calm).

Joining Individual and Group Practice Components

However, even with the usability limitations noted for synchronous group discussions, there were unexpected benefits from joining individual Web-based training and with group discussion. For instance, after participating in group discussions, participants reported surprise that they had learned more from the individual Web-based training than they realized. Others reported increased confidence in their parenting abilities due to the integration of the individual Web-based training with group discussions.

While group interaction was originally planned to provide a social component to support parents in their change efforts, these unexpected outcomes suggested other benefits. In addition to support, does group work amplify the individual training component? For example, does group work create greater opportunity to reflect on and reassess participants' own resources and capacities for acting on knowledge gains made in the individual Web-based training?

Community Participant Study Outcomes

Following the trial demonstration, the group component of the program was redeveloped for asynchronous delivery to encourage greater interactivity and reflection. The intervention was then researched with community participants (Wilkerson et al., 2020). Community participants were engaged in four groups, and 19 out of 23 participants completed the intervention. Caregivers' mean age was 44 years. Sixteen were biological parents, 15 were female, four were African American, and 15 were non-Hispanic White. Youth were predominantly male, and almost half exhibited poor school performance.

Dependent variables in this research included parenting self-efficacy, parenting style (lax or authoritarian), and youth oppositional defiant behaviors. Pretest–posttest surveys demonstrated moderate changes for increased parent self-efficacy and moderately large changes for decreased likelihood of oppositional defiance disorder. Group discussion demonstrated active use of individual training module content centering on parenting style and reduction of overreactive and coercive parenting behaviors.

A PRACTICE MODEL FOR DIGITAL HYBRID PSYCHOEDUCATION

The community participant research focused on the contribution of peer support in a hybrid psychoeducation intervention (Wilkerson et al., 2020). Further development of the practice model requires definition, key concepts, assumptions, and conceptual explanations for change. In the case of analog psychoeducation, Lukens and McFarlane (2004) noted inconsistencies in the definition of psychoeducation and made this recommendation: "Efforts are needed to further articulate the common and situation-specific aspects of psychoeducational curriculum where possible, as well as structure, duration, and organization of content" (p. 220).

In the case of a hybrid practice model, the intersection of individual training and group work is highlighted in this section. I use a case illustration and participant feedback from the community participant study to illustrate key concepts and components of the hybrid model.

Model Definition

A first step in developing the model is definition: *Digital hybrid psychoeducation* is a professionally facilitated intervention that integrates, synergizes, amplifies, and personalizes individual Web-based training with online group work. This definition extends Lukens and McFarlane's (2004) definition of psychoeducation by highlighting the aspect of group work within the hybrid model and includes several key concepts, beginning with professional facilitation.

Professionally Facilitated

The key concept professionally facilitated recognizes that online hybrid psychoeducation is neither self-directed nor self-paced, as online psychoeducation has previously been described (Abbott et al., 2008; Barak & Grohol, 2011). The voluntary nature of self-directed and self-paced participation presents drawbacks for online programs that segment group and individual Web-based training into unintegrated components of intervention (Wilkerson, 2016). Drawbacks that have affected group participation in these intervention designs include low attendance (Cristancho-Lacroix et al., 2015), low levels of content contributions (Steed, 2005), and lurking (van Mierlo, 2014). The hybrid model assumes that professional facilitation is a crucial factor for joining individual and group work to ensure that users actively alternate their participation between individual and group components.

Integration, Synergy, Amplification, and Personalization

The concepts of integration, synergy, amplification, and personalization are interrelated. Integration of individual and group work is prerequisite to synergizing, amplifying, and personalizing individual Web-based training outcomes through group work. *Amplifying* refers to the use of group work to deepen participant interaction with the individual Web-based training curriculum.

Integration

In the community participation study (Wilkerson et al., 2020), the elements of individual Web-based training and group work were joined and integrated in several ways. The most basic method was by facilitating alternating participation in these components. Participants completed an individual training module and were then directed to the asynchronous discussion forum. Group participation was also professionally facilitated so that materials for discussion were prioritized and sequenced based on intervention training goals. Facilitation for the group discussion also included (a) emailing participants to ensure they observed new posts, replies, or relevant observations related to their own posts and (b) scheduling beginnings and endings for each of the discussions that followed Web-based individual training modules.

Synergy

Synergizing individual and group work assumes a joint effect is created that is greater than the sum of the separate effects of individual training and group work. The seminal work of Cunningham and colleagues (1993, 1995) provided a method for synergizing these components using PBL guided by attributional questions. Cunningham et al. (1993) found that PBL resulted in better attendance, homework completion, and program satisfaction for program participants. PBL replaces didactic instruction with the presentation of a problem that group participants assess, explain, evaluate, and solve. Critical to this process is that the problem addresses participants' real-life concerns in a relevant learning domain, which, in this intervention, was parent management.

In the hybrid model's application of PBL, following each of the individual Web-based training modules, participants enter an asynchronous group discussion forum in which they are presented a video vignette that illustrates parent–child conflict that is mismanaged by the parent. The video vignette is followed by an attributional question that poses a problem for discussion. An *attribution* is defined as

> an *inference about the cause* of a *particular person's behaviour(s)* or of an *observed* action or *event. Attribution can* be *explanatory,* in *which the viewer seeks a reason that a particular event occurred,* or *interpersonal,* in *which one explains the actions* of *oneself or others.* (The Free Dictionary, n.d., italics added)

Cunningham and colleagues (1998) presented several examples of attributional questions they used in their program:

- What lessons does a strategy teach?
- What message does a strategy communicate to the child or family?
- What difference might the approach make (for the child, parent, siblings, or family) if applied over a period of years?
- Is the effort required to maintain the strategy justified? (p. 13)

The use of PBL guided by attributional questions concerning the social effect, communication, long-term outcome, and effort was adapted for the community participant research (Wilkerson et al., 2020) to synchronize individual training with group work.

Amplification

Individual training modules included examples of the application of heuristic strategies to respond to common parenting management disturbances like negative reciprocity and punishment traps. The amplification of individual training content through group work assumes that the PBL strategy used for synchroni-zation motivates participants to apply individual training content to their own experiences to assess, explain, evaluate, and solve parent mismanagement issues in their group discussion.

Personalization

Cunningham and colleagues' (1993, 1998) use of PBL guided by attributional questions was expanded through individual training modules with the introduc-tion of self-assessment in which participants could identify their own parenting styles in an engaging manner that introduced a central and compelling goal for change. The method is demonstrated in the following case demonstration.

CASE ILLUSTRATION

This case illustration provides examples of integration, synchronization, personal-ization, and amplification of individual Web-based training through group work. This example focuses on a husband and wife who participated in the digital group psychoeducation program (Wilkerson et al., 2020) following on-the-ground office sessions.

Their presenting problem concerned conflict with their 16-year-old son that centered on his poor school performance. The son was seen individually until treatment focus shifted to his parents' ongoing disagreements regarding their respective parenting styles. Father and son criticized the mother as the problem due to her authoritarian style, whereas the mother criticized her husband as the problem due to his lax style. The couple's lack of progress in treatment combined with the long distance they traveled for office appointments led to their referral to the digital group psychoeducation program.

Integrating, Synergizing, and Personalizing Hybrid Components: Self-Assessments

Like analog psychoeducation, self-assessments can be used in digital psychoedu-cation to help participants develop a basic understanding of a stressor or problem, measure their own level of distress, and develop goals for change. Following the intervention's orientation module, the couple completed a self-assessment that was developed for them to personalize their understanding of individual training skills as well as their discussions with peers. One of three parenting styles could be identified through the assessment: (1) task-centered (TC), (2) relationship-focused (RF), or (3) balanced. These style designations were developed to provide participants a more engaging interpretation of authoritarian (TC) or lax (RF) parenting dimensions. The term "balanced style" was then used to create a goal for change that joined TC and RF parenting in a more intuitively effective style to balance an overemphasis on one or the other two styles.

Following self-assessment, the individual training module presented video vignettes that illustrated the RF and TC styles and provided the descriptions given in Box 9.1. The module then presented heuristic strategies for effective management and illustrated their use in video vignettes of an RF and a TC parent using these strategies and demonstrating a balanced/authoritative style. Participants were then invited to introduce themselves in the discussion group and share their goals for change (see Box 9.2).

The couple completed their introductions in the asynchronous group, and the mother identified her parenting style based on self-assessment:

> I am a task-centered mom. I am willing to change, but really, I have tried many times in the past two years. It doesn't seem to work. I think I am seeking a better way to change by joining this program and learn from each other.

She added the following background:

> My husband and I have a teenager. We have had problems with him for over two years. His grades have slipped significantly. Every time we ask him to do his homework/assignment or prepare for a test, he always argues with us. Or he says he will do it, but he doesn't do it. Then when his grades are not good, he blames us for pushing him. He always says, "If you guys don't push me, I will get it done." But the fact is, even if we don't say anything, he still doesn't do it. Making excuses, blaming us, and avoiding his responsibilities has become an ongoing issue at our home.

The father also used the self-assessment to identify his parenting style for the group members:

> I am a relationship-focused father. Unfortunately, I am still not getting along with my 16-year-old son. Even though his behavior and grades are not acceptable, I am not blaming him. I think that something is wrong with me or our parenting. I just don't know what to do. From my point of view, if he is not making some serious change, his life will be miserable. It makes me so anxious.

Box 9.1: Parenting Style Descriptions

As you compare the relationship-focused (RF) and task-centered (TC) parenting styles, you will see that both have strengths.

Parents with an RF parenting style can be leaders in:	Parents with a TC parenting style can be leaders in:
• Protecting their kids	• Making decisions
• Soothing their kid's hurts	• Providing rules and structure
• Expressing love and empathy	• Keeping life organized
• Providing good things and good times	• Making sure things get done

Most parents have some mixture of these two parenting styles. However, when conflict, stress, or problems appear, we often do more of what we're best at. For example, RF-style parents will do more connecting, whereas TC-style parents will do more regulating. Although this is not always a problem, as we saw in the video clips, parents can get out of balance. Parent trouble zones can be best managed when both the RF and TC styles are blended: This is called the balanced (B) parenting style.

Whatever we do to address the issues in the parent trouble zones, we want to pay attention to both the parent–child relationship and the tasks of managing behaviors. When we balance our parenting styles, we are opening the main pathways through which parents become leaders and influence their children. These leadership pathways are:

• RF (i.e., the connection pathway)
• TC (i.e., the regulation pathway)

However, maintaining these pathways can be difficult during conflict with our child or teen. We have seen how the RF parenting style can get into trouble by overlooking task regulation and how the TC style can get into trouble when the relationship and connection are overlooked.

The couple's use of the self-assessment from the first individual training module in their initial group discussion posts provides a basic illustration of integration, synchronization, and personalization of hybrid individual and group components. It can also be observed that while they identified their differing parenting styles, their disagreements about parent management were not clearly stated; instead,

Box 9.2: Introductions

To get started in our discussion forum, please follow these two steps:

Step 1: *Please introduce yourself to the group.*

- For your introduction, write a short description about yourself, your child, and any challenges you are experiencing and would like to share.

- It's fine to use a few short sentences; of course, do not include any personal identifying information.

  Here's an example: "My name is Frank, and I have an 11-year-old daughter. She won't listen, she's disrespectful, and, frankly, I don't know what to do."

- When you are ready to post, click the "Reply" button below on the bottom, right-side menu bar.

Step 2: *Please share how you intend to use the program. For example, in the current module, "Parenting Styles," you discovered your preferred style.*

- You might want to change your style. You could share this goal and rate "how much" you'd like to change. For instance, you could share on a scale of 1 to 10, with 10 being the most change.

- Also, you could rate (once a day, every few days, etc.) how frequently you think you should log-in to the individual and group parts of the program to reach your goal.

the father noted, "I am not blaming him. I think that something is wrong with me or our parenting."

Parenting conflict was identified by other community participants who used the self-assessment, and, in some cases, they provided more specific goals. In the following example, a mother rated her style as TC and wanted to develop a balanced style. She also acknowledged that the father held an opposite attitude about their son:

> I have a 13-year-old son and a five-year-old daughter. I am recently divorced, and since my divorce, my son has become really withdrawn. He doesn't talk to me and ignores all the rules in our house. He will even flat out tell me no or walk out of the house when I tell him to do his chores or work on his homework. His grades are slipping, and I am worried that some of his friends are experimenting with drugs. His father has noticed the same problems but thinks that it is normal teenage rebelliousness and that we must give him some time. However, he is only with his father two weekends a month, so I don't know if he sees everything.

> I am a "task-centered" parent, according to the survey. I would really like to change and be more balanced. I think my desire to change is about an 8 or 9. I want to improve my relationship with my son and try to prevent my daughter from having the same problems as she gets older.

In another example, a mother completed the self-assessment, established goals, and suggested her parenting style was criticized by her husband and parents:

> According to the survey, I am a relationship-focused parent. I know even a year ago, my score for relationship-focused would be off the chart high because I desire more than anything to be close to my son and love making him happy. However, I know that being relationship-focused is not enough and in some ways is hurting my son more than helping him.
>
> My goal is a balanced parenting style. I want to be able to have a relationship with my son but also have him listen to me and have my husband and my parents' respect. I am also looking to the future and know that if my son doesn't stop behaving in the negative ways that he is behaving now, he will have these negative behaviors as an adult and struggle in relationships, college, and jobs. I want him to grow up and be happy; productive; and healthy mentally, emotionally, physically, and spiritually. I am willing to do whatever it takes to help him help himself.

These examples of the use of self-assessment to integrate, synchronize, and personalize individual and group components in the hybrid model also illustrate the importance of engaging and connecting with participants. The concepts RF and TC parent styles were readily accepted and applied by participants in their initial posts. These concepts continued to be applied by participants throughout later group discussions and were observed to amplify application of Web-based individual training.

Synchronizing and Amplifying Hybrid Components: PBL Guided by Attributional Questions

Following introductions, participants were posed a first attributional question that asked about the long-term outcome of a father's use of negative reciprocity (threatening to break his daughter's belongings) in reaction to his daughter's destructive behavior. Group participants viewed the father–daughter conflict in a video vignette and responded to the following two questions:

1. What lesson(s) is this dad teaching his daughter when he handles her anger this way?

2. Is there a different lesson this dad could be teaching when he handles problems like we saw in the video? How would he need to act to teach that lesson?

Participant posts demonstrated a recognition of the long-term effect associated with the father's response in the video vignette, and some of them amplified discussion with descriptions of their own parenting behavior, as in this example:

> I must admit it that I have become this type of parent. I wasn't raised in a setting like this, but it's how I react. Not always yelling but more of the "how about I break something of yours, would you like that?" attitude. Now let me say I have never done any of this, but I feel that way. I have tried all types of parenting, and nothing has ever worked with my daughter. On the other hand, I have given in to her for many of years as I was a single parent, and she is my only child. It feels like it has come full circle to bite me in the butt.

In another example, the parent reacted to the father in the video vignette and shared her own difficulties with managing anger when her children misbehave:

> Instead of getting instantly mad and yelling, he should've discussed the issue calmly. Now I know that sometimes that's just not going to happen. I know there have been times when one of my kids have broken or spilled something and left it there to be discovered later. I just flew off the handle.

In these examples, participants can also be observed to be providing explanations to make their recognition of the parent management issues more meaningful while also suggesting a training need for increased coping persistence in the face of challenges.

Couple's Discussion

The couple's responses in the PBL discussions demonstrated their application of attributional questions to their own conflicts over parent management. The father's posts were lengthy reflections on the nature of punishments and the importance for youth to agree that a punishment is warranted: "At least make kids understand why they are being punished. If kids don't understand, then you'd better not punish them because unreasonable punishments will break the relationship." In a follow-up post he repeated this belief about punishments, amplifying its meaning with an underlying message to his wife along with his goal:

> I believe that if we parents can make appropriate punishments, kids will accept them willingly and correct their behavior gradually. In terms of how to find good punishments, that's why I am here, and I wish to get the right answer for my family and for my son.

The mother later responded with a post that recognized that developmental differences cause adults to manage negative consequences differently than youth. She then considered whether compliance can be better managed when parents work together, which was also a message about the couple's disagreements:

> That might be one of the differences between an adult and a teen. A punishment may not always make children happy, but that doesn't mean this punishment is not a good one. I think the important thing is if you do it consistently, and parents are on the same page when you think this is the right thing to do. After a teen tries several times, they will eventually realize the lesson they have learned from that.

In another post, she can also be observed to amplify the parenting styles module presentation and its meaning for the couple's parenting conflict:

> Sometimes, it's just hard to act consistently. It's even harder for both wife and husband to be on the same page. Maybe that's why our teens are having issues with us? Maybe this is a difference between task-focused parent and relation-focused parent? A task-focused parent cares more about problem solving, while a relation-focused parent cares more about feelings.

Later Discussions

The couple's discussions continued to demonstrate the integration of individual and group components; however, two participants left the program at about the halfway mark, limiting the group's development. The couple, though, continued to use discussions to obliquely discuss their own disagreements about parent management. For example, the father posted to the group about the use of a family issues meeting for problem solving and implied this was unsuccessful due to his wife's use of aversive behaviors, remarking that parents need to practice patience:

Having a family meeting periodically is very, very important, and it's a very effective solution. But it depends on how the parents handle the meeting because the meeting could make things worse. That's what happened in our family. The purpose of family meetings is not for giving orders to kids and only having kids listen to whatever parents say. The purpose of a family meeting is listening to each other, understanding each other, and learning from each other. Every time we had a family meeting, it always turned into arguments. My son disagreed with us, my wife was really mad at his disrespectful attitude, and I tried to stop the conflict. As parents, if we could be little bit patient, then things will be much better.

Wrapping Up

As the program was ending, the mother amplified the training in the individual Web-based modules in group discussion, when she stated her plan to use several techniques recommended in the module "Avoiding Responsibilities":

Stay calm, help not blame, praise, have patience, and be part of it would be key elements. I liked the ideas in module 2 about having periodic family meetings, keeping a family issue tracking sheet, and noticing a job well done. I will try to use these techniques.

A final post by the mother provided explanation to the group of the meaning of the program for her own changes and her changes in relationship to parenting with the father and son:

A year or so ago, if I rated the compliance rate, I was sure it would probably only be about 25%. A lot of things we had been asking our son to do, he would listen to very few. Now, I rated again. I got 50%. I am very positive this rating will continue to increase with the facilitator and all the other parents' help through this program and discussions.

I am a task-centered parent. My concept before was this should be the way to raise a son. A boy needs to be task centered and responsible. So, a lot of time, I did what the dad did on the first video clip we watched. I can see myself in video clip: the tone of voice, similar word being used, etc. I started to seek a different approach. Asking friends, other parents, coworkers, counselors, anyone who could give us ideas. My husband and I listened and tried. Now I can see myself doing more often what the dad is doing on the second video clip we watched. It does help. My son listens more. As he gets older, we give him more room to handle things on his own, under mutually agreed consequences, and praise him when he does right. Things have gotten a little better than a year ago. Our goal is to increase his compliance rate by participating in this program, learn from other parents, and continue working with our son.

Postintervention

Following the program, both parents completed posttest surveys of parenting self-efficacy, lax parenting, and overreactive parenting as well as posttests of their son's oppositional defiant behaviors. The posttests the couple completed for their son demonstrated a significant decrease in oppositional defiant behaviors, whereas the mother's posttests demonstrated significant increase in parenting self-efficacy and decrease in overreactive parenting behaviors. The father's posttests demonstrated significant increase in self-efficacy only.

At six weeks, participants completed a Learning Activity Survey (LAS; King, 2009) that identified whether they experienced a perspective transformation in their parenting values, beliefs, opinions, or expectations following the program. Their LAS responses are illustrated in Table 9.1. The final question asked what parts of the program accounted for perspective transformation. They described a resolution of their parenting conflict with one another. In Table 9.1, it can also be observed that the mother identified a greater number of individual and group components to have influenced her perspective transformation in comparison with the father, which was in line with couple posttests that demonstrated greater changes for her parenting behaviors than the father.

CONCLUSION

Chan and Holosko (2016) observed the need for digital social work interventions to include theoretical or conceptual explanations for change. This chapter introduced a model for digital hybrid psychoeducation and addressed two questions: (1) What are the conceptual explanations for change that develop from the integration of individual and group work within digital hybrid psychoeducation? (2) Can integrating online group work with individual training in a hybrid format amplify practice components of intervention like Web-based individual skills training?

Table 9.1: Mother and Father's Responses at Six Weeks Postintervention on the Learning Activity Survey

When thinking about your experiences in the Parent Management Training program . . .
CHECK ALL THAT APPLY

Mother's Responses	Father's Responses
• I had an experience that caused me to question the way I normally act. • I had an experience that caused me to question my ideas about social roles (for example, what a mother or father should do or how a child should act). • As I questioned my ideas, I realized I no longer agreed with my previous beliefs or role expectations. • I thought about acting in a different way from my usual beliefs and roles. • I tried to figure out a way to adopt these new ways of acting. • I gathered the information I needed to adopt these new ways of acting. • I adopted these new ways of acting.	• Or instead, as I questioned my ideas, I realized I still agreed with my beliefs or role expectations. • I tried to figure out a way to adopt these new ways of acting. • I acted and adopted these new ways of acting.

Since you began the program, do you believe you have experienced a time when you realized that your values, beliefs, opinions, or expectations about parenting/family life had changed? If yes, what happened?

Mother's Responses	Father's Responses
• I learned how to accept some of my son's behaviors and to change my reactions	• My discussions with parents and others

What part of Module 1: "Parent Styles" influenced the change?
CHECK ALL THAT APPLY

Mother's Responses	Father's Responses
• Videos (single mom and daughter who wanted to go to concert; parents arguing over daughter's grounding) • Self-assessment (on parenting style) • Parent management content in module • Group discussion forum • Facilitator's questions in the discussion forum	• Videos (single mom and daughter who wanted to go to concert; parents arguing over daughter's grounding) • Parent management content in module • Group discussion forum • Facilitator's questions in the discussion forum

Continued

| What part of Module 2: "Avoiding Responsibilities" influenced this change? *CHECK ALL THAT APPLY* ||
Mother's Responses	Father's Responses
• Videos (dad, son, and poor grades) • Quizzes • Parent management content in module group discussion forum • Facilitator's questions in the discussion forum • Downloadable handouts: "Calming Technique," "Family Issues Tracking Sheet," "Job Well Done"	• Videos (dad, son, and poor grades) • Quizzes • Parent management content in module group discussion forum

| What part of Module 3: "Stubborn Noncompliance" influenced this change? *CHECK ALL THAT APPLY* ||
Mother's Responses	Father's Responses
• Videos (daughter watched TV and didn't do homework, boy's messy room, daughter cursing mom) • Quizzes • Parent management content in module	• Videos (daughter watched TV and didn't do homework, boy's messy room, daughter cursing mom) • Parent management content in module

| Thinking back to when you realized that your views or perspective had changed, what did your participation in the Parent Management Training program have to do with the change you experienced? ||
Mother's Responses	Father's Responses
• I began seeking the ideas of my husband and others and changed my attitudes toward my son's misbehavior	• I can be a parent and not be in conflict between my wife and son

Conceptual explanations for change included the use of multiple methods to integrate, synchronize, and personalize individual and group work, including a PBL strategy using attributional questions. The case illustration of a couple's long-standing conflict over how to manage their son's growing oppositional and defiant behaviors illustrated these key concepts.

The second question considers whether the group component can amplify individual skills training. In the case example of the couple, this was illustrated in the mother's discussion posts and, to a lesser extent, the father's posts. The postintervention LAS also demonstrated the influence of joined individual and group components on their perspective transformations, with the mother presenting a greater number of components to be important for her transformation.

In comparison with office-based analog delivery, the case also illustrated the effectiveness of the hybrid model for aiding the couple in achieving a successful resolution of long-standing conflict and reduction of their son's oppositional behaviors. The logistical advantages of digital intervention eliminated time and travel for office visits at a point when the couple was no longer making progress. Consequently, the couple persisted in the digital intervention and was able to successfully resolve their conflict while their son's oppositional and defiant behaviors were improved.

REFERENCES

Abbott, J.-A. M., Klein, B., & Ciechomski, L. (2008). Best practices in online therapy. *Journal of Technology in Human Services, 26*, 360–375. https://doi.org/10.1080/15228830802097257

Barak, A., & Grohol, J. M. (2011). Current and future trends in internet-supported mental health interventions. *Journal of Technology in Human Services, 29*, 155–196. https://doi.org/10.1080/15228835.2011.616939

Barak, A., Hen, L., Boniel-Nissim, M., & Shapira, N. (2008). A comprehensive review and a meta-analysis of the effectiveness of internet-based psychotherapeutic interventions. *Journal of Technology in Human Services, 26*, 109–160. https://doi.org/10.1080/15228830802094429

Chan, C., & Holosko, M. J. (2016). A review of information and communication technology enhanced social work interventions. *Research on Social Work Practice, 26*, 88–100. https://doi.org/10.1177/1049731515578884

Cristancho-Lacroix, V., Wrobel, J., Cantegreil-Kallen, I., Dub, T., Rouquette, A., & Rigaud, A.-S. (2015). A Web-based psychoeducational program for informal caregivers of patients with Alzheimer's disease: A pilot randomized controlled trial. *Journal of Medical Internet Research, 17*, Article e117. https://doi.org/10.2196/jmir.3717

Cunningham, C. E., Bremner, R., & Boyle, M. (1995). Large group community-based parenting programs for families of preschoolers at risk for disruptive behaviour disorders: Utilization, cost effectiveness, and outcome. *Journal of Child Psychology and Psychiatry, 36*, 1141–1159. https://doi.org/10.1111/j.1469-7610.1995.tb01362.x

Cunningham, C. E., Bremner, R., & Secord, M. (1998). *COPE leader's manual: The community parent education program.* COPE Works.

Cunningham, C. E., David, J. R., Bremner, R., Rzasa, T., & Dunn, K. (1993). Coping modeling problem solving versus mastery modeling: Effects on adherence, in-session process, and skill acquisition in a residential parent training program. *Journal of Consulting and Clinical Psychology, 61,* 871–877.

de Graaff, E., & Kolmos, A. (2003). Characteristics of problem-based learning. *International Journal of Engineering Education, 19,* 657–662.

DuPaul, G. J., Evans, S. W., Mautone, J. A., Owens, J. S., & Power, T. J. (2020). Future directions for psychosocial interventions for children and adolescents with ADHD. *Journal of Clinical Child & Adolescent Psychology, 49,* 134–145. https://doi.org/10.1080/15374416.2019.1689825

The Free Dictionary. (n.d.). *Attribution.* Retrieved November 7, 2022, from https://medical-dictionary.thefreedictionary.com/attributional

Furr, S. R. (2000). Structuring the group experience: A format for designing psychoeducational groups. *Journal for Specialists in Group Work, 25,* 29–49. https://doi.org/10.1080/01933920008411450

Harvey, J., & Weary, G. (1984). Current issues in attribution theory and research. *Annual Review of Psychology, 35,* 427–459. https://doi.org/10.1146/annurev.ps.35.020184.002235

Hill, J. R., Song, L., & West, R. E. (2009). Social learning theory and web-based learning environments: A review of research and discussion of implications. *American Journal of Distance Education, 23,* 88–103. https://doi.org/10.1080/08923649028857713

King, K. (2009). *The handbook of the evolving research of transformative learning based on the Learning Activities Survey.* Information Age Publishing.

Lukens, E. P., & McFarlane, W. R. (2004). Psychoeducation as evidence-based practice: Considerations for practice, research, and policy. *Brief Treatment and Crisis Intervention, 4,* Article 205. https://doi.org/10.1093/brief-treatment/mhh019

Rains, S. A., & Young, V. (2009). A meta-analysis of research on formal computer-mediated support groups: Examining group characteristics and health outcomes. *Human Communication Research, 35,* 309–336. https://doi.org/10.1111/j.1468-2958.2009.01353.x

Reese, R. J., Slone, N. C., Soares, N., & Sprang, R. (2015). Using telepsychology to provide a group parenting program: A preliminary evaluation of effectiveness. *Psychological Services, 12,* 274–282. https://doi.org/10.1037/ser0000018

Renkl, A., Hilbert, T., & Schworm, S. (2009). Example-based learning in heuristic domains: A cognitive load theory account. *Educational Psychology Review, 21,* 67–78. https://doi.org/10.1007/s10648-008-9093-4

Steed, A. (2005). *The creation and formative evaluation of an attachment-based parenting education website* (Publication No. 28108907) [Master's thesis, Brigham Young University]. ProQuest Dissertations and Theses Global.

Tursi, M. F. de S., Baes, C. von W., Camacho, F. R. de B., Tofoli, S. M. de C., & Juruena, M. F. (2013). Effectiveness of psychoeducation for depression: A systematic review. *Australian & New Zealand Journal of Psychiatry, 47*, 1019–1031. https://doi.org/10.1177/0004867413491154

van Mierlo, T. (2014). The 1% rule in four digital health social networks: An observational study. *Journal of Medical Internet Research, 16*, Article e33. https://doi.org/10.2196/jmir.2966

Weinberg, H. (2020). Online group psychotherapy: Challenges and possibilities during COVID-19—A practice review. *Group Dynamics: Theory, Research, and Practice, 24*, 201–211. https://doi.org/10.1037/gdn0000140

Wiggins, G. P., & McTighe, J. (2011). *The understanding by design guide to creating high-quality units*. ASCD.

Wilkerson, D. A. (2016). Lurking behavior in online psychosocial discussion forums: Theoretical perspectives and implications for practice. *Journal of Technology in Human Services, 34*, 256–266. https://doi.org/10.1080/15228835.2016.1193456

Wilkerson, D. A., Gregory, V. L., Jr., & Kim, H.-W. (2020). Online psychoeducation with parent management training: Examining the contribution of peer support. *Child & Family Social Work, 25*, 448–459. https://doi.org/10.1111/cfs.12701

Yalom, I. D. (2020). *The theory and practice of group psychotherapy* (6th ed.). Station Hill Press.

Index

In this index, the following abbreviations are used: f for figure, n for note, and t for table.

About the Editors

David A. Wilkerson, PhD, MSW, is an associate professor and director of the Office of e-Social Work Education and Practice at Indiana University School of Social Work in Indianapolis. His practice experience with youth and families in the field of mental health led to his research interest in digital social work education and practice. His work addresses a gap in intervention designs, enabling peer support to develop and contribute to the outcomes of online psychoeducation interventions. He has applied these interests in research with caregivers of behaviorally challenging adolescents and caregivers of persons with dementia. His contributions to the scholarship of teaching and learning have also focused on digital practice and include student decision making in the matter of adoption of telepractice and continuing education in telepractice basics for practitioners responding to COVID-19. In another application of digital practice, he is participating in the development of a state-funded, university–community collaboration to provide rural library patrons with accessible online well-being resources and support.

Liam O'Sullivan, MA, NQSW, is the executive director of Care Alliance Ireland, an award-winning alliance of more than 95 nonprofit organizations supporting family caregivers in the Republic of Ireland. He earned his social work qualification in 1998 from Trinity College Dublin and has worked in statutory social work and in several nonprofit organizations. His work with Care Alliance since 2004 has included bringing National Carers Week to Ireland, developing collaborative and impactful relationships with third-level institutions in family caregiver research, and establishing an online family caregiver support group that engages and supports thousands. He has been actively involved in the international family caregivers' movement, initially with the establishment of Eurocarers and, more recently, as a trustee of the International Alliance of Carer Organizations. He has additional qualifications in youth and community studies; social research methods; and, most recently, implementation science. He has a particular interest in good governance and in bridging the gap between research policy and practice.

About the Contributors

Neil Ballentyne, MPhil, is principal lecturer in social work at Te Pūkenga, the New Zealand Institute of Skills and Technology, where he teaches in a blended learning social work program. He is also a doctoral candidate at the University of Otago, working on a thesis on the datafication of social welfare and the rise of the international movement for data justice.

Ebony Barnes, MS, is project director for the Center for the Advancement of Youth Development at the University of Memphis in Tennessee. Her work with youth is both varied and multifaceted, ranging from youth coordinator for a nonprofit system of care to elementary school teacher for Shelby County Schools, to project coordinator for the Center for the Advancement of Youth Development with the University of Memphis Department of Social Work. She has worked with specialized communities, such as youth with emotional and behavioral disorders, youth impacted by trauma, and youth at risk for detrimental social and educational outcomes.

James R. Brown, PhD, LCSW, is associate professor at the Indiana University School of Social Work in Bloomington. He has 13 years of social work practice experience serving rural children and youth through prevention and intervention services. His work as a practitioner influenced him to examine aspects of school safety, particularly school bullying from the perspectives of multiple stakeholders, including parents. He currently is implementing free-use, technology-based interventions to help parents and youth address bullying.

Kerry Cuskelly, RSW, MSW, MSc, is principal social worker in adult mental health. She completed her MSW at Trinity College Dublin in Ireland and master's degrees in advanced healthcare practice as well as digital healthcare transformation at University of Limerick in Ireland. She is a lecturer at Ireland's University College Dublin, University College Cork, and Maynooth University, where she addresses critical and radical social work, policy practice, critical mental health, activism in social work, and social work and technology. She is a published author and has a particular interest in qualitative systematic reviews and practitioner research.

Christian Deck, LCSW, CTMH, is lecturer with the Indiana University School of Social Work in Indianapolis, teaching primarily in the online MSW program. His research focuses include e-simulations, telebehavioral health practice, online social work education, social work futures, and the enhancement of e-social work distance education through program development and technology design. He is a clinical social worker licensed in Indiana and conducts online practice with college students.

Susan Elswick, EdD, LCSW, LSSW, RPT-S, IMH-E, is full professor at the University of Memphis School of Social Work in Tennessee and a clinical social worker licensed in Tennessee, Mississippi, and Arkansas with more than 16 years in practice. Her research focuses on the development of trauma-responsive, school-based mental health programs; expressive art therapies/experiential therapies; and the use of informatics and technology in the field of social work. Her research has been funded by the Substance Abuse and Mental Health Services Administration, Tennessee state-level awards, and Health Resources and Services Administration, and through numerous community and regional partnership awards.

Dale Fitch, PhD, MSSW, is associate professor in the University of Missouri School of Social Work and core faculty in the University of Missouri Institute for Data Science & Informatics in Columbia. Following a 15-year practice career, his research focuses on the use of information technology in human services organizations.

Kristin Funk, LCSW, LCAC, is currently a PhD student and research assistant at the Indiana University School of Social Work in Indianapolis. She is a clinical social worker and clinical addictions counselor licensed in Indiana. Her research focuses on digital equity and rural social work.

Virgil Gregory, Jr., PhD, LCSW, LCAC, MSCR, is associate professor at the Indiana University School of Social Work in Indianapolis. He has practiced as a clinical social worker using cognitive–behavioral therapy (CBT) in the treatment of persons with mood, anxiety, psychotic, and substance use disorders. His research, which has a translational emphasis, includes the evaluation and implementation of CBT in the treatment of opioid use disorder and affective disorders and in persons of African descent. His research methods include psychometric validation, systematic reviews, meta-analyses, and clinical trials.

John M. Keesler, PhD, is associate professor with the Indiana University School of Social Work in Bloomington. His practice experience spans more than a decade and includes direct care, behavioral health, and administration among nonprofit organizations supporting both people with intellectual and developmental disabilities and their families. Rooted in his social work practice, his scholarship examines the impact of adversity and trauma; integration and evaluation of trauma-informed care; and efforts to promote quality of life, with an emphasis on the disability service industry and rural communities.

Khadija Khaja, PhD, MSW, is associate professor at Indiana University School of Social Work in Indianapolis. Her research, teaching, and service have focused on human rights and international social work policy and practice, including the impact of war and terrorism on Muslim communities, child welfare, and women's health and the growth of White nationalist movements. Her professional presentations, peer-reviewed publications, and book chapters have been internationally recognized. She has received numerous awards, such as Outstanding Woman Faculty Leader Award, Translating Research into Practice Scholar, Dr. Joseph Taylor Excellence in Diversity Award, Trustee Teaching Award, and Chancellors Excellence in Multicultural Teaching Award.

Imelda Ojeda, MSW, MPA, is community social worker and academic associate at the Arizona State University School of Social Work in Phoenix. There, she is an instructor in diversity and oppression, program evaluation, and professional seminars. Originally from Guadalajara, Mexico, she migrated to Arizona, where she received a bachelor's degree in psychology and a double master's degree in social work and public administration from Arizona State University. She works in nonprofit administration and development with a focus on access to healthcare. She also cohosts Social Worker's Break Room podcast and leads grassroots efforts as an activist and advocate for immigrant rights, reproductive justice, and health equity.

Christy Peterson, MPPA, is currently a PhD candidate in the applied behavioral analysis program at the University of Memphis in Tennessee. Her research interests include culturally centered empowerment methods and use of protective factors associated with youth development. A major goal of this work is to identify and promote the use of innovative culturally centered group interventions that reduce risk for disparities in behavioral health, socioeconomic, and incarceration outcomes among young people of color. She has served as a project coordinator for the University of Memphis SMART Center and has managed multiple federal, state, and local projects.

Gregory Washington, PhD, LCSW, is director of the Center for the Advancement and Youth Development and a full professor in the School of Social Work at the University of Memphis in Tennessee. He is clinical social worker and has been licensed in Illinois, Georgia, Arkansas, and Tennessee, where he has practiced individual, family, and group therapy. He also is a Substance Abuse and Mental Health Services Administration–funded researcher and community clinical practitioner. A major goal of his scholarship is to identify and promote the use of innovative culturally centered interventions that reduce risk for disparities in behavioral health and incarceration outcomes among people of color.

Lisa Werth, LCSW, LCAC, is developer of substance use early intervention programs in Indiana. Having a strong clinical background combined with significant skill in program development, she is the creative mind behind the evidence-based curricula, Get S-M-A-R-T, at Calla Collaborative Health in Lafayette, Indiana.

Samantha Wolfe-Taylor, PhD, LCSW, CTH, is assistant professor and associate director of the Office of e-Social Education and Practice at Indiana University School of Social Work in Indianapolis. She is a practicing certified telehealth clinician in Indiana. Her teaching and research focus on distance education, online simulations, and telehealth. She manages the e-social work practice graduate certificate program and online simulation education for the Indiana University School of Social Work.